FOREIGN AFFAIRS

Special Collection

POLLUTION AND TRASH

ENERGY

Introduction

Gideon Rose

"I am the Lorax. I speak for the trees," a famous environmentalist rant began, almost half a century ago. Dr. Seuss' creation had to speak for the trees, "for the trees have no tongues"; he spoke as well for the Brown Bar-ba-loots in their Bar-ba-loot suits, and all the rest of nature's flora and fauna, who were under attack by, essentially, industrialized modernity. The conclusion of the book was stark: "Unless someone like you cares a whole awful lot, nothing is going to get better. It's not."

Some of the fears expressed back in 1971 have proved unfounded, and some of the then nascent environmental movement's proposed remedies have not worn well. But given what's happening around the world, complacent optimism seems destined to appear as misguided as frantic pessimism, for various reasons. Although we're not particularly well known for it, we at Foreign Affairs care a great deal about the state of the physical world and all its inhabitants, and have run a substantial number of articles about environmental, conservation, and climate issues. So we decided this spring that it was time to pull together some of the highlights of our coverage in this special collection.

Reading them over, it is hard not to be shaken by the scale of the damage being wrought on the planet and its non-human inhabitants by rapid, unregulated growth around the globe. But it is also hard not to recognize how much sensible public policy could do to address the problem. Call us naive technocrats, but we really don't believe that there is necessarily a stark, zero-sum choice between economic progress and environmental protection. Many of the pieces lay out promising ideas for ways to allow modern human society to move forward while limiting the collateral damage on the natural world.

In the end, I think Dr. Seuss' conclusion is partly right. Unless we care a whole awful lot, nothing is going to get better. But caring by itself isn't enough: it's important to care about the right things, and to think intelligently about them. We hope this is a useful guide in that effort.

Where the Wild Things Were

How Conservation Efforts are Faltering

Steven Sanderson

On the eve of the 2002 World Summit on Sustainable Development in Johannesburg, I argued that wild nature was in deep distress and that the international institutions charged with the planet's care were managing it poorly ("The Future of Conservation," September/October 2002). Seven years on, the situation is even worse. Humans control the Earth's biosphere and directly manage perhaps half of global plant matter. Their collective ecological impact, however, has taken on a pernicious life of its own, seemingly beyond the will, and perhaps even the capacity. of sovereign political actors to affect.

The Rio de Janeiro summit in 1992 yielded the Convention on Biodiversity (CBD), which was designed to promote the "conservation of biological diversity [and] the sustainable use of its components." As the International Year of Biodiversity approaches in 2010, a charitable appraisal might argue that the CBD has held its own. Ten percent of the world's terrestrial surface is now at least nominally under some kind of protection. National biodiversity assessments and the Millennium Ecosystem Assessment have provided useful information on the "state of nature" in various places.

STEVEN SANDERSON is President and Chief Executive Officer of the Wildlife Conservation Society.

The world knows more and is doing more about conservation than in the past.

Nevertheless, the loss of biodiversity—wildlife, genetic material, ecosystems, and evolutionary processes—has not abated. The United States has still not ratified the CBD, and the UN system for conservation is still weak, lacking sanctions for states that fail to live up to their commitments. Trade in protected wildlife continues and poaching runs rampant. Funding for conservation remains vanishingly small, and important animal populations and entire species are in grave danger.

Climate change, meanwhile, has begun to rival habitat loss as the greatest threat to the biosphere. After somehow maintaining most of its animal species throughout human history, for example, Africa now faces unprecedented losses of wildlife and wild places thanks to global warming. Savannah elephants have no exit corridors from East African drought; changes in water availability threaten natural areas and force the rural poor to resettle; migrating birds arrive at the wrong time, finding little food or nesting opportunities; small populations of animals are simply blinking out.

Melting glaciers and changing patterns of rain and snowfall are transforming the Andean, Rocky Mountain, and Himalayan watersheds. The headwaters of the Amazon, the Ganges, and the Brahmaputra rivers are in peril, along with the human and wildlife diversity they sustain. The Arctic is warming fast, surrendering methane and CO_2 to the atmosphere from the not-so-permafrost. Troubling images of drowning polar bears overshadow an even greater concern: credible estimates warn that five out of every six migratory birds are vulnerable to climate change, and some Arctic habitats could suffer a 90 percent depletion of waterfowl.

The linkages between climate change and conservation, moreover, go in both directions. Healthy wildebeests, Afghan Marco Polo sheep, and American bison are all necessary for the world's grasslands, which in turn are an important store for organic CO_2. Tropical forests represent a vast sink for carbon, and their destruction may account for 20 percent of annual CO_2 emissions. Peatlands lock up one-third of global soil carbon in three percent of global territory, representing a cost-effective area for climate change mitigation—yet they are suffering losses from fire, drainage, and agricultural conversion and, consequently, emitting up to two gigatons of CO_2 per year. Mapping the greatest stores of organic carbon would help connect protection of that carbon to protection of ecologies at great risk.

In short, the time is ripe for a new vision, one that takes both biodiversity and climate change seriously and explores the crucial connections between them. The Copenhagen process is already moving in this direction, and some new global financial mechanisms are also emerging. The World Bank's climate investment funds are designed to reduce deforestation in order to mitigate climate change. The Global Environmental Facility, an organization that provides grants to developing countries for projects related to promoting biodiversity and other environmental issues, could make a greater contribution if given more funding and more agile management. Both the UN and the World Bank have limited but valuable new financial facilities for reducing emissions from land-use change.

So far, however, these initiatives lack policy coherence and the power to overcome obstacles thrown up by recalcitrant stakeholder nations. They are burdened by institutional legacies, stultifying bureaucracy, and the continuing grievances of North-South relations. Few voices are heard in favor of more comprehensive conservation of global carbon stocks or the wildlife they protect. Above all, no global actor has proposed even a rudimentary road map to a global low-carbon future.

For years, Washington has largely stood apart from the climate change debate. The U.S. role in the lead-up to next month's climate summit in Copenhagen has been cautious and noncommittal, as the Obama administration looks warily over its shoulder at years of hostility in Congress toward the Kyoto protocol and its successors. If climate legislation ever emerges from Congress, it will have struggled its way past powerful forces trying to prevent a truly global bill or at least deflect its purpose from combating climate change to subsidizing special interests in the agricultural, energy, and other sectors.

Realism cannot turn into defeatism, however. There have been landmark foreign policy acts in the past that managed to satisfy both domestic and global interests, and there could be again in the future. The Food for Peace program begun in 1954, for example, has been simultaneously good for agricultural surplus disposal, foreign assistance, and hunger relief. Leadership from Washington now could help spur movement toward a low-carbon economy and marry it to existing support for protected areas and global public health.

The problems of climate change and biodiversity loss are global, but the solutions to them must begin at the local level. Conservation is about saving wildlife and wild places in specific locales. Small programs can become large building blocks if the global community stands ready to encourage them. In October, for example, the government of Cambodia established the Seima Protection Forest as the first reserve dedicated to the combined goals of conserving both carbon and endangered wildlife. This act transformed a former logging concession along Cambodia's eastern border with Vietnam into a Yosemite-sized protected area that safeguards not only threatened primates, tigers, and elephants but also massive stores of carbon.

Seima should serve as a model for how efforts known as REDD (Reducing Emissions from Deforestation and Degradation) can work on the ground, providing inspiration for similar projects under way in Bolivia, Guatemala, Chile, Democratic Republic of Congo, Tanzania, Madagascar, and Indonesia. Globalizing such an initiative and offering it political and financial support would validate the actions of a far-sighted government willing to lead. Should the Copenhagen conference and other forums and powerful actors follow such a path, the future of conservation might eventually appear more promising than it looks today.

The Globalization of Animal Welfare

More Food Does Not Require More Suffering

Miyun Park and Peter Singer

T he Universal Declaration of Human Rights, adopted in 1948, articulates the idea that it is wrong to exclude any member of the human species from the circle of moral concern. This enlightened vision was a tremendous advance over earlier, more restricted views about who matters morally; yet it still excludes a far larger number of beings who can both enjoy life and suffer: nonhuman animals. They, or at least those capable of feeling pain, which at a minimum includes all vertebrates, are also entitled to concern. Pain is pain, irrespective of the species of the being that experiences it.

Concern for the welfare of animals is not a new idea. In the fourth century BC, the Chinese Taoist philosopher Zhuangzi said that compassion should permeate relations not only between humans but also between all sentient beings. Buddhist teachings consider caring for all sentient beings a central ethical precept. The Indian emperor Ashoka, who ruled in the third century BC, issued edicts against the unnecessary killing and mutilation of animals,

MIYUN PARK is Executive Director of Global Animal Partnership.

PETER SINGER is Ira W. DeCamp Professor of Bioethics at Princeton University and Laureate Professor at the University of Melbourne. He is the author of *Animal Liberation*, among other books.

including hunting for sport. He also established animal hospitals and promoted, but did not require, a vegetarian diet. In seventeenth-century Japan, Tokugawa Tsunayoshi, the so-called Dog Shogun, enacted various rules protecting animals, especially dogs. The Hebrew Bible requires that the Sabbath be a day of rest for oxen, as well as for humans, and other texts command Jews to relieve the suffering of animals, even if they belong to an enemy. The Koran, too, encourages Muslims to treat animals with kindness; the Prophet Muhammad is said to have cut off the sleeve of his shirt rather than disturb a cat who was sleeping on it.

The modern animal welfare movement started in the West. Beginning in the early nineteenth century, first in the United Kingdom and later in other European states and North America, governments passed laws to protect animals from at least some forms of cruelty, such as whippings and beatings, and from being deprived of food and water. Western states went on to extend legal protection to animals in industries, such as those used in experiments, and, later, to those raised on farms and slaughtered for human consumption. The European Union today has a number of protections for agricultural animals, including the banning of sow stalls for pregnant pigs, intensive confinement of young calves, and barren cages for egg-laying hens. Meanwhile, national governments and the global community have increasingly voiced concern for farm animals, no matter where they may be raised.

But despite these advancements in domestic policy, including various but limited animal protection laws, a regulatory framework for animal welfare has largely been absent on the international level. Although there have long been international agreements to protect certain species from hunting—for example, the 1946 agreement that established the International Whaling Commission—no comparable agreements exist to govern the treatment of animals raised to be eaten by humans or to produce eggs or milk.

In the past decade, however, the welfare of farm animals has become an issue of international concern. In part, the shift has been caused by the growth in international trade in animals and animal products, and in part, by Westerners' reactions to what they perceive as cruel practices both in their own countries and outside their borders. Between 1980 and 2006, total meat exports increased more than threefold, dairy exports more than doubled, and exports of eggs nearly doubled. This growing trade in animal products has heightened awareness of welfare concerns, as has the export of animals themselves. Last June, for example, an Australian television program aired undercover video showing the slaughter of domestic cattle who had been exported to Indonesia. Workers were shown knocking the animals to the ground and strapping them down— fully conscious, in panic, eyes bulging—to await the slaughterer's knife. Such gruesome scenes were simply unacceptable to the Australian public; shortly after the program aired, Canberra suspended the export of Australian cattle to Indonesia until the Indonesian government permitted inspections to ensure that slaughterhouse conditions would be made more humane.

A new movement is emerging. With an increasing number of animals being raised for international markets, and with a growing ability for people to watch previously unseen footage of animal handling, policymakers, businesspeople, nongovernmental organizations, and ordinary citizens are showing greater interest in how animals are treated, wherever they may be. It is no longer sufficient for governments to be concerned for the welfare of animals within their own borders: animal welfare is quickly becoming an issue of international concern.

WHERE'S THE BEEF?

Today, economic growth and development around the world are leading to a rise in the demand for animal products. According to the World Bank, increased global demand caused total meat production in the developing world to almost triple between 1980 and 2002—from 45 million to 134 million tons—with the greatest escalation taking place in countries experiencing rapid economic growth, led by China. According to the UN's Food and Agriculture Organization (FAO), in developing countries since the early 1960s, milk consumption has almost doubled, meat consumption has more than tripled, and egg consumption has increased by a factor of five. (Yet even despite the increased consumption in the developing world, the average person in an industrialized country still consumes far more animal products each year: 181 pounds of meat, 459 pounds of dairy, and 29 pounds of eggs, as compared with 68 pounds of meat, 110 pounds of dairy, and 18 pounds of eggs for each person in the developing world.)

The world's farm animal population has grown to meet this rising demand. In 2009 alone, more than 60 billion land animals— nearly nine times as many as the human population—were slaughtered for food. (This number included approximately 52 billion chickens, 1.34 billion pigs, 656 million turkeys, 521 million sheep, 403 million goats, and 298 million cattle.) In addition, around 1.18 trillion eggs were produced for food that year.

These huge numbers raise concerns about pollution, the soaring demand for grain and soybeans to feed these animals, and the significant contribution that farm animal production has on global warming. At the same time, the conditions under which the animals live pose problems for their welfare. The vast majority of the world's animal products are supplied by intensive confinement systems, which deny animals the opportunity to live in a way suited to the normal behavior of their species. As the world's appetite for meat, eggs, and milk has grown, the intensive confinement model of animal production, initially developed in the years after World War II in Europe and North America, has continued to supplant more traditional farming practices. Today, industrial systems—those that purchase at least 90 percent of their animal feed from other enterprises and house a single species in intensive conditions—produce around two-thirds of the world's poultry, meat, and eggs, and more than half the pork. And these industrial methods place severe limits on animals, in terms of both space and their ability to engage in natural behavior.

Given the sheer numbers of chickens that are raised for meat and eggs each year, the poultry industry is arguably the most egregious violator of animal welfare. Egg-laying hens, for example, are typically kept in barren, wire-mesh enclosures known as battery cages. These cages are so small that even if there were just one hen in each cage, she would be unable to fully stretch and flap her wings—and there are often at least four, if not more, hens per cage. Under such crowded conditions, the birds are unable to establish their usual social hierarchy. Subordinate hens have no way of isolating themselves from their more dominant cagemates and, as a result, are likely to have their feathers and bodies pecked by the dominant birds, resulting in injury and sometimes even death. But instead of providing the birds with more space or genetically selecting for traits to minimize feather-pecking behavior, many egg producers simply sear off portions of the birds' beaks, often with a hot blade and rarely, if ever, with anesthesia. In *The State of the Animals 2001*, a group of leading animal scientists called the procedure a "stop-gap measure masking basic inadequacies in environment or management."

The European Union banned the use of barren battery cages beginning in January 2012. European producers must now raise hens in cage-free environments or, at a minimum, use enriched cages that include nesting boxes and scratching posts, which allow hens to satisfy at least some of their primary behavioral instincts. Although these cages are an improvement, they still keep hens in intensive confinement without the means to behave in the ways that their instincts dictate.

The overwhelming majority of chickens reared for meat are also raised in restrictive conditions, often in large sheds that can hold more than 20,000 birds, packed so densely that each chicken has only as much space as the equivalent of a single sheet of letter-sized paper. In addition to the limitations imposed on their welfare by such confinement practices, the widespread use of selective breeding has an adverse impact on the well-being of tens of billions of animals each year. Simply put, chickens are forced to grow much fatter and much faster than is natural or healthy: in 1925, chickens reached 2.5 pounds in about 16 weeks; today, most commercially raised birds grow to 5.5 pounds in less than seven weeks. Such unnatural and rapid growth rates leave many chickens debilitated, suffering from bone deformities, gait abnormalities, ruptured tendons, and metabolic diseases—despite their being slaughtered when they are, in effect, still juveniles. Reaching slaughter weight at approximately 42 days of age, many birds cannot walk properly and suffer from other ailments because their immature bones cannot support their abnormally heavy bodies.

Of the mammals eaten by humans, pigs are raised in the greatest number—and may be the most intelligent of all animals commonly eaten. Commercial farming methods have relegated these animals to confinement in large sheds on bare concrete or slatted flooring without any mental stimulation or basic comforts, causing frustration, boredom, and physical distress. Female pigs, when they are about to give birth, build a nest from straw or leaves and twigs in order to create a comfortable and safe place where they can nurse their litter. But in many of today's industrial production facilities, pregnant pigs are still often caged in sow stalls so narrow that they cannot turn around or even walk more than a step forward or backward, without any straw or bedding material. Right before they give birth, they are often moved into farrowing crates, which are metal enclosures scarcely larger than their own bodies and constructed to physically separate mother from piglets. It is in these

barren and restrictive crates, which leave the pigs virtually immo-
bilized, that they give birth and nurse their young—although only
for a fraction of the time they would in the wild, as their piglets are
prematurely weaned and soon taken away for "fattening." The sows
are then once again impregnated. Although sow stalls for gestating
pigs have already been banned throughout the European Union
and are slowly being phased out in some U.S. states, they are still
widely used elsewhere, and restrictive farrowing crates remain the
common agricultural model.

These methods, developed over the past 60 years in order to
reduce the need for skilled labor, produce a standard product irrespective of season or weather. And in the pursuit of efficiency and
economies of scale, they have now spread from Western countries
to many developing nations, particularly those in Asia and Latin
America. The result has been an unmitigated disaster for animals:
more animals in more places are confined in restrictive conditions
utterly unlike their natural environments and are pushed beyond
their physiological limits to produce ever-greater numbers of eggs,
gallons of milk, and pounds of flesh. It is a tragic turn of events
that just as these methods are being modified or even phased out in
the countries where they were first invented, they are being introduced in their old, unmodified forms in other countries around the
world. The exportation of industrialized animal-production models has inflicted misery on animals on an unprecedented scale—not
to mention causing higher grain prices for the poor, greater greenhouse gas emissions, and a serious threat to human health, as seen
by the rise of various zoonotic diseases and the pollution of land,
air, and water.

BATTLE OF THE COWSHED

The replication in developing nations of the worst forms of intensive
animal farming is grim news. But there is hope: people in the industrialized world are beginning to show concern about the treatment of
animals beyond the borders of their countries. At the same time,
some developing countries already have animal welfare legislation,

although enforcement varies greatly, and others, including China, are discussing it. Meanwhile, international regulation is making some progress, as are corporate policies in favor of better farm animal welfare. The question now is whether these gains can be consolidated into a centralized and uniformly-agreed-on set of rules.

The European Union has been a leader in passing legislation intended to improve the welfare of farm animals across national borders. To a large extent, this effort has been driven by public attitudes: in March 2007, the European Commission released a survey called "Attitudes of EU Citizens Towards Animal Welfare," which found that more than 34 percent of those polled felt that animal welfare was of the highest possible importance and gave it a score of ten out of ten points, whereas only two percent deemed animal welfare unimportant. (Overall, those surveyed gave animal welfare an average rating of 7.8 points.) And the European public is not merely content with existing regulations. Although the majority of the EU's most significant animal welfare rules (for example, bans on sow stalls, barren battery cages, and individual confinement stalls for calves raised for veal) were enacted in the late 1990s and early years of this century, a resounding majority (77 percent) of those responding to the 2007 European Commission poll wanted further improvements to protect farm animals.

There is broad public interest in animal welfare in the United States, too. For example, 64 percent of those responding to a 2008 Gallup survey favored "strict laws" governing the treatment of farm animals. A 2007 survey sponsored by the American Farm Bureau Federation found that 95 percent of those polled said that it was important to them how farm animals were cared for, with 76 percent of respondents saying that the well-being of these animals was more important than low meat prices. And when these questions have been put to an actual vote, the results have validated such sentiments: in California, for example, a 2008 referendum to ban the standard battery cage and sow and veal stalls passed with a 63 percent majority. Yet the United States lacks any federally mandated protections for animal welfare, in no small part due to effective and entrenched agricultural lobbies.

In China, where food production is not stringently regulated and animals are often raised in dire conditions, public attitudes also favor protections for animals raised for food. A 2005 poll conducted there by the International Fund for Animal Welfare found that 90 percent of respondents believed that they had a moral duty to minimize animal suffering, and 77 percent favored legislation to do so.

And there are signs that attitudes among China's commercial and political power brokers are beginning to shift. In 2007, the director of the Beijing Chaoyang Anhua Animal Product Safety Research Institute and the president of the Chinese General Chamber of Commerce signed a memorandum of understanding on humane slaughter with the World Society for the Protection of Animals. The agreement calls for efforts, including training, to ensure the humane transport, handling, stunning, and slaughter of farm animals in China. As of August 2009, more than 2,300 people from nearly 950 companies from different parts of China had received training on animal welfare. Given the size and scale of China's animal agricultural industry, these numbers may seem insignificant; what is important is that business leaders, scientists, and other stakeholders in the country have made such a commitment and are making available educational modules on the treatment of farm animals.

Also in 2007, a team of Chinese legal experts submitted a draft proposal of an animal protection law to the Standing Committee of the National People's Congress. The proposed law would be China's first piece of national legislation on animal welfare and would afford basic protections to animals on farms, in laboratories, and in the entertainment industry, as well as to pets, service animals, and wild animals. Although the law has not yet passed, its basic principles, which acknowledge the need to protect animals and regulate the treatment of them, are a sign of changing attitudes. Chang Jiwen, one of the law's drafters and a researcher with the Law Institute of the Chinese

Academy of Social Sciences, told the Xinhua News Agency in 2009 that he is "convinced—along with the enhancement of people's awareness of animal welfare—laws and regulations in this respect will become more sophisticated and complete."

WELFARE GOES GLOBAL

Although national legislation plays a key role in improving the welfare of animals raised for food, it is not the only answer. Indeed, even in those countries with animal protection laws, monitoring and enforcement mechanisms are limited. In a growing number of cases, the consumer marketplace is driving new policies, and international organizations are helping raise consciousness and fill the gaps left by national laws.

The need to improve the welfare of farm animals has been accepted by a number of such multilateral bodies, including the World Organization for Animal Health (known by its initials in French, OIE). Created in 1924 to combat the global spread of animal diseases, the OIE, aware of the link between the treatment of animals and their well-being, has expanded its attention beyond animal health to include animal welfare. The acceptance on such an international level of the importance of animal welfare is a strong indication of the global community's interest in farm animal well-being. In 2008, more than 400 participants met in Cairo at the OIE's second Global Conference on Animal Welfare, where they put forth a resolution stating that ethics is as important as science in the development of animal welfare standards. For the OIE, a scientific authority on animal health and disease, to acknowledge the ethical significance of the mistreatment of animals indicates a momentous shift in opinion at the highest level.

Animal production practices not only influence the welfare and health of the animals themselves but also affect food security, the environment, and community sustainability. In recognition of this, the FAO has joined the global call for improved welfare, recognizing the myriad effects of how animals are raised for food. In 2008, the FAO convened a forum on animal welfare practices, which led to a report stating that as human and farm animal populations continue to rise, "the resulting escalation of animal production raises a number of ethical issues, including environmental sustainability and secure access to food, which must be considered alongside the growing concern about animal welfare." It went on to say, "Animal welfare is coming to be recognized as highly relevant to success in international development."

Soon after its 2008 meeting, the FAO launched the Gateway to Farm Animal Welfare, a Web portal that contains information on diverse aspects of animal agriculture, including animal welfare, in various countries and agricultural sectors. It serves as a single access point for scientific reports, case studies, training opportunities, expert directories, events, and more. The gateway aims to facilitate information sharing around the world, primarily for professionals and producers in less developed countries. On the portal, the FAO explains the importance of focusing on animal welfare: "In many regions, a secure supply of food for people depends on the health and productivity of animals, and these in turn depend on the care and nutrition that animals receive." But, as the FAO goes on to note, "animal welfare practices, despite their evident positive impacts, are insufficiently applied" both on traditional and on industrial farms.

The private sector is also highlighting farm animal welfare as a necessary component of sound business models. In 2006, the International Finance Corporation of the World Bank published "Creating Business Opportunity Through Improved Animal Welfare," which pointed out that consumers around the world are increasingly demanding that their food be produced humanely and safely, which in turn means that "animal welfare is also important for commercial reasons, both directly, by increasing a business's overall sustainability, and indirectly, by addressing society's expectations of how animals should be treated and how food should be produced."

Just last year, the International Organization for Standardization, or ISO, a network of the national standards institutes from 163 countries, issued its "ISO 26000" guidelines, which serve as the internationally accepted standard on social responsibility for both the public and the private sectors. The new document marks the first time that the ISO has included references to animal welfare, requiring those observing the standard to respect "the welfare of animals, when affecting their lives and existence, including by providing decent conditions for keeping, breeding, producing, transporting and using animals."

Although such initiatives represent welcome progress, more work needs to be done. Given that farm animal production affects diverse communities, human and nonhuman alike, a collaborative strategy that unites the public and private sectors is necessary. Global Animal Partnership, an international charity dedicated to farm animal welfare, founded in 2008, embodies this multistakeholder approach. (One of the co-authors of this essay is executive director of the organization.) It brings together farmers and ranchers, animal welfare advocates, animal behavioral scientists, and food retailers to agree on common principles and to speak out with a unified voice for continuous improvement in animal agriculture. Recognizing the diversity of animal production methods, the charity's flagship initiative is an assessment program that contains different sets of progressively higher welfare requirements covering nearly every aspect of on-farm production. The 5-Step Animal Welfare Rating Standards program, as opposed to binary certification schemes, encourages innovation and empowers producers to move up the so-called welfare ladder. Participating farmers and ranchers adhere to production standards and subject themselves to auditing and certification by independent third parties. In less than three years, more than 1,750 farms and ranches that together raise more than 140 million animals each year have sought this certification. The program's multitiered structure allows a wide variety of producers, from small farms to large-scale operations, to participate. Each tier in the program has its own set of comprehensive standards, covering basic provisions, such as food, water, and shelter, and enhancements that encourage foraging and other natural behaviors. These tiers lead to progressively higher welfare practices, including prohibitions against the transportation of live animals and against physical alterations, such as beak trimming or castration. The multitiered system gives producers incentives to improve their farming practices and modify their production systems in ways that lead to better animal welfare. Higher ratings serve as further information for consumers and, in many cases, allow certified producers to charge higher prices. Other stakeholders also benefit from the program: retailers are able to offer wider product selection to meet customer demands, consumers are given transparent and more accurate sources of information on how the animals were raised for the meat they purchase, and, of course, the animals raised in these systems enjoy better lives. Global Animal Partnership completed a pilot program last year with Whole Foods Market, North America's largest natural food retailer, and is now in discussions with restaurants, producers, and other grocers in a number of countries around the world.

Given the sheer magnitude of intensive confinement agriculture—in terms of the number of individual animals involved and in terms of the impact on animal welfare, human health, and the planet's limited resources—the sense of urgency cannot be overstated. Whether one spends his or her days in a corporate boardroom in India, a government office in Russia, a university classroom in Brazil, or a farm in Canada, all who are involved in the global food industry, as producers or consumers, have an obligation to find remedies to the problems caused by the growth in intensive confinement animal agriculture around the world. It is time for a global commitment to reduce animal suffering and to mitigate the many unintended and undesirable consequences of raising animals for food.

Africa's Anti-Poaching Problem

How Wildlife Trade Bans Are Failing the Continent's Animals

Alexander Kasterine

D ecades after more than 100 countries agreed to ban the rhinoceros horn trade in 1979, poachers are killing record numbers of the endangered species. In just 2013 alone, they slaughtered some 1,000 rhinos in South Africa, up from 668 in 2012. If the hunting continues at current rates, one of the conservation movement's most famous mascots could be extinct within the next two decades. And rhinos are not alone. Many other animals—including elephants and tigers—are also facing the prospect of extinction, all in spite of long-standing trade bans.

In South Africa, police and national defense forces have become increasingly engaged in efforts to protect threatened wildlife, and the government has earmarked roughly $7 million in extra funding to ramp up security in its national parks. Yet poaching there has continued, just as it has throughout the continent. Last year alone, poachers killed a total of 22,000 elephants, the majority for tusks that were sold to feed rising demand in Asia.

Through the Convention on International Trade in Endangered Species of Flora and Fauna (CITES), an international agreement

ALEXANDER KASTERINE is Head of the Trade and Environment Unit at the UN/WTO International Trade Center in Geneva. The article reflects the personal views of the author.

South Africa's Poaching Predicament

South Africa's police force has become increasingly engaged in efforts to protect threatened wildlife, yet poaching has continued to thrive. [Source: Save the Rhino/South African Department of Environmental Affairs]

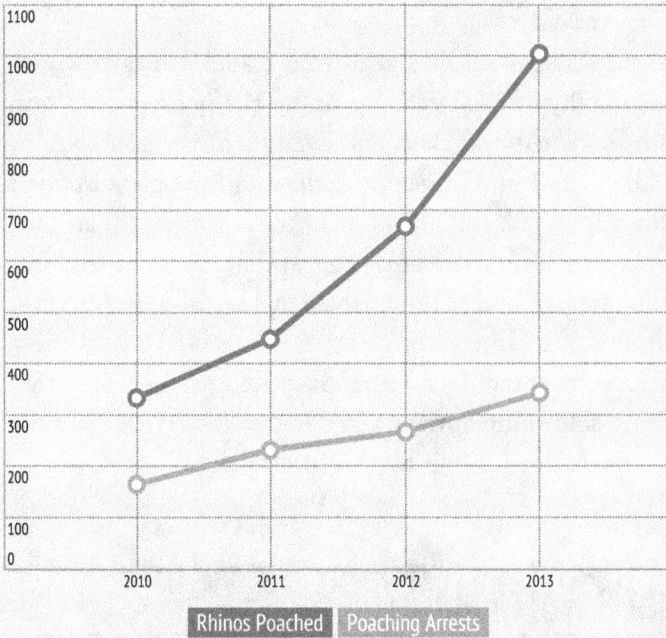

Rhinos Poached | Poaching Arrests

among 179 countries, governments can vote to ban the trade of products from species threatened with extinction. But such trade bans are failing in large part because they have run into the same basic problem as the war on drugs. Prohibitions on trading wildlife products such as tusks and timber have ultimately made them more valuable. And criminal organizations have moved in and taken over the market, imposing high costs—through violence and corruption—on weak societies.

In some ways, this is an old story. As the American economist Thomas Schelling has argued, the United States' prohibition of alcohol in the 1920s advantaged criminals by giving them "the same kind of protection that a tariff gives to a domestic monopoly." As the demand for alcohol increased, prohibition guaranteed "the absence of competition from people who are unwilling to be criminal, and an advantage to those whose skill is evading the law." Today, the United States spends an estimated $30 billion annually to combat the drug trade, yet illegal narcotics remain readily available on American streets.

Both the illegal wildlife and drug trades are now worth huge sums, the bulk of which ends up lining the pockets of criminal organizations, corrupt officials, and even terrorist groups. According to the UN Office on Drugs and Crime and the global policing organization Interpol, the illegal drug trade was worth an estimated $435 billion in 2013. Estimates suggest that the illicit wildlife trade, including logging and fishing, is worth around $130 billion—more than three times the size of Kenya's entire GDP. And the profits have been substantial. Last year, Vixay Keosavang, a wildlife trader from Laos, sold rhino horn at $65,000 per kilo. He bought the horn in southern Africa for one-tenth of that price.

What's Worth More?

In recent years, the price of a kilo of rhino horn has surpassed the approximate prices of a kilo of gold, a kilo of platinum, and a kilo of cocaine in the United States. [Sources: The Guardian, U.S. Drug Enforcement Administration]

$1,500 $26,000 $40,000 $43,000 $65,000

Elephant Ivory | Cocaine | Gold | Platinum | Rhino Horn

As the money has rolled in, poachers and smugglers have grown more sophisticated, investing in miniature armies. All across Africa, it is increasingly common for park rangers to skirmish with poachers. According to the charity Thin Green Line, poachers in Africa kill some 1,000 park rangers each year. And the fight is far from fair: The U.S. Congressional Research Service has reported that many poachers now use "night vision goggles, military-grade weapons, and helicopters." By comparison, the rangers are often poorly equipped. And that makes trading in wildlife all the more attractive.

THE PATH TO LEGALIZATION

Conservation groups such as the World Wildlife Fund have long advocated for stiffer sentences and fines to deter poachers and traders. They are right that penalties could be tougher. Last year, an Irish court fined two traffickers just 500 euros ($676) for smuggling rhino horn worth 500,000 euros ($676,600). However, even high penalties do not necessarily deter all types of crime. Drug runners can face the death penalty in Southeast Asia, yet a seemingly endless stream of impoverished people sign up to act as drug mules anyway.

The appetite for illegal wildlife goods, meanwhile, shows no signs of abating. Ever since Asia's economies took off in the 1990s, demand has soared. The prices of such items as rhino horns have followed, rising from roughly $1,000 per kilo in 1990 to around $65,000 per kilo today. Many Asian consumers believe that when used as a medicine, the horns can help cure cancer and detoxify the body. It does not matter how scientifically dubious such claims may be; they are simply a matter of faith. Just as drug addicts will go to any length for a fix, no matter the cost, those who believe that rhino horn can cure cancer will go to nearly any length to get their medicine. Never mind that such horns are made of the same material as human toenails.

Many buyers in Asia are motivated by prestige as well. In Vietnam and elsewhere, serving bush meat caught in the wild is a status symbol—as is owning elephant tusks, shahtoosh shawls made from endangered Tibetan antelope, and live orangutans as household pets. And such goods derive much of their appeal from being scarce and expensive—making demand for them insensitive to price hikes.

Outright bans, then, are not the answer. For this reason, the South African government plans to propose lifting the ban on

Captured Contraband

As Asian economies have boomed, demand for illicit wildlife products has soared. So, too, have seizures of illegal ivory -- over 100,000 kilograms were interdicted between 1989 and 2011 in these ten Asian nations. [Source: National Geographic/ETIS, measurements are from 1989 to 2011]

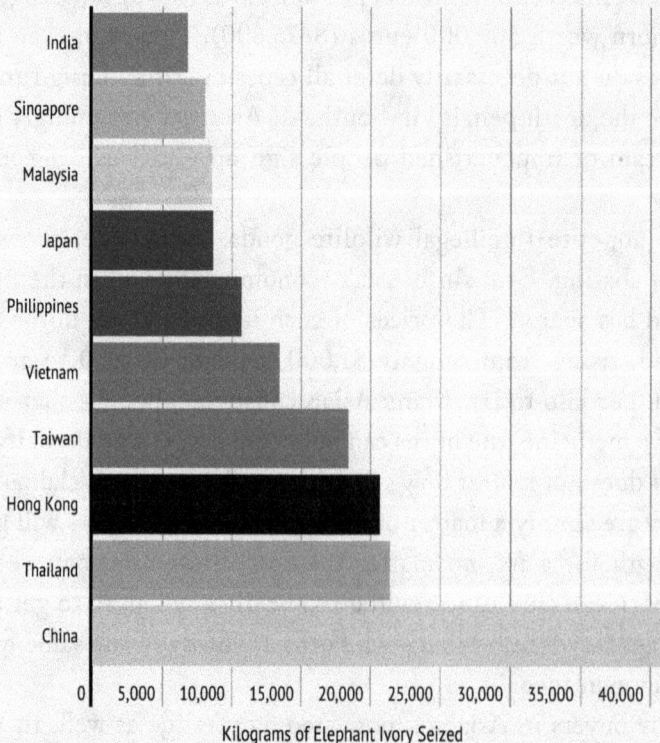

Kilograms of Elephant Ivory Seized

trading rhino horn at the next CITES meeting in 2016. South African officials argue that a legal trade would take profits away from criminal syndicates. Just as taxes on cigarettes fund education and health programs in the United States, similar levies would also provide ample funds for campaigns to combat poaching and reduce demand. Meanwhile, regular de-horning of the animals would increase the global horn supply, lowering prices and the attraction of poaching. Rhinos produce nearly one kilogram of horn each year, which can easily be harvested through a simple veterinary procedure. Farming the animals ethically, moreover, would allow consumers to demand horn products from sustainably managed sources.

To legalize the rhino trade, South Africa will need a two-thirds majority among CITES members. It can expect to run into stiff opposition from a group that will likely include the United States, Kenya, and a number of European countries. Animal welfare groups will also push hard against legalization. That said, CITES already permits the trading of live rhinos and some limited hunting. In January, the Dallas Safari Club auctioned the right to hunt an old rhino in Namibia for $350,000. (One bidder withdrew his offer of $1 million—money that could have gone toward protecting rhinos—after receiving a death threat from an animal welfare extremist.) Such hunting fees can provide a critical source of revenue; in Namibia, they finance one-third of the government's wildlife protection budget.

Peru embarked on a similar legalization process in 1979. To save the vicuña—a camelid that resembles a small llama—from extinction at the hands of hunters who prized its fine wool, the Peruvian government gave local communities the right to shear and market the animal's wool. Now local herders protect the animals and also earn money from sale of their wool. Since then, the country's vicuña population has grown from 5,000 animals—on the verge of extinction—to more than 200,000 today. CITES approved the policy in 1994.

Such a process of legalization, however, would not necessarily be a magic bullet. For a legal trade to work, governments would have to enforce a tight system of export permits and harvest quotas. Policing would still be needed to protect animals and forests. The success of a legal trade would also hinge on animal reproductive rates and the level of poverty in rural areas where the incentives to poach are high. But policymakers should heed the lessons of the drug wars. Bans fail because borders remain porous and officials corrupt. There is no wall high enough to counteract enormous financial rewards for breaking the rules to feed a voracious market.

Like the drug wars, restrictions on the animal trade reflect not only policy positions but also certain moral beliefs. Yet moralizing conservation organizations are typically based in wealthy countries and overlook the huge financial burdens that enforcement imposes on poor countries with already scarce resources. Such groups also minimize the potential benefits of taxing the wildlife trade, in the form of precious funds that would otherwise go to criminal outfits. Individual countries, then, will have to make some informed decisions on their own. They would do well to consider what the United States has achieved in its war on drugs—now in its fourth decade.

Networking Nature

How Technology Is Transforming Conservation

Jon Hoekstra

C onservation is for the first time beginning to operate at the pace and on the scale necessary to keep up with, and even get ahead of, the planet's most intractable environmental challenges. New technologies have given conservationists abilities that would have seemed like super powers just a few years ago. We can now monitor entire ecosystems—think of the Amazon rainforest—in nearly real time, using remote sensors to map their three-dimensional structures; satellite communications to follow elusive creatures, such as the jaguar and the puma; and smartphones to report illegal logging.

Such innovations are revolutionizing conservation in two key ways: first, by revealing the state of the world in unprecedented detail and, second, by making available more data to more people in more places. Like most technologies, these carry serious, although manageable, risks: in the hands of poachers, location-tracking devices could prove devastating to the endangered animals they hunt. Yet on balance, technological innovation gives new hope for averting the planet's environmental collapse and reversing its accelerating rates of habitat loss, animal extinction, and climate change.

JON HOEKSTRA is Chief Scientist at World Wildlife Fund. Follow him on Twitter @Jon_Hoekstra.

CELL PHONES FOR ELEPHANTS

In 2009, I visited the Lewa Wildlife Conservancy, in northern Kenya. A cattle ranch turned rhinoceros and elephant preserve, Lewa has become a model for African conservation, demonstrating how the tourism that wildlife attracts can benefit neighboring communities, providing them with employment and business opportunities. When I arrived at camp, I was surprised—and a little dismayed—to discover that my iPhone displayed five full service bars. So much for a remote wilderness experience, I thought. But those bars make Lewa's groundbreaking work possible.

More than a decade earlier, Iain Douglas-Hamilton, who founded the organization Save the Elephants, had pioneered the use of GPS and satellite communications to study the movements of elephants. At Lewa, Douglas-Hamilton outfitted elephants with tracking collars that connect to the Safaricom mobile network as easily as my cell phone did. These connections allow Lewa's researchers to effectively call the tracking collars of the conservancy's elephants and download their location data on demand, all the while plotting their migration between Lewa and the forests flanking Mount Kenya.

Today, Lewa uses the collars for more than research, piloting a program to reduce human-elephant conflict that results when elephants raid crops and to provide safer passage for elephants when they move through agricultural and other settled areas. Using accumulated data on elephant migration routes, the conservancy identified and protected ideal migration corridors. It even constructed a highway underpass to reduce the risk of elephants colliding with cars. Lewa also straps tracking collars on problem elephants with a history of raiding crops. If one of the elephants approaches a farm or village, its collar sends a text message to wildlife rangers, who can then quickly locate the animal and move it away in order to prevent any damage. True to their reputation for intelligence, the elephants quickly learn to mind such virtual fences and keep clear of farms.

The Lewa project shows how a relatively simple, low-cost tracking device can transform wildlife conservation. Using data from such devices, conservationists can shape protected areas around predictable migratory patterns—avoiding needless, often fatal confrontations between endangered species and human civilization. For example, Magellanic penguins that forage along the coast of Argentina have long been vulnerable to running into oil when they swim through shipping lanes. Once covered in oil, most penguins struggle to maintain their body temperature and die of hypothermia, and the survivors suffer from health and reproductive problems. In the mid-1990s, P. Dee Boersma, one of the world's foremost authorities on penguin conservation, discovered that Argentina's oil pollution was killing as many as 40,000 penguins each year. She used GPS tracking devices, at a time when the technology was on the cutting edge and costly, to document where the birds were foraging. She then worked with Argentinian authorities to move the shipping lanes further offshore, dramatically reducing a mortality rate that could have easily led to the penguins' extinction.

Tracking collars such as those used on Lewa's elephants or the Magellanic penguins can cost as much as $5,000 each. But Eric Dinerstein, a leading scientist at World Wildlife Fund, has collaborated with engineers at a cell-phone company to make a GPS tracking device that can be manufactured for less than $300. The use of stronger and smaller components has also made it possible to tag and track a wider variety of species, from jaguars in dense jungle to albatross soaring over the open ocean.

COUNTING BY TREES

The tropical forests of the Amazon and the Congo are among the last of the planet's vast wildernesses. They are menageries of innumerable species. And they act as the planet's lungs, inhaling carbon dioxide—an overabundance of which causes climate change—and exhaling oxygen. For this reason, scientists know that forest conservation is an immediate and effective strategy for slowing climate change. Estimates suggest that the cutting and burning of tropical forests accounts for around ten percent of the carbon emissions that are heating the climate.

In 2005, the UN Framework Convention on Climate Change created REDD+, a program to compensate developing countries that reduce their overall carbon emissions through forest conservation. The system recognizes only huge-scale conservation achievements that can be measured and verified—often ten million acres or more. Hundreds of millions of donor dollars are now earmarked for countries that can estimate the avoided carbon emissions across vast areas with high levels of mathematical rigor. But such schemes have consistently run into one big technical stumbling block: it has been difficult to precisely measure, report, and verify the emissions-reduction benefits of variable stretches of forest. Early, labor-intensive methods of measuring a forest's capacity to store carbon relied on satellite imagery to measure the overall area and ground surveys to size up individual trees in sample plots. The process was costly, and the accuracy of the estimates varied.

Scientists are now using remote sensors, laser-imaging technologies, and advanced statistical algorithms to see both the forest and the trees at the same time and in extraordinary detail—right down to the chemical signatures of individual trees. As their costs decline and their precision increases, these forest-scanning methods could unlock billions of dollars for innovative conservation programs that can prove their carbon, social, biodiversity, and even financial values.

Greg Asner, an ecologist at Stanford University and the Carnegie Institution for Science, is the leading pioneer of such forest-surveillance systems. His most recent project builds on a technology called "light detection and ranging" (LIDAR). Mounted on a small airplane, the system beams powerful lasers through tree canopies to the forest floor, which bounce back carrying highly detailed data about the structure of the forest. Asner's plane also carries a separate set of hyperspectral sensors that can recognize a range of seemingly invisible characteristics, including a tree's photosynthetic pigments, its basic structural compounds, and even the water content of its leaves. Researchers can use this data not only to estimate carbon storage capacities but also to analyze forest diversity and assess tree health. With a single airplane, these paired technologies can scan over 120,000 acres, or as many as 50 million trees, in a single day. And the equipment is so sophisticated that it can distinguish among 200 different tree species. Scientists are already integrating information gathered by the LIDAR system with national forest inventories in Nepal, Panama, Thailand, and dozens of other countries to establish their forests' base lines of carbon storage. Diplomats at the United Nations and the World Bank recently agreed on the key rules for estimating the carbon storage capacity of individual forests, anticipating a coming wave of climate-mitigation finance.

Researchers are also making use of high-resolution satellite imagery. In 2012, the biologist Michelle LaRue reported the findings of her satellite-based census of emperor penguins in Antarctica. Using high-resolution images collected by the QuickBird satellite, LaRue was able to count individual birds over huge areas of ice. Her study, the first of its kind, discovered seven previously unknown colonies and estimated the global population of emperor penguins at nearly 600,000 individuals—nearly 50 percent greater than previous estimates compiled from various ground-based observations of accessible penguin colonies. More accurate population assessments such as these will enable conservationists to verify whether conservation efforts are succeeding and target scarce resources toward the species in the greatest danger.

In a similar vein, the geologist John Amos, who founded the activist organization SkyTruth, now uses satellite imagery and digital mapping to document the environmental impact of mining, oil and gas development, and illegal fishing. He compiles series of satellite images of a single area to create animated visualizations of changes to the landscape over time. His findings have helped quantify the damage done by mountaintop removal, mining, and fracking. Amos' analysis of satellite imagery of the Deepwater Horizon oil spill in 2010 accurately estimated that the spill was far larger than official reports initially claimed. And advanced imaging technologies are now enabling SkyTruth to detect and document illegal fishing activity in remote waters, which will aid enforcement efforts.

CAPITAL INVESTMENTS

Humanity's survival depends on the planet's stores of natural resources: its fish, water, wood, minerals, and arable land. But the replenishment of these goods depends on the world's natural capital: its forests, grasslands, topsoil, lakes, rivers, and oceans. Increases in agricultural productivity and the expansion of critical infrastructure have improved the lives of billions of people but have left this natural capital dangerously depleted. As the overall demand for goods and services has continued to grow, human consumption of natural resources has become unsustainable. Since the mid-1970s, people have been consuming more resources than the world's natural capital can replenish and producing more pollution than it can absorb. In 2010, the nonprofit organization the Global Footprint Network calculated that humanity now requires roughly 1.5 earths to sustain its current level of consumption each year. Put another way, humanity now uses up a year's supply of the earth's natural resources by mid-August. After that, it is drawing down against the future capacity of natural capital.

The Natural Capital Project, a joint venture of World Wildlife Fund, Stanford University, the Nature Conservancy, and the University of Minnesota, has generated the technology needed to manage natural capital and predict how changes in land management, infrastructure, and resource use will affect levels of water, timber, and fish, as well as natural defenses against floods and erosion. The project's flagship technology is an open-source software package called InVEST, which uses relatively simple data inputs to produce maps, trend lines, and balance sheets that measure natural capital. These analyses can inform land-use, development, and conservation decisions by making the potential tradeoffs of various options clearer. InVEST calculates and visualizes how development choices will affect natural capital and, with it, the flows of goods and services to people from the environment.

Today, the Chinese government is using InVEST to establish a national network of "ecosystem function conservation areas" that will balance the potential environmental toll of development with targeted conservation projects. China plans to use the software to restrict development in designated areas that will cover about 25 percent of the country. InVEST is enabling Beijing to identify which areas can provide the biggest returns in natural capital— helping it avoid erosion, conserve water resources, prevent desertification, and protect biodiversity.

In 2011, World Wildlife Fund and the Indonesian government used the software to quantify the impact of different land-use and development scenarios on the forest ecosystems of Sumatra. Their studies compared the costs and benefits of alternative development plans by taking into account the carbon storage potential of local forests, the habitat for tigers, and the fresh water supply. Following this study, the Millennium Challenge Corporation recommended that InVEST be used to guide $332 million in environmental investments under a $600 million U.S.-Indonesian compact.

The private sector is using similar software, with many companies recognizing that their long-term profitability hinges on a sustainable supply of water, agricultural commodities, and other renewable resources that form the bases of their supply chains. For example, Coca-Cola and World Wildlife Fund recently renewed a strategic partnership that includes goals for incorporating natural-capital considerations into how Coca-Cola uses water and sources the commodities in its products. A number of considerations informed these goals, including data collected to better understand how Coca-Cola uses water throughout its supply chain and manufacturing processes. To date, Coca-Cola has improved its system-wide water efficiency by more than 21 percent, in addition to setting a goal to sustainably source key agricultural ingredients, such as cane sugar, corn syrup, and palm oil, by 2020. One of the company's first major steps toward sustainable sourcing was its work in helping create Bonsucro, which sets global standards for sustainable sugar-cane production. In 2011, a sugar mill in São Paulo, Brazil, became the first to achieve Bonsucro certification, and Coca-Cola was the first buyer of the mill's certified sugar.

FILLING HOLES

Biotechnology may have the most far-reaching and controversial implications for conservation. De-extinction—the notion that extinct species could be reconstituted from remnants of their DNA—has garnered significant media attention in recent years, as genetic sequencing and cloning technologies have made such a lofty goal appear ever more plausible. To paraphrase the author Stewart Brand, whose Revive & Restore initiative is working to bring back the passenger pigeon, extinction punches holes in the fabric of nature; de-extinction creates the opportunity to fill those holes, restoring biodiversity and making ecosystems more resilient.

Two of the most talked-about candidates for revival are the thylacine, a marsupial tiger that was hunted to extinction in Tasmania in the 1930s, and the North American passenger pigeon, which was once the world's most abundant species but disappeared due to excessive hunting and the clearing of its forest habitat. Scientists have already brought back an odd species of mouth-brooding frog in Australia that swallows its own eggs and regurgitates its offspring when they hatch. Now, scientists could reconstitute many more species by replacing the DNA of closely related creatures with DNA from extinct species.

But reconstituting some extinct species is only the beginning. Synthetic biology is an emerging discipline that applies the tenets of engineering to modify, redesign, and even construct bacteria for specific purposes. Biologists are using advanced techniques in genetic sequencing and bioengineering to rewrite genetic code, manipulate the fundamental building blocks of biological functions, and assemble them within microbes that behave like tiny machines. Sophisticated equipment that was once available only to professional researchers in well-funded laboratories is now accessible to entrepreneurs in garage start-ups and to do-it-yourself hobbyists in community laboratories. This accessibility is rapidly accelerating the pace of innovation and expanding the scope of potential applications.

Synthetic biology could radically expand the possibilities for conservation. Consider, for example, the problem of desertification and land degradation. Every year, about 30 million acres of land succumb to desertification, rendering that land less productive for farming and threatening biodiversity. Around the world, as many as 5.4 billion acres of land—an area larger than the size of South America—have been degraded by land clearing, soil erosion, or unsustainable farming practices. Rehabilitating that land could help farmers meet rising food demands and could restore natural habitats. But it takes far longer to naturally revive soils and regrow natural vegetation than it takes to destroy them—and the planet cannot afford to wait.

Synthetic biologists are already seeking a faster solution. As part of the 2011 International Genetically Engineered Machine Competition, Christopher Schoene, a doctoral candidate in biochemistry at Imperial College London, came up with a way to use synthetic biology to accelerate the rehabilitation of damaged lands. Working with a small group of fellow students, Schoene designed a project to engineer microbes that could find plant roots and stimulate their growth to improve their absorption of water and essential nutrients. If such advances progress past the proof-of-concept stage, they could slow or counteract land degradation, since roots hold soil in place.

Of course, many important questions about the risks of such technologies have yet to be answered. Engineered microbes could have many negative impacts on natural organisms outside the laboratory. They could evolve such that their intended functions diminish or adapt in ways that pose unintended consequences. Nevertheless, the fundamental technologies are coming into place. Synthetic biology, as it advances, could be used to supercharge nature, helping it bounce back faster and stay stronger in the face of human pressures.

RISKY BUSINESS

Excitement about the possibilities of technology must be tempered by a recognition of their risks. For example, an explosion of wildlife crime in Africa is resulting in the slaughter of hundreds of rhinoceros for their horns and thousands of elephants for their tusks. Technology is helping conservationists defend against the poachers through improved monitoring and surveillance. But the information that conservationists are using for good could present a significant risk if it fell into criminal hands. Data security thus becomes as important as physical security in the bush.

Biotechnology applications could have any number of unintended consequences. Efforts to revive extinct species are controversial because they could create a moral hazard, making extinction risks seem less urgent. Some critics of biotechnology warn of a Jurassic Park scenario, in which a genetically engineered organism escapes from the lab and wreaks ecological havoc in the natural world. Such a fear is not unjustified given the economic and ecological damage invasive species have caused when introduced in places where they have few competitors or predators. Costly examples include the zebra mussel, which clogs water intakes in the Great Lakes, and the chestnut blight that nearly wiped out the American chestnut tree at the turn of the century. Synthetically engineered genes could also spread from modified plants or bacteria to other species, resulting in unexpected consequences: such a gene transfer is one of the primary mechanisms behind the rapid spread of antibiotic resistance among bacteria. Current evidence suggests that so-called horizontal gene transfers among genetically modified organisms are infrequent. Nonetheless, bioengineers will need to adopt safety measures to manage and diminish such risks. And scientists need to deepen their understanding of the ecology of engineered organisms and how they interact with other species in the environment.

Some of the most promising applications of technology to conservation may also be limited by a lack of basic infrastructure. Although I enjoyed excellent cell-phone connectivity in northern Kenya, many of the world's most important natural areas remain wild and off the grid. That means technologies that rely on connections to telecommunications and power networks won't work there—at least until those networks expand. The proliferation of more affordable satellite uplinks, microcell towers, and solar power has the potential to help overcome such limitations.

At the end of the day, however, technology is merely a tool—one that can help but also do harm. To maximize its potential benefits, conservationists and technologists will need to come together to determine how technology should and should not be used. But as rising populations and surging consumer demand stress the planet's ability to sustain vital resources, humanity needs all the help it can get. Technology may not be a panacea for the world's many environmental ills, but it could still help tip the balance toward a sustainable future.

Animal Rights, Animal Wrongs

The Case for Nonhuman Personhood

Steven M. Wise

Around the world, what the media often refer to as "the animal rights movement" is taking off. Mass protests, fierce lobbying, litigation, and draft treaties have led to new legislation at the national, provincial, and city levels. It is now forbidden to use great apes in biomedical research, to bullfight in Catalonia, and to operate factory farms and slaughterhouses without adhering to the stricter rules governing the treatment and living conditions of livestock. However, with a few exceptions, these efforts are not truly about "animal rights" but about "animal welfare."

One reason for this difference is that worldwide, animals are regarded as "legal things," incapable of having rights and treated as articles of property. In contrast, humans are deemed "legal persons," possessing intrinsic value and the capacity for an infinite number of legal rights as the owners of "legal things." Another reason is that the term "animal" encompasses the enormously diverse biological kingdom of animalia, which comprises more than 1.25 million known species (with more to be discovered) that fall along a vast continuum of consciousness, sentience, general intelligence, and autonomy. It

STEVEN M. WISE is President of the Nonhuman Rights Project. He has practiced animal protection law for 30 years throughout the United States. He is the author of four books, including *Rattling the Cage: Toward Legal Rights for Animals* (2000) and *Drawing the Line: Science and the Case for Animal Rights* (2003).

includes 60,000 vertebrates: 5,500 mammals, 10,000 birds, 6,200 amphibians, 30,000 fish, and 8,200 reptiles. The million-plus known invertebrates include about 950,000 varieties of insects, 81,000 mollusks, and 40,000 crustaceans.

At one end of this spectrum of mental capacity and awareness are animals such as sponges, jellyfish, and sea anemones that scientists believe are unlikely to be conscious or have an ability to feel pain or suffer. These are therefore unlikely to be appropriate subjects of animal welfare legislation (which focuses on preventing unnecessary pain and suffering), though they may be protected by environmental or conservation laws.

At some point along this continuum, however, a primitive level of consciousness and sentience kicks in. A great number of animals fall in this category, such as cows and sheep. These animals have been the subject of welfare legislation ever since the beginning of the nineteenth century, when early animal welfare movements in the United Kingdom sought to end cruel practices such as beatings and other inhumane treatment. Since then, the animal rights movement has struggled to make further progress with these types of animals. In 2000, an international group of venerable animal welfare organizations proposed the Universal Declaration on Animal Welfare (UDAW), which sought to reduce unnecessary cruelty toward the suffering of animals. In 2005, an intergovernmental steering committee was assembled to improve UDAW's chances of adoption. It received endorsements from a number of national veterinary associations, the World Organization for Animal Health, the United Nations Food and Agriculture Organization, and the Council of the European Union. UDAW's organizing values embrace the principles that animated the nineteenth-century anticruelty legislation.

Animals at the continuum's other end—including great apes, cetaceans (whales, dolphins, and porpoises), and elephants—possess a complex consciousness and self-consciousness, exquisite sentience, robust general intelligence, and a powerful sense of autonomy. They, too, have long received some protection from unnecessary cruelty. But rapid scientific advances over the last half century have demonstrated that their advanced levels of cognition leave them inadequately protected by anticruelty and similar legislation.

For example, chimpanzees can reflect upon their thoughts. They have powerful memories, can anticipate and prepare for the future, and even have a sense of moral agency—they ostracize those who violate social norms and respond negatively to inequitable situations. When playing economic games, chimpanzees spontaneously make fair offers and have a simple understanding of numbers. They have a material, social, and symbolic culture. For example, through a discipline known as "chimpanzee archaeology," it was discovered that some 4,300 years ago, chimps living in the rainforests of the Ivory Coast used stone tools to crack nuts. They passed this cracking technique over 200 generations of chimpanzees. These and other scientific advances have catalyzed a new and growing twenty-first-century "animal rights movement" that demands legal rights to protect these animals' fundamental interests.

The Nonhuman Rights Project, which I lead, is a pioneer when it comes to pushing for animal rights. We are working with legal groups on three other continents to assist them in achieving legal personhood for "nonhuman animals." We filed the first animal rights cases in the United States in 2013, in which we argued that four chimpanzees—Tommy, Kiko, Hercules, and Leo—were being held unlawfully by their alleged owners and were entitled to be released pursuant to a common-law writ of habeas corpus (one of the attractions of a common-law writ of habeas corpus is that it allows us to file suit on behalf of another who is being imprisoned). Our goal is to have these and other autonomous and self-determining animals declared to be legal persons, at least when it comes to unlawful detention.

The roots of the animal rights movement do not lie in the anticruelty legislation of the nineteenth century; they reach deeper into the worldwide antislavery movements that began in the eighteenth century and flowered into the broad international human rights movement of the twentieth century.

These newer animal rights campaigners' demands for fundamental legal rights for nonhumans are often misinterpreted as demanding "human rights" for nonhuman animals. But that is not correct; the new animal rights practitioners recognize that our subjects are not human. We are demanding legal rights that are appropriate to the levels of cognition that scientists are able to determine through their work with nonhuman animals both in the wild and in captivity. Therefore, chimpanzees are entitled to "chimpanzee rights," elephants to "elephant rights," and orcas to "orca rights."

The Nonhuman Rights Project spent years determining in which jurisdiction it would file its initial cases, finally settling on New York State. We identified seven chimpanzees and decided to file suit on behalf of two. But they both died, as did a third, before we could sue. We decided to pursue our case on behalf of the four survivors.

The Universal Declaration of Human Rights speaks, among other things, to humanity's dignity, entitlement to equal and inalienable rights, recognition as a legal person, and rights to life, liberty, equality, security, and freedom from enslavement. There is no rational reason why autonomous and self-determining nonhuman animals should not also possess equal and inalienable rights, recognition as a legal person, and rights to life, liberty, equality, security, and freedom from enslavement.

Over the centuries, we humans have slowly and painfully developed a core of near universal values and principles intended to protect our most fundamental interests. It is time we recognize that we share the planet with other species with similar fundamental interests and that our failure to protect those interests both wrongs the animals and subverts the core values and principles that protect our own.

The Day the Earth Ran Out

The Causes and Consequences of Earth Overshoot Day

Carter Roberts

Many readers will be familiar with the worrisome, white-knuckle wait that comes when you drain your checking account long before payday, the anxiety that builds until the coffers are replenished. That is what all of humanity has signed on for, effective today.

Earth Overshoot Day marks the moment when, according to Global Footprint Network, an independent think tank based in the United States, Switzerland, and Belgium, humanity's demand for natural resources exceeds the earth's ability to renew them in a year. As of today, just 34 weeks into 2013, we are officially in ecological overdraft.

Scientists and data-crunchers at Global Footprint Network calculate Earth Overshoot Day by dividing the earth's current biocapacity (the area of land and water available to produce renewable resources and absorb CO_2 emissions) by the world's ecological footprint (the area of land and water required to meet humanity's demand for resources and absorb waste). They then multiply the quotient by 365, the number of days in a calendar year. That number reveals Earth Overshoot Day. This year, that day arrived two

CARTER ROBERTS is President and CEO of World Wildlife Fund.

days sooner than it did last year. It has come earlier, by about three days each year, since 2001.

Both biocapacity and ecological footprint are measured in global hectares, a common unit that encompasses the average productivity of all the biologically productive land and sea area in the world in a given year. Measurements are drawn from Global Footprint Network's National Footprint Accounts, datasets for more than 230 countries, territories, and regions that contain more than 6,000 annually gathered data points per country. Although not yet perfect, these accounts provide the most comprehensive available aggregate indicator of human pressure on ecosystems.

Earth Overshoot Day is an approximation, but it is yet one more sign that humanity is consuming the planet's finite resources at an unsustainable rate. In 2013, humanity requires the equivalent of approximately 1.5 earths to produce the goods and services our lifestyles demand in one year and to absorb the attendant CO_2 emissions and other greenhouse gases. If the United Nations' moderate projections for growth in population and consumption are correct, we will need two earths before 2050. And that is not even counting on overshooting being aggravated as increased pressure on ecosystems makes less productive land and water available; some ecosystems will collapse even before a particular resource is completely gone.

To be sure, technology has improved biological productivity, but production is still well behind demand. On a global scale, the average person's ecological footprint has increased since 1961. And available biocapacity per person has nearly halved in the same time. In aggregate, adding up cropland, forest, grazing land, fishing grounds, built-up land, and land available for carbon sequestration—our accounts are overdrawn. At the same time, energy needs are on the rise, and agriculture production must somehow double by 2050 to keep pace with demand.

It is not shocking that some nations overshoot more than others. The per capita ecological footprint of high-income nations dwarfs that of low- and middle-income countries. The footprint of a typical American is ten times that of a typical resident of an African nation. China's per capita footprint is smaller than those of countries in Europe and North America but still exceeds the resources that are available per person worldwide. In all, more than 80 percent of the world's population lives in countries that use more than their own ecosystems can renew. Today's Japan requires 7.1 Japans to support itself, Italy needs 4 Italys, and Egypt needs about 2.5 Egypts.

Obviously, a challenge of this magnitude requires action from every corner of society—governments, nongovernmental organizations (NGOs), businesses, and consumers. But where to begin? With the U.S. Congress stalemated, the most traction might come from working with businesses, especially those that are major purchasers of commodities. Simple improvements to efficiency, reductions of waste, and the creation of sustainable supply chains would make a huge difference. At World Wildlife Fund, of which I am the president and CEO, we have signed memoranda of understanding with many of the major companies that are involved in the trade of the commodities that most impact deforestation and marine systems. These agreements involved assessing the risks and opportunities within each company's supply chains for those commodities that WWF has identified as the most important drivers for environmental conservation. In some cases, companies also promised to reduce carbon emissions. Further, earlier this month, CEOs from 15 companies responsible for producing 70 percent of global farmed salmon announced their commitment to deliver 100 percent Aquaculture Stewardship Council–certified products by the year 2020, in collaboration with the United Nations, the UN Food and Agriculture Organization, WWF, and others.

Businesses are utterly dependent on a reliable supply of natural resources, healthy communities, and the goodwill of a public that increasingly votes for sustainability with its wallet. So, out of pure self-interest, they should care about resource depletion. But that is not the only reason. As counterintuitive as it might seem, this is their moment to shine. Business, arguably more than any other sector, has the influence, money, and agility to begin leading the planet back toward sustainability, and ultimately press governments to enact regulations that matter.

In fact, there are four steps companies should take right now to let go of the myth of infinite resources and help ensure that the earth will still be available to sustain us in a generation or two. First, they should identify resource footprints, set targets for shrinking them, and measure performance against them. Companies manage what they measure. Setting hard targets can catalyze an entire enterprise toward resource efficiency.

Second, they should leverage their influence. A business is only as sustainable as its supply chain, and simply inviting suppliers to follow a company's lead will not guarantee sustainability. The most effective companies are demanding sustainability as a condition for doing business. Environmental certifications, such as those from the Forest Stewardship Council, the Marine Stewardship Council, Bonsucro, and others, offer ready-made solutions for making supply chains sustainable.

Third, companies should give consumers the sustainability consumers demand. A 2011 study by Cone Communications and Echo showed that 94 percent of consumers want products that are more environmentally responsible. And 93 percent want to know what companies are doing about sustainability. Consumers, especially in emerging markets like China, India, and Brazil, expect companies to take a part in solving environmental issues.

Finally, companies should forge partnerships. No organization can achieve sustainability alone. The area of overlapping interests on a Venn diagram of business, NGOs, and government is surprisingly large. Capitalizing on those interests with long-term, collaborative relationships is crucial to curbing ecological overshooting.

A few companies—Unilever, Wal-Mart, and Coca-Cola among them—have begun to demonstrate that it is possible to seek both profitability and sustainability. But capitalism on the whole is mostly concerned with the near term. At this point, though, so should we be when it comes to the earth's health. Humanity urgently needs markets with the foresight, wisdom, and discipline to help us live within our planet's means. In the absence of strong regulatory frameworks, companies need to set the pace for this work, and then drive for better government practice over time.

Like a twenty-something living on a credit card until payday, humanity will certainly coast to 2014, when a new "resource year" begins. It is not too late to bring our longer-term resource spending back in line with our finite resources, at least according to current measures. But Earth Overshoot Day is an unsettling reminder that we are closing in on the point of no return. It is time for businesses, and eventually governments, to seize this opportunity for leadership and begin producing more with less. And the rest of us must consume better, wiser, and more conservatively, before we overspend ourselves out of existence.

Environmental Alarmism, Then and Now

The Club of Rome's Problem—and Ours

Bjorn Lomborg

Forty years ago, humanity was warned: by chasing ever-greater economic growth, it was sentencing itself to catastrophe. The Club of Rome, a blue-ribbon multinational collection of business leaders, scholars, and government officials brought together by the Italian tycoon Aurelio Peccei, made the case in a slim 1972 volume called *The Limits to Growth*. Based on forecasts from an intricate series of computer models developed by professors at MIT, the book caused a sensation and captured the zeitgeist of the era: the belief that mankind's escalating wants were on a collision course with the world's finite resources and that the crash would be coming soon.

The Limits to Growth was neither the first nor the last publication to claim that the end was nigh due to the disease of modern development, but in many ways, it was the most successful. Although mostly forgotten these days, in its own time, it was a mass phenomenon, selling 12 million copies in more than 30 languages and being dubbed "one of the most important documents of our age" by *The New York Times*. And even though it proved to be

Bjorn Lomborg is an Adjunct Professor at the Copenhagen Business School and head of the Copenhagen Consensus Center. He is the author of *The Skeptical Environmentalist* and *Cool It.*

phenomenally wrong-headed, it helped set the terms of debate on crucial issues of economic, social, and particularly environmental policy, with malign effects that remain embedded in public consciousness four decades later. It is not too great an exaggeration to say that this one book helped send the world down a path of worrying obsessively about misguided remedies for minor problems while ignoring much greater concerns and sensible ways of dealing with them.

THAT '70S SHOW

If the 1950s and early 1960s had been a period of technological optimism, by the early 1970s, the mood in the advanced industrial countries had begun to turn grim. The Vietnam War was a disaster, societies were in turmoil, economies were starting to stagnate. Rachel Carson's 1962 book *Silent Spring* had raised concerns about pollution and sparked the modern environmental movement; Paul Ehrlich's 1968 book *The Population Bomb* had argued that humanity was breeding itself into oblivion. The first Earth Day, in 1970, was marked by pessimism about the future, and later that year U.S. President Richard Nixon created the Environmental Protection Agency to address the problem. This was the context in which *The Limits to Growth* resonated; its genius was to bring together in one argument the concerns over pollution, population, and resources, showing how so-called progress would soon run into the natural world's hard constraints.

Founded in 1968 and grandly declaring itself to be "a project on the predicament of mankind," the Club of Rome had set as its mission the gathering of the world's best analytic minds to find a way "to stop the suicidal roller coaster man now rides." This led it to Jay Forrester, an MIT professor who had developed a computer model of global systems, called World2, that allowed one to calculate the impact of changes in several variables on the planet's future. The club appointed a team led by two other MIT researchers, Donella Meadows and Dennis Meadows, to create an updated version, World3, and it was the output of this model that was presented in book form in *The Limits to Growth*. In an age more innocent of and reverential toward computers, the reams of cool printouts gave the book's argument an air of scientific authority and inevitability; hundreds of millions of logical microcircuits seemed to banish any possibility of disagreement.

The model was neither simple nor easy to understand. Even the graphic summary was mind-numbingly convoluted, and the full specifications of the model were published a year later, in a separate book of 637 pages. Still, the general concept was straightforward. The team "examined the five basic factors that determine, and therefore, ultimately limit, growth on this planet—population, agricultural production, natural resources, industrial production, and pollution." Crucially, they assumed that all these factors grow exponentially—a step so important that the whole first chapter of the book is dedicated to explaining it. They asked readers to consider the growth of lilies in a pond:

> Suppose you own a pond on which a water lily is growing. The lily plant doubles in size each day. If the lily were allowed to grow unchecked, it would completely cover the pond in 30 days, choking off the other forms of life in the water. For a long time the lily plant seems small, and so you decide not to worry about cutting it back until it covers half the pond. On what day will that be? On the twenty-ninth day, of course. You have one day to save your pond.

In the standard scenario, shown in Figure 1, the authors projected the most likely future that would play out for humanity. With the years 1900 to 2100 on the horizontal axis, the graph shows levels of population, pollution, nonrenewable resources, food, and industrial output on the vertical axis. As death rates drop significantly (because of improvements in medical knowledge) and birthrates drop slightly, population increases. As each person consumes more food and products, meeting the total demand "requires an enormous input of resources." This depletes the resource reserves available, making it ever harder to fulfill next year's resource demands, and eventually leads to the collapse of the economic system. Because of lags in the effects, population keeps growing until a staggering increase in the death rate driven by a lack of food and health services kills off a large part of civilization. The culprit is clear: "The collapse occurs because of nonrenewable resource depletion."

What if the world gets better at conserving resources or finding new ones? It doesn't matter. Run the model again with double or infinite resources, and a collapse still occurs—only now it is caused by pollution. As population and production explode, pollution does, too, crippling food production and killing off three-quarters of the population.

What if pollution is kept in check through technology and policy? It still doesn't matter. Run the model again with unlimited resources and curbs on pollution, and the prediction remains bleak. As production soars, the world's population does, too, and with it demands for food. Eventually, the limit of arable land is reached, and industry is starved as capital is diverted into ever-feebler attempts to increase agricultural yields. With food production back at the subsistence level, death rates shoot up, and civilization is again doomed.

Figure 1

The Future According to *The Limits to Growth*

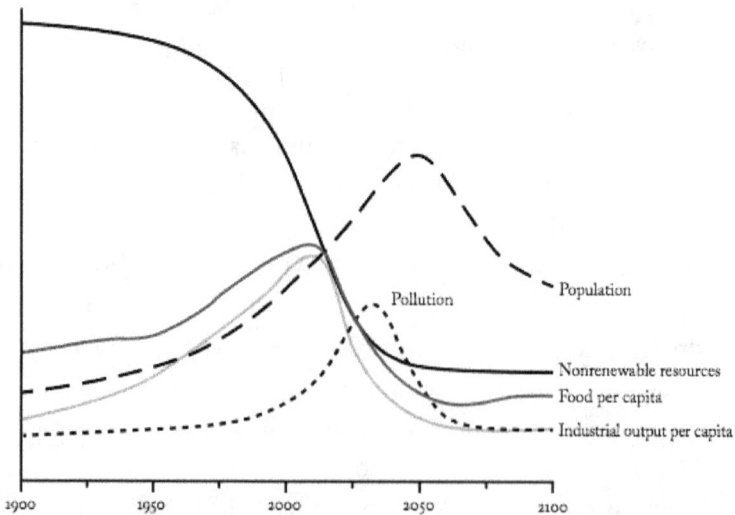

Pollution

Population

Nonrenewable resources
Food per capita
Industrial output per capita

1900   1950   2000   2050   2100

SOURCE: Adapted from *The Limits to Growth* (Universe Books, 1972), 124.

The authors concluded that the "basic behavior mode of the world system is exponential growth of population and capital followed by collapse." And "when we introduce technological developments that successfully lift some restraint to growth or avoid some collapse, the system simply grows to another limit, temporarily surpasses it, and falls back."

Unlike previous gloomy forecasts, this one offered no easy way out. Carson wanted to stop the use of pesticides; Ehrlich wanted to slow population growth. But *The Limits to Growth* seemed to show that even if pollution and population growth were controlled, the world's resources would eventually be exhausted and food production would decline back to the subsistence level. The only hope was to stop economic growth itself. The world needed to cut back on its consumption of material goods and emphasize recycling and durability. The only hope to avoid a civilizational collapse, the authors argued, was through draconian policies that forced people to have fewer children and cut back on their consumption, stabilizing society at a level that would be significantly poorer than the present one.

Since most people saw such a solution as wildly unrealistic, the real takeaway was simple: the world was screwed. And so *Time* magazine's 1972 story on *The Limits to Growth* was headlined "The Worst Is Yet to Be?" It read:

> The furnaces of Pittsburgh are cold; the assembly lines of Detroit are still. In Los Angeles, a few gaunt survivors of a plague desperately till freeway center strips, backyards and outlying fields, hoping to raise a subsistence crop. London's offices are dark, its docks deserted. In the farm lands of the Ukraine, abandoned tractors litter the fields: there is no fuel for them. The waters of the Rhine, Nile and Yellow rivers reek with pollutants.
>
> Fantastic? No, only grim inevitability if society continues its present dedication to growth and "progress."

The Limits to Growth got an incredible amount of press attention. *Science* gave it five pages, *Playboy* featured it prominently, and *Life* asked whether anyone wanted to hear "the awful truth."

Publications such as *The Economist* and *Newsweek* chimed in with criticisms, but in 1973, the oil embargo made the book look prescient. With the oil shock and soaring commodity prices, it seemed that the world was fast-forwarding to the Club of Rome future.

OOPS

Forty years on, how do the predictions stack up? Defenders like to point out that *The Limits to Growth* carefully hedged its bets, with its authors claiming that they were not presenting "exact predictions" and that they were "deliberately . . . somewhat vague" on time frames because they wanted to focus on the general behavior of the system. But this is sophistry. It was obvious from the way the book was both presented and understood that it made a number of clear predictions, including that the world would soon run out many nonrenewable resources.

Assuming exponentially increasing demand, *The Limits to Growth* calculated how soon after 1970 various resources would be exhausted. Their conclusion was that before 2012, the world would run out of aluminum, copper, gold, lead, mercury, molybdenum, natural gas, oil, silver, tin, tungsten, and zinc—12 of the 19 substances they looked at. They were simply and spectacularly wrong.

They singled out mercury, claiming that its known global reserves in 1970 would last for only 13 years of exponential growth in demand, or 41 years if the reserves magically quintupled. They noted that "the prices of those resources with the shortest static reserve indices have already begun to increase. The price of mercury, for example, has gone up 500 percent in the last 20 years." Since then, however, technological innovations have led to the replacement of mercury in batteries, dental fillings, and thermometers. Mercury consumption has collapsed by 98 percent, and by 2000, the price had dropped by 90 percent.

They predicted that gold might run out as early as 1979 and would certainly do so by 1999, based on estimations of 10,980 tons of known reserves in 1970. In the subsequent 40 years, however,

81,410 tons of gold have been mined, and gold reserves are now estimated to be 51,000 tons.

Known reserves of copper in 1970 came to 280 million tons. Since then, about 400 million tons have been produced globally, and world copper reserves are now estimated at almost 700 million tons. Since 1946, new copper reserves have been discovered faster than existing copper reserves have been depleted. And the same goes for the other three most economically important metals: aluminum, iron, and zinc. Despite a 16-fold increase in aluminum consumption since 1950, and despite the fact that the world has consumed four times the 1950 known reserves in the years since, aluminum reserves now could support 177 years of the present level of consumption. *The Limits to Growth* also worried about running out of oil (in 1990) and natural gas (in 1992). Not only have those not run out, but their reserves, measured in terms of years of current consumption, are larger today than they have ever been since 1970, even though consumption has increased dramatically.

WHAT THEY MISSED

The basic point of *The Limits to Growth* seemed intuitive, even obvious: if ever-more people use ever-more stuff, eventually they will bump into the planet's physical limits. So why did the authors get it wrong? Because they overlooked human ingenuity.

The authors of *The Limits to Growth* named five drivers of the world system, but they left out the most important one of all: people, and their ability to discover and innovate. If you think there are only 280 million tons of copper in the ground, you'll think you'll be out of luck once you have dug it out. But talking about "known reserves" ignores the many ways available resources can be increased.

Prospecting has improved, for example. As recently as 2007, Brazil found the Sugar Loaf oil field off the coast of São Paulo, which could hold 40 billion barrels of oil. Extraction techniques have also been improving. The oil industry now drills deeper into the ground, farther out into the oceans, and higher up in the Arctic. It drills horizontally and uses water and steam to squeeze out more from existing fields.

And shale gas can now be liberated with new fracking technology, which has helped double U.S. potential gas resources within the past six years. This is similar to the technological breakthrough of chemical flotation for copper, which made it possible to mine ores that had previously been thought worthless, and similiar to the Haber-Bosch process, which made nitrogen fixation possible, yielding fertilizers that now help feed a third of humanity.

Aluminum is one of the most common metallic elements on earth. But extracting it was so difficult and expensive that not so long ago, it was more costly than gold or platinum. Napoleon III had bars of aluminum exhibited alongside the French crown jewels, and he gave his honored guests aluminum forks and spoons while lesser visitors had to make do with gold utensils. Only with the invention of the Hall-Héroult process in 1886 did aluminum suddenly drop in price and massively increase in availability. Most often, however, ingenuity manifests itself in much less spectacular ways, generating incremental improvements in existing methods that cut costs and increase productivity.

None of this means that the earth and its resources are not finite. But it does suggest that the amount of resources that can ultimately be generated with the help of human ingenuity is far beyond what human consumption requires. This is true even of energy, which many think of as having peaked. Costs aside, for example, by itself, the Green River Formation in the western United States is estimated to hold about 800 billion barrels of recoverable shale oil, three times the proven oil reserves of Saudi Arabia. And even with current technology, the amount of energy the entire world consumes today could be generated by solar panels covering just 2.6 percent of the area of the Sahara.

Worries about resources are not new. In 1865, the economist William Stanley Jevons wrote a damning book on the United

Kingdom's coal use. He saw the Industrial Revolution relentlessly increasing the country's demand for coal, inevitably exhausting its reserves and ending in collapse: "It will appear that there is no reasonable prospect of any release from future want of the main agent of industry." And in 1908, it was Andrew Carnegie who fretted: "I have for many years been impressed with the steady depletion of our iron ore supply. It is staggering to learn that our once-supposed ample supply of rich ores can hardly outlast the generation now appearing, leaving only the leaner ores for the later years of the century." Of course, his generation left behind better technology, so today, exploiting harder-to-get-at, lower-grade ore is easier and cheaper.

Another way to look at the resource question is by examining the prices of various raw materials. The *Limits to Growth* camp argues that as resource constraints get tighter, prices will rise. Mainstream economists, in contrast, are generally confident that human ingenuity will win out and prices will drop. A famous bet between the two groups took place in 1980. The economist Julian Simon, frustrated by incessant claims that the planet would run out of oil, food, and raw materials, offered to bet $10,000 that any given raw material picked by his opponents would drop in price over time. Simon's gauntlet was taken up by the biologist Ehrlich and the physicists John Harte and John Holdren (the latter is now U.S. President Barack Obama's science adviser), saying "the lure of easy money can be irresistible." The three staked their bets on chromium, copper, nickel, tin, and tungsten, and they picked a time frame of ten years. When the decade was up, all five commodities had dropped in price, and they had to concede defeat (although they continued to stand by their original argument). And this was hardly a fluke: commodity prices have generally declined over the last century and a half (see Figure 2).

In short, the authors of *The Limits to Growth* got their most famous factor, resources, spectacularly wrong. Their graphs show resource levels starting high and dropping, but the situation is precisely the opposite: they start low and rise. Reserves of zinc,

Figure 2
The Decline of Commodity Prices

SOURCE: The index was calculated by merging *The Economist's* industrial commodity price index with the International Monetary Fund's commodity industrial inputs price index and adjusting for inflation.

Figure 3
The Growth of Natural Resource Reserves

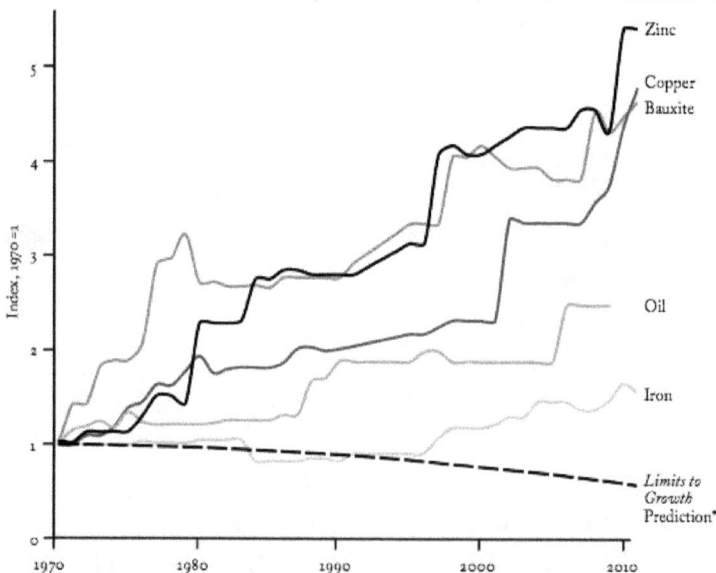

* *The Limits to Growth* considered various natural resources all together.
SOURCE: Julian L. Simon, Guenter Weinrauch, and Stephen Moore, "The Reserves of Extracted Resources: Historical Data," *Natural Resources Research* 3, no. 4 (1994): 325–340, updated with data from the U.S. Geological Survey.

copper, bauxite (the principal ore of aluminum), oil, and iron have all been going spectacularly up (see Figure 3).

MORE, MORE, MORE

What of the other factors in the analysis? Their devastating collapse was predicted to occur just after 2010, so it may be too soon for that to be definitively falsified. But the trends to date offer little support for the gloom-and-doom thesis.

The growth in industrial production per capita to date was slightly overestimated by *The Limits to Growth*, possibly because resources have gotten cheaper rather than more expensive and more and more production has moved into the service industry. But mainstream forecasts of long-term GDP growth, a plausible proxy, are positive as far as the eye can see, in sharp contrast to what *The Limits to Growth* expected. The Intergovernmental Panel on Climate Change, for example, the only major group to have set out informed GDP scenarios through 2100, estimates that global GDP per capita will increase 14-fold over the century and increase 24-fold in the developing world.

The amount of population growth was somewhat underestimated, mainly because medical advances have reduced death rates even faster than expected (despite the unforeseen HIV/AIDS crisis). But the population growth rate has slowed since the late 1960s, unlike the World3 predictions, because birthrates have fallen along with development.

And predictions about the last two factors, agricultural production and pollution, were way off—which is important because these were the two backup drivers of collapse if a scarcity of resources didn't do the job. Global per capita food consumption was expected to increase by more than 50 percent in the four decades after 1970, peak in 2010, and then drop by 70 percent. Calorie availability has indeed increased, if not quite so dramatically (by somewhat more than 25 percent), but the collapse of the food supply is nowhere in sight, and there is every reason to believe that the gains will continue and be sustainable. Malnutrition has not been vanquished, and the absolute number of people going hungry has in fact increased slightly recently (in part because some crops have been diverted from food to biofuel production due to concerns about global warming). But over the past 40 years, the fraction of the global population that is malnourished has dropped from 35 percent to less than 16 percent, and well over two billion more people have been fed adequately. The world is nowhere close to hitting a ceiling on the usage of arable land; currently, 3.7 billion acres are being used, and 6.7 billion acres are in reserve. Nor have productivity gains maxed out. The latest long-range UN report on food availability, from 2006, estimated that the world would be able to feed ever-more people, each with ever-more calories, out to midcentury.

As for its pollution predictions, *The Limits to Growth* was simultaneously scary and vague. Pollution's increase was supposed to trigger a global collapse if the decrease of food or resources didn't do so first, but how exactly pollution was defined was left unclear. Individual pollutants, such as DDT, lead, mercury, and pesticides, were mentioned, but how those could kill any significant number of people was unspecified, making it a bit tricky to test the prediction. Air pollution might be considered a good proxy for overall pollution, since it was the biggest environmental killer in the twentieth century and since the Environmental Protection Agency estimates that its regulation produces 86-96 percent of all the social benefits from environmental regulation more generally. In the developing world, outdoor air pollution is indeed rising and killing more people, currently perhaps over 650,000 per year. Indoor air pollution (from using dirty fuels for cooking and heating) kills even more, almost two million per year (although that number has been decreasing slightly).

Even in the developed world, outdoor air pollution is still the biggest environmental killer (at least 250,000 dead each year), although environmental regulation has reduced the death toll dramatically over the past half century. Indoor air pollution in the developed world kills almost nobody. Whereas the Club of Rome imagined an idyllic past with no pollution and happy farmers and a future world choked by fumes and poisons from industrialization run amok, the reality is quite different. Over the last century, pollution has neither spiraled out of control nor gotten more deadly, and the risk of death from air pollution is predicted to continue to drop (see Figure 4).

WHO CARES?

So the *Limits to Growth* project got its three main drivers spectacularly wrong and the other two modestly wrong. The world is not running out of resources, not running out of food, and not gagging on pollution, and the world's population and industrial output are rising sustainably. So what? Why should anyone care now? Because the project's analysis sunk deep into popular and elite consciousness and helps shape the way people think about a host of important policy issues today.

Take natural resources and the environment. Ask someone today whether he cares about the environment and what he is doing about it, and you are likely to hear something like, "Of course I

Figure 4
Pollution, Prediction Versus Reality

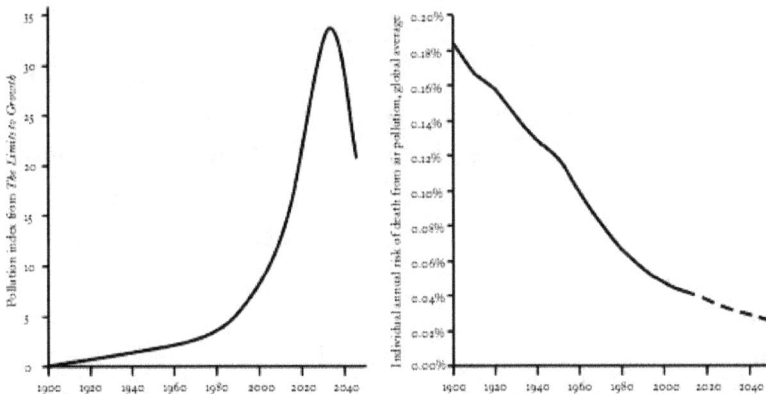

SOURCE: Adapted from *The Limits to Growth.*

SOURCE: Estimates by Guy Hutton in Bjørn Lomborg's forthcoming book, *The Twentieth-Century Scorecard* (Cambridge University Press).

care; I recycle." The caring part is all to the good and a major positive change from a few decades ago. But the recycling part is often just a feel-good gesture that provides little environmental benefit at a significant cost.

Recycling is not a new idea. It made sense for companies and people to recycle precious commodities long before the *Limits to Growth* project came along, and they did so. Copper, for example, was recycled at a rate of about 45 percent throughout most of the past century, for purely practical, and not environmental, reasons. Why wasn't the rate higher? Because some used copper comes in great bundles and is easy to reprocess, making the recycling effort worthwhile, whereas other used copper is dispersed in small, hard-to-get-at pieces, making recycling inefficient.

When people think of recycling today, however, they often think of paper. This, too, is not a new idea; trash has been a resource for centuries, with the extent of its culling and reprocessing depending on the current market prices of the goods in question. Throughout the past century, about 30-50 percent of all paper was recycled, before the advent of public information campaigns or peer pressure.

But now, in the wake of jeremiads such as *The Limits to Growth*, recycling tends to be seen less as an economic question and more as a matter of personal and civic virtue. Children learn to "reduce, reuse, and recycle" as part of their official moral education. They are told that by doing so, they are "saving trees." Yet in fact, well-managed forests for paper production in countries such as Finland and Sweden are continuously replanted, yielding not fewer trees but more. Artificially encouraging the recycling of paper lowers the payoff for such forests, making them more likely to be converted into agricultural or urban land. Nor does recycling paper save the rain forests, since it is not made with tropical timber. Nor does recycling paper address a problem of municipal waste: incineration can recapture much of the energy from used paper with virtually no waste problems, and even without incineration, all U.S. municipal waste from the entire twenty-first century could be contained in a single square dump that was 18 miles on each side and 100 feet high.

The effort to recycle substances such as paper and glass, however, consumes money and manpower, which are also scarce resources and could be expended on other socially valuable efforts, such as building roads or staffing hospitals. And so as the price of paper has declined and the value of human work has risen dramatically, today we pay tribute to the pagan god of token environmentalism by spending countless hours sorting, storing, and collecting used paper, which, when combined with government subsidies, yields slightly lower-quality paper in order to secure a resource that was never threatened in the first place.

What is true about resources, moreover, is also true about two of the other supposed drivers of collapse, population and pollution. Spurred by analyses such as that presented in *The Limits to Growth*, much time and effort over the years has been diverted from useful activities to dubious or even pernicious ones. The specter of an ever-increasing population chewing up ever-dwindling resources, for example, helped scare people into draconian responses such as the one-child policy in China and forced sterilizations in India. These actions were not warranted, and other policies could have done a better job, at lower cost and with more preferable outcomes. Increasing education for women, reducing poverty, and ensuring higher economic growth, for example, would have reduced family sizes with many more ancillary benefits.

Scary scenarios of pollutants such as DDT and pesticides killing off humanity, meanwhile, have led to attempts to ban them and to the widespread growth of the organic-food movement. But although it is true that the use of such products has costs—in large doses, DDT is likely harmful to birds, and even well-regulated pesticides probably cause about 20 deaths each year in the United States—it also yields substantial benefits. DDT is the cheapest and one of the most effective ways to tackle malaria. The ban on DDT in much of the developed world (which in itself might have made sense) led to pressures from nongovernmental organizations and aid agencies for bans elsewhere, and these campaigns, now abandoned by the World Health Organization, have likely contributed to several million unnecessary deaths.

In the developed world, the push to eliminate pesticides has ignored their immense benefits. Going completely organic would increase the cost of agricultural production in the United States by more than $100 billion annually. Since organic farming is at least 16 percent less efficient, maintaining the same output would require devoting an additional 50 million acres to farmland—an area larger than the state of California. And since eating fruits and vegetables helps reduce cancer, and since organic farming would lead to higher prices and thus lower consumption, a shift to purely organic farming would cause tens of thousands of additional cancer deaths.

Paying more than $100 billion, massively increasing the amount of the country's farmland, and killing tens of thousands of people seems a poor return for avoiding the dozens of American deaths due to pesticides annually. Yet this is how the *Limits to Growth* project and similar efforts have taught the world to think, making people worry imprudently about marginal issues while ignoring sensible actions for addressing major ones.

DO THE RIGHT THING

The problematic legacy of *The Limits to Growth* is not just the unnecessary recycling of paper and a fascination with organic produce. More generally, the book and its epigones have promulgated worst-case environmental-disaster scenarios that make rational policymaking difficult.

Alarmism creates a lot of attention, but it rarely leads to intelligent solutions for real problems, something that requires calm consideration of the costs and benefits of various courses of action. By implying that the problems the world faces are so great and so urgent that they can be dealt with only by massive immediate interventions and sacrifices—which are usually politically impossible and hence never put into practice—environmental alarmism actually squelches debate over the more realistic interventions that could make a major difference.

One of the most insightful original reviews of *The Limits to Growth*, by the economist Carl Kaysen in these pages, actually, was cleverly titled "The Computer That Printed Out W*O*L*F*." After mercilessly picking apart the flaws in the book's argument, it noted that in the fable of the boy who cried "wolf," "there were in the end, real wolves," just as "in the world today, there are real and difficult problems attendant on economic growth as we now experience it." The challenge is differentiating between false alarms and real ones and then coming up with prudent efforts at risk management.

Take pollution. Thanks to works such as *Silent Spring* and *The Limits to Growth*, worrying about pesticides captured much of the early environmental debate and virtually monopolized the policy agenda of the Environmental Protection Agency during the 1970s. Unfortunately, this did nothing to address the real wolf of indoor and outdoor air pollution. The latter may still kill some 135,000 Americans each year—more than four times the number who die in traffic accidents. But because it is less interesting and has no celebrity backers, it remains an ignored wolf—as is indoor pollution, which kills about two million people annually in the developing world.

But the Club of Rome did not just distract the world's attention. It actually directed that attention in precisely the wrong direction, identifying economic growth as humanity's core problem. Such a diagnosis can be entertained only by rich, comfortable residents of highly developed countries, who already have easy access to the basic necessities of life. In contrast, when a desperately poor woman in the developing world cannot get enough food for her family, the reason is not that the world cannot produce it but that she cannot afford it. And when her children get sick from breathing in fumes from burning dung, the answer is not for her to use environmentally certified dung but to raise her living standards enough to buy cleaner and more convenient fuels. Poverty, in short, is one of the greatest of all killers, and economic growth is one of the best ways to prevent it. Easily curable diseases still kill 15 million people every year; what would save them is the creation of richer societies that could afford to treat, survey, and prevent new outbreaks.

By recommending that the world limit development in order to head off a supposed future collapse, *The Limits to Growth* led people to question the value of pursuing economic growth. Had its suggestions been followed over subsequent decades, there would have been no "rise of the rest"; no half a billion Chinese, Indians, and others lifted out of grinding poverty; no massive improvements in health, longevity, and quality of life for billions of people across the planet. Even though the Club of Rome's general school of thought has mercifully gone the way of other 1970s-era relics, such as mood rings and pet rocks, the effects linger in popular and elite consciousness. People get more excited about the fate of the Kyoto Protocol than the fate of the Doha Round—even though an expansion of trade would do hundreds or thousands of times as much good as feeble limitations of emissions, and do so more cheaply, quickly, and efficiently for the very people who are most vulnerable. It is past time to acknowledge that economic growth, for lack of a better word, is good, and that what the world needs is more of it, not less.

Is Growth Good?

Resources, Development, and the Future of the Planet

Frances Beinecke; Dennis Meadows; Jørgen Randers; John Harte; Bjorn Lomborg

ENVIRONMENTALISTS DO NOT OPPOSE GROWTH

Frances Beinecke

In 1970, U.S. President Richard Nixon signed the Clean Air Act into law, launching one of the most successful public health and environmental programs in history. In the first decade that followed, in Los Angeles, the amount of pollution from ozone—the main component of smog—exceeded government health standards on 200 days each year. By 2004, that number had dropped to 28 days. In the 1970s, also as a result of polluted air, nearly 90 percent of American children had lead in their blood at levels higher than what the Centers for Disease Control and Prevention deemed safe, and parents were alarmed by studies showing that lead

FRANCES BEINECKE is President of the Natural Resources Defense Council.

DENNIS MEADOWS is President of the Laboratory for Interactive Learning and Professor Emeritus of Systems Policy at the University of New Hampshire. As a faculty member at the Massachusetts Institute of Technology in 1970-72, he directed the Club of Rome project and co-authored *The Limits to Growth*.

JØRGEN RANDERS is a Professor at BI Norwegian Business School. He is a co-author of *The Limits to Growth* and its two sequels.

JOHN HARTE is Professor of Ecosystem Sciences at the University of California, Berkeley.

MARY ELLEN HARTE is a biologist and columnist who writes on climate change and population.

interfered with cognitive development. Today, only two percent of children have such high levels of lead in their bodies.

By controlling hazardous emissions, the Clean Air Act delivered these and many other health benefits. And it did so without curbing economic growth. The United States' GDP has risen by 207 percent since the law was passed over four decades ago. And because the law sparked innovation—from catalytic converters, which convert toxic exhaust fumes from automobiles into less dangerous substances, to smokestack scrubbers—pollution reductions have proved relatively inexpensive. According to the U.S. Environmental Protection Agency, for every dollar the United States has spent on cutting pollution through the Clean Air Act, it has gained more than $40 in benefits.

Yet in his recent article ("Environmental Alarmism, Then and Now," July/August 2012), Bjørn Lomborg argues that the modern environmental movement has been distracted by unproductive goals and a desire to thwart economic growth. As evidence, he cites *The Limits to Growth*, a book published in 1972 by a group of scientists associated with the Club of Rome. The book cautioned that exponential increases in population, consumption, and pollution would exhaust the earth's finite natural resources and trigger the collapse of the world system. Lomborg rightly points out that the Club of Rome's worst forecasts never materialized, but he believes the book had a perverse effect on the way people think. "By recommending that the world limit development in order to head off a supposed future collapse," he writes, "*The Limits to Growth* led people to question the value of pursuing economic growth."

Lomborg assumes that those who acknowledge that the planet has finite resources must necessarily oppose economic progress. This framing reveals the limitations of Lomborg's argument. The question the environmental movement asks is not, "How can we arrest growth?" The question is, "What kind of growth do we want?" For decades, heads of state, economists, captains of industry, and environmental leaders have opted for the type of growth that allows economic output to rise, makes the air cleaner, and preserves the planet's resources at the same time.

The public call for environmental protection did not begin with the publication of a slender volume from the Club of Rome. It emerged from what people saw with their own eyes: raw sewage in the Great Lakes, smog so thick that it obscured the George Washington Bridge, oil despoiling Santa Barbara's pristine beaches, old-growth forests stripped bare in Oregon. It was Americans' desire to protect their families and their resources that ignited the modern environmental movement and inspired the passage of the Clean Air Act, the Clean Water Act, the Safe Drinking Water Act, and other landmark legislation.

Lomborg, however, claims that the Club of Rome's dire warnings distracted people from making real progress. "Spurred by analyses such as that presented in *The Limits to Growth*, much time and effort over the years has been diverted from useful activities to dubious or even pernicious ones." As an example, he says that instead of banning DDT, a known carcinogen, the United States should have focused on air pollution. He claims that because air pollution does not enjoy "celebrity backers," it has been "ignored." The lives saved by the Clean Air Act prove him wrong. For 40 years, the environmental movement has sought to make the air safer to breathe, the water cleaner to drink, and the wilderness better protected. Only those who forget the sight of yellow-brown haze or burning rivers would call this a distraction.

GETTING IT RIGHT

Today, a new set of images reveals the hazards not of economic growth per se but of the unsustainable exploitation of natural resources. These are not predictions from a 40-year-old report but measurements of real developments. Right now, 90 percent of the world's large fish, such as tuna, swordfish, and marlin, have disappeared thanks to overfishing. This is alarming not just for the sake of the species themselves but also for industry and food supplies: the National Ocean Economics Program reports that between 1997 and 2007, California's commercial fishing revenues dropped by 43 percent because fish stocks were plummeting. Meanwhile, 90 percent of West Africa's rain forests have been destroyed, and between 2000 and 2005 alone, the world lost rain-forest acreage equal to the size of Germany. The amount of carbon dioxide in the air has increased by 23 percent over the last 50 years, driving climate change and intensifying such extreme weather events as the 2010 floods in Pakistan, which affected 20 million people, and the 2011 floods in Thailand, which caused more than $45 billion in damage.

Accounting for the world's natural capital is not alarmist; it is wise. Clean air, a stable climate, plentiful fish, lush forests, fresh water, and energy resources are the building blocks of prosperity. Identifying how to tap them without exhausting them will open the door to economic growth.

Consider, for instance, the automobile industry. The United States can continue to waste oil, a limited and expensive resource, by burning it in inefficient engines that use outdated technologies. Or it can build cars that travel farther on less gasoline. The Obama administration has opted to encourage the latter by raising the fuel-efficiency standard to 54.6 miles per gallon by 2025. Within 20 years, better-performing cars will reduce U.S. oil use by more than the amount that the country imported from Iraq and Saudi Arabia in 2010. They will also save drivers more than $80 billion a year at the pump and, by 2025, halve the amount of carbon pollution emitted by vehicles in the United States.

Even if the United States finally starts to clean up its automobile fleet, demand for cars is rising around the globe. Right now, there are about 800 million vehicles in use; by 2050, that number will rise to 2.5 billion. If the world is to meet this demand without sending oil prices through the roof, endangering public health with dirty tailpipes, and intensifying climate change, then it must start finding ways to make this growth greener.

The same holds for rising energy needs. Two-thirds of the buildings that are projected to exist in India in 2030, for instance, have not yet been built. David Goldstein, a scientist at the Natural

Resources Defense Council, has argued that if India incorporates energy-saving features from the beginning of construction, it can reduce energy use by 50 percent at no additional cost. In other words, it makes more economic sense to start with efficient buildings than to retrofit them later. The production of efficient buildings and cleaner cars will generate billions of dollars for manufacturers and employ millions of people. That constitutes growth, but because it will use less energy and generate less pollution, it will be more sustainable growth.

Lomborg fails to account for these gains because he persists in thinking that environmental leaders oppose economic growth. He is mistaken. At the recent Earth Summit in Rio de Janeiro, nobody called for an end to growth. Instead, the 50,000 heads of state, mayors, business executives, and citizens who gathered there affirmed that, despite Lomborg's claims to the contrary, infinite growth in the consumption of finite resources is simply not possible. Those of us who are concerned for the environment want economic growth. After all, prosperity often leads to greater environmental protection. We just want to do it right.

PATTERNS, NOT PREDICTIONS
Dennis Meadows

According to Bjørn Lomborg, *The Limits to Growth*, a short book written 40 years ago (and of which I am a co-author), is "mostly forgotten." Nevertheless, he believes that the book "helped set the terms of debate on crucial issues . . . with malign effects that remain embedded in public consciousness four decades later."

Among those "malign effects" is the growing recognition that current economic policies can produce problems greater than their benefits. Lomborg rejects that perception, concluding, "It is past time to acknowledge that economic growth, for lack of a better word, is good, and that what the world needs is more of it, not less."

The expansion of economic output over the past 250 years has produced enormous gains in human welfare. But conditions have changed. Humanity must now become more nuanced in its policies. We noted this in *The Limits to Growth*, writing, "Any human activity that does not require a large flow of irreplaceable resources or produce severe environmental degradation might continue to grow indefinitely."

Lomborg quotes only the first edition of our book, long out of print. Thus, readers cannot easily form their own conclusions. In *Limits to Growth: The 30-Year Update*, we used more recent data but still reached the original conclusions.

Lomborg's critique of our report boils down to the assertion that we predicted the exhaustion of resources before the year 2000. But we said repeatedly in *The Limits to Growth* that it is impossible to predict the future of social systems precisely. Instead, our goal was to understand long-term patterns of development for world population, capital, and other physical variables. We showed 12 different scenarios of the future, seven portraying collapse and five showing possibilities for a sustainable future. We declared unambiguously that the scenarios were "not exact predictions of the values of the variables at any particular year in the future. They are indications of the system's behavioral tendencies only." We were interested in patterns, not predictions.

Unlike Lomborg, most readers noted this point. As the physicist Graham Turner wrote in a 2008 paper for Australia's Commonwealth Scientific and Industrial Research Organization (CSIRO) comparing *The Limits to Growth*'s predictions with "thirty years of reality," the book "was not intended to be predictive or for making detailed forecasts, but to provide a means for better understanding the behaviour of the world economic system."

Lomborg claims that *The Limits to Growth* "worried about running out of oil (in 1990) and natural gas (in 1992)." But as Matthew Simmons, who was an energy adviser to U.S. President George W. Bush and a member of the National Petroleum Council, wrote in a 2000 white paper on energy, "Nowhere in the book was there any mention about running out of anything by 2000. Instead, the book's concern was entirely focused on what the world might look like 100 years later. There was not one sentence or even a single word written about an oil shortage, or limit to any specific resource, by the year 2000."

Lomborg errs because his critique overwhelmingly draws on numbers he took from one data table in the first edition of *The Limits to Growth*. He presents those numbers as predictions generated by our computer model, even though our citations indicated that this table presented 1970 data compiled by the U.S. Bureau of Mines and other sources. We used the numbers solely to illustrate important differences between linear and exponential growth; they had no connection to our scenarios. What is more, Lomborg ignores the fact that we eliminated this table completely from the second and third editions of our book with no effect whatsoever on our results.

Lomborg makes many other important mistakes. His discussion of his Figure 2, on commodity prices, ignores the rise in the commodity price index since the year 2000, which may herald a permanent shift in the trend. His Figure 3, on natural resource levels, confuses resource reserves with their crustal abundance. The first can be increased by raising prices; the second cannot. His Figure 4 compares the effects of short-lived air pollution with our scenario values for long-lived toxics, a category from which we explicitly excluded air pollution.

Ignoring climate change, Lomborg suggests that conventional policies can solve society's problems. Many scientific studies contradict that view, most recently a report from IAP, a global network of 105 scientific academies. In June, IAP published a joint statement acknowledging that the global system is "on track to alternative futures with severe and potentially catastrophic implications for human well-being."

The Limits to Growth said this in 1972, and Turner's CSIRO report has reconfirmed our concern. After analyzing empirical information on the development of global society, Turner concluded, "The analysis shows that 30 years of historical data compares favorably with key features of [*The Limits to Growth*'s] business-as-usual scenario called the 'standard run' scenario, which results in collapse of the global system midway through the 21st Century."

To avert that result, we proposed deliberate measures for slowing physical expansion. Lomborg, by contrast, argues that human ingenuity alone will allow the world to overcome its environmental challenges. The problem is that he ignores the role ingenuity often plays in blocking constructive change. Irrespective of the problems it may cause humanity, every policy brings wealth, influence, and satisfaction to some. When that policy is challenged, its beneficiaries typically use their ingenuity to stymie useful alternatives. One may hope they will fail. But boosterism on the part of conventional economists only makes their task easier.

IT'S A SMALL WORLD

Jørgen Randers

The Limits to Growth has been aggressively criticized since it first appeared in 1972 (I am one of its co-authors). But much of the criticism has been directed at straw men, so much so that during the 1970s and 1980s, a number of people who had never read the book gradually came to believe that it contained a number of statements that its authors had never actually made. One of them is the widely repeated allegation that the book predicted the end of oil before 1990, which it did not. Bjørn Lomborg's essay, which reproduces many of the arguments long used against those statements, is a classic example of the faulty criticism of the book.

The reason *The Limits to Growth* was attacked so fiercely on imaginary grounds is simple: as the chemist Ugo Bardi noted in his book *The Limits to Growth Revisited*, the study challenged central tenets of the worldview held and cherished by many Westerners. But despite Lomborg's claims, some of the major trends discussed in *The Limits to Growth* have in fact matched real developments since 1972. For example, the global population reached only six billion in 2000, as forecast in the "business-as-usual" scenario in *The Limits to Growth*, not seven billion, as most demographers had predicted in 1972.

The fundamental message of *The Limits to Growth* was that the world is small, and that if we want to live well and long on a small planet, we need to limit our ecological footprint. The sad fact is that despite the study's warnings, humans are already overwhelming the earth's carrying capacity. Today, humans emit twice as much greenhouse gases per year as the world's oceans and forests can absorb. This so-called overshoot cannot last. If human society does not reduce the size of its footprint, the ecological systems that underpin its well-being will collapse. The world must now either accept long-term chaos for the sake of short-term comforts or make short-term sacrifices for the sake of long-term comforts. Unfortunately, around the world and particularly in market democracies, decision-makers too often disregard long-term consequences.

The Limits to Growth was supposed to help humanity make wiser policy choices. It warned that it was necessary to take action before distant problems became immediate crises and to spend on solutions while the sailing was still smooth. But the world's elites feared that such a change in the status quo would end both economic growth and their own privileged positions. And so the critics of *The Limits to Growth* instead tried to deny the problems it addressed and attacked the messenger.

Rather than joining in the critical effort to reduce man-made greenhouse gas emissions, Lomborg revives a number of straw men and inaccurate claims about what *The Limits to Growth* said. The study did not predict that oil and other resources would run out before 2000. It did not assume that population and GDP would grow exponentially; their growth rates vary and were computed as an outcome of other drivers in the model. Nor did *The Limits to Growth* state that air pollution could or would kill humanity. Rather, it tried to estimate how strong the effect of persistent long-term pollutants would be on human health and food production. In other words, the study did not simply forecast the end of the world as we know it; it encouraged a wise human response to create a sustainable world.

Lomborg's assessment of the present state of affairs is even more troubling. He sees a world that is well on its way toward solving its environmental crisis and cites the progress that it has made in curbing air pollution. But by ignoring emissions of carbon dioxide, Lomborg overlooks the single greatest long-term threat to the environment. Emissions of carbon dioxide matter much more than those of shorter-lived pollutants, such as sulphur dioxide, since those are washed out of the atmosphere in weeks. Carbon dioxide has a half-life of 100 years, and emitting it causes lasting damage to the planet's climate.

In my recent book and Club of Rome report, *2052: A Global Forecast for the Next Forty Years*, I argue that emissions of greenhouse gases will cause the world's temperature to rise to two degrees Celsius higher than in preindustrial times by 2052. In the following decades, the world will be three degrees Celsius warmer and probably warm enough to trigger a further and uncontrollable increase in the global average temperature caused by the gradual melting of the tundra. In short, this future is unpleasantly similar to the "persistent pollution scenario" from *The Limits to Growth*, with carbon dioxide as the persistent pollutant.

The rise in greenhouse gas emissions will be the critical factor that shapes the future of life on earth. These emissions could easily be reduced if humanity decided to take action. But held back by myopic decision-making, humanity will not likely change its behavior. In modern, democratic market economies, investments mainly flow to what is profitable, not to what is needed. And regulators, who could in principle consider both economic growth and larger social needs, do not receive the necessary political mandates from shortsighted voters who want low taxes and cheap prices. Society can address the environment's problems only if it regains some control over the flow of investments.

ALARMISM IS JUSTIFIED
John Harte and Mary Ellen Harte

In his essay, Bjørn Lomborg begins by criticizing the notion that the primary constraint on economic growth is the finiteness of resources, as if that remains the belief of the scientific community. Environmental scientists have long recognized, however, that the main limit to growth is not running out of resources but rather running out of space for the byproducts of that growth. Humans are filling the world's atmosphere with greenhouse gases, tainting its aquifer and surface water with deadly pollutants, eroding its soils, and allowing damaging toxics to build up in human bodies.

Obsessed with the numerical accuracy of projections made decades ago in *The Limits to Growth*, Lomborg ignores the importance of that study's qualitative insights, still valid today, concerning the interconnections between humanity and the natural world. The book illustrated the many ways in which increases in the human population and consumption levels undermine the sustainability of human society, including through pollution, the depletion of both renewable and nonrenewable resources, and industrial production. Lomborg also ignores some of the study's accurate quantitative insights: recent analyses by scientists show that *The Limits to Growth* was eerily correct in at least some of its most important projections. In a reexamination of the study, the ecologists Charles Hall and John Day showed that if a timeline were added to the book's predictions with 2000 at the halfway point, "then the model results are almost exactly on course some 35 years later in 2008."

The Limits to Growth countered the blissful ignorance of many economists and business magnates who wanted to believe in the convenient pipe dream of unlimited growth, denying the finiteness of the natural environment. Many policymakers did understand the value of the study, however, and tried to inculcate its basic concepts into our civilization, but without success. The scientific community thus still has educational work to do, and finishing it is essential to securing a future for our civilization.

WHAT THE SCIENCE SAYS

Lomberg promotes numerous misconceptions in his essay. Bemoaning The Limits to Growth's results as neither "simple nor easy to understand," Lomborg fails to grasp what many reputable scientists and policymakers have long known: that predicting the details of complex phenomena is difficult. In that light, *The Limits to*

Growth was just a first stab at analyzing the elaborate dynamics that cause continued economic growth to threaten the sustainability of human society.

Lomborg further displays scientific ignorance when he talks about pesticides. His estimate of 20 U.S. deaths annually from pesticides ignores both the ecological harm they cause and the human health problems, including cancer, hormone disruption, and neurological effects, associated with pesticide exposure. His argument that DDT is a cheap, effective solution to malaria overlooks the ability of mosquitoes, like other pests, to evolve resistance. Pesticides can be valuable tools when used as scalpels, but when they are used as bludgeons, the evolution of resistance often undoes their efficacy. This is why many epidemiologists fear that society is regressing from the happy era of working antibiotics.

Lomborg also perpetuates the denial of the multiple ways in which civilization is underpinned by a healthy environment. Yes, we can continue to expand into previously untapped arable land, but only at the cost of undermining the giant planetary ecosystems that assure humanity will have clean air, clean water, and a sustainable and benign climate. Yes, we can forgo recycling and grow plantations for paper, but only at the expense of biodiversity. Indeed, as increasing population growth and overconsumption degrade the environment, none of the economic growth that Lomborg hopes for will be possible. Moreover, the capacity of society and its institutions to maintain, let alone improve, the quality of life—a capacity that Lomborg takes for granted—will be at risk.

Lomborg retells the story of how the biologist Paul Ehrlich, the physicist John Holdren, and one of us lost a bet in 1990 after the economist Julian Simon wagered that the prices of a number of commodities would drop over a ten-year period. But had the bet been extended a few more years, the scientists would have won, because the prices of those commodities had, on average, risen. Simon later challenged ecologists to a new set of bets on the future; Ehrlich and the climatologist Stephen Schneider accepted the challenge and picked 15 environmentally significant trends, such as the concentration of greenhouse gases in the atmosphere and the amount of biodiversity on the planet. To our surprise, once he recognized the trends, Simon saw the writing on the wall and promptly backed out of the bet; he would have lost more than $10,000. Indeed, the limitations on the human enterprise extend beyond minerals. World hunger is increasing, as is the cost of basic food staples. The temporary advances of the environmental movement, such as the creation of more ecological reserves to protect biodiversity, are proving less and less effective faced with the sheer weight of further population growth and increasing consumption.

THE RIGHT KIND OF INNOVATION

Lomborg is correct that innovation is an important tool. Yet he seems to display a curious lack of confidence in human ingenuity when it comes to solving the environmental problems that science has identified to be of most concern to the future of humanity. He praises the very actions that cause climate disruption and pollution, such as offshore oil drilling, but has no such confidence that technological achievements can sharply reduce the world's dependence on fossil fuels. He revels in a food-production system that is awash in overused fertilizers, harmful pesticides, herbicides, and antibiotics, and is a major destroyer of the biodiversity on which it depends, but sees no hope for new inventions that could bring down the cost of organically produced food. Unfortunately, Lomborg seems to support ingenuity only in the cause of the trends he likes, rather than in the cause of technologies that could create a more sustainable future.

In fact, the scientific community knows how to transition to renewable clean energy to create a safer, more politically stable world and prevent destructive climate change without decreasing the quality of life. We know how to stem the problem of overpopulation by supplying family-planning knowledge and contraceptives to the more than 100 million women who lack them in developing countries. Where the world most needs the ingenuity that Lomborg assures us exists is in replacing an economic system hooked on perpetual growth and overconsumption by the rich with one that is much more equitable and sustainable.

Unlike Lomborg, most scientists understand the pernicious exponential effects of overpopulation on the environment. In 1993, 58 academies of science stated that "continuing population growth poses a great risk to humanity," and it now looks like the population could roughly double from its 1993 size by the end of this century. Other recent scientific statements have sounded an equally "alarmist" note, and with good reason. In March, for example, the participants at the "Planet Under Pressure" meeting, a gathering of climate-change scientists, declared that "the continued functioning of the Earth system as it has supported the well-being of human civilization in recent centuries is at risk. Without urgent action, we face threats to water, food, biodiversity and other critical resources: these threats risk intensifying economic, ecological and social crises, creating the potential for a humanitarian emergency on a global scale." To translate the warnings of the scientific community into action, the world desperately needs courageous political leadership to counter the powerful interest groups that continue to deny the unsustainability of humanity's current existence.

The Limits to Growth helped educate a generation, and now more than ever, those concerned for humanity need to promote the solutions that can make society more sustainable. The denial of science is a perfectly harmless activity done in the privacy of one's own home, but when scientific misconceptions are laid out in the pages of the public media, as in Lomborg's essay, it is a threat to the world's well-being.

LOMBORG REPLIES

The Limits to Growth predicted catastrophe: humanity would deplete natural resources and pollute itself to death. Its solution was less economic growth, more recycling, and organic farming. My essay documented how the book's predictions were wildly off, mainly because its authors ignored how innovation would help people overcome environmental challenges.

Because the book's goal was so dramatic—averting the end of the world—its recommendation was for society to simultaneously do everything in its power to forestall that outcome. Today, much of the environmental movement continues to evince such alarmism and, consequently, is unable to prioritize. Developed countries focus as much on recycling, which achieves precious little at a high cost, as they do on attaining the much larger benefits from tackling air pollution, a massive, if declining, threat. Meanwhile, some environmentalists' demands are simply counterproductive. Avoiding pesticides, for example, means farming more land less efficiently, which leads to higher prices, more hunger, more disease (because of a lower intake of fruits and vegetables), and less biodiversity.

My essay argued that although the *The Limits to Growth*'s analysis has been proved wrong, much of its doomsaying and policy advice still pervades the environmental debate 40 years later. These four critiques, instead of refuting my argument, in fact vindicate it.

First, only Dennis Meadows really tries to defend *The Limits to Growth*'s predictions of collapse, and he does so with little conviction. Second, at least some of the responses accept in principle that society needs to prioritize among its different environmental goals and that economic growth will make achieving them easier—in Frances Beinecke's words, "prosperity often leads to greater environmental protection." Third, all four of the critiques of my essay rely on the language of doom to motivate action, which, to the detriment of the environment, convinces society that it must pursue all its environmental goals at once, regardless of the costs and benefits. Finally, by focusing on the threats of economic growth to the environment, the authors generally neglect that growth has lifted billions of people out of grinding poverty and that others may remain poor because of the developed world's environmental concerns, real or imagined.

WRONG AGAIN

Defending *The Limits to Growth*, Meadows curiously complains that I address only the original book, which is "long out of print."

He then posits that my case rests on one table from that book, on resource depletion, which he says I misrepresent. That is incorrect on several counts.

First, it is patently false to claim, as Meadows does by way of a quotation from Matthew Simmons, that "nowhere in the book was there any mention about running out of anything by 2000." (Jørgen Randers makes a similar point.) *The Limits to Growth* quoted approvingly the first annual report by the U.S. government's Council on Environmental Quality, in 1970: "It would appear at present that the quantities of platinum, gold, zinc and lead are not sufficient to meet demands. At the present rate of expansion . . . silver, tin and uranium may be in short supply even at higher prices by the turn of the century." Meadows' own table publicized "the number of years known global reserves will last at current global consumption," showing that gold, lead, mercury, silver, tin, and zinc would not last to the year 2000. The instances go on.

According to the book's model, the main driver of the global system's so-called collapse would be the depletion of resources, and averting that outcome was the book's widely publicized rallying cry. So focusing on that aspect of the book can hardly be called a misrepresentation. What is more, claiming that this is my only critique ignores that I also showed how the book got pollution wrong and how its analysis of collapse simply did not follow.

Meadows and Randers both claim that in their model, pollution consisted of long-lived toxics, not air pollution. In fact, they were much more vague on this question in 1972. In the best case for their predictions of deadly pollution, they meant air pollution, which today accounts for about 62 percent of all environmental deaths, according to the World Bank and the World Health Organization. But if they indeed meant long-lived toxics, their prediction that "pollution rises very rapidly, causing an immediate increase in the death rate" has been clearly disproven by the declining global death rate and the massive reductions in persistent pollutants.

John Harte and Mary Ellen Harte put forth a similarly weak defense of *The Limits to Growth*, as they do not challenge my data.

They quote an article by the ecologists Charles Hall and John Day to say that *The Limits to Growth*'s results were "almost exactly on course some 35 years later in 2008." This is simply wrong when it comes to resource levels, as the data in my original article shows, and indeed the cited article contains not a single reference for its claims about oil and copper resource reductions.

Harte and Harte further argue that the increase in the cost of resources during the last ten years is evidence of "the limitations on the human enterprise." Meadows claims that this uptick may "herald a permanent shift in the trend." Yet neither carries through the argument, because the empirical data from the past 150 years overwhelmingly undermine it. The reason is that a temporary increase in the scarcity of a resource causes its price to rise, which in turn encourages more exploration, substitution, and innovation across the entire chain of production, thereby negating any increase in scarcity.

Harte and Harte demonstrate the unpleasant arrogance that accompanies the true faith, claiming that I "deny" knowledge, promote "scientific misconceptions," and display "scientific ignorance." They take particular issue with my assertion that DDT is a cheap solution to malaria, stating that I overlooked the issue of biological resistance. In fact, all malarial treatments face this problem, but DDT less so than the others. Whereas many malarial treatments, such as dieldrin, work only by killing insects, DDT also repels and irritates them. Dieldrin strongly selects for resistance, whereas DDT works in three ways and even repels 60 percent of DDT-resistant mosquitoes.

FALSE ALARM

All four critiques contain grand dollops of doom. Beinecke invokes "alarming" environmental problems from overfishing to the destruction of the rain forests and global warming. These are real issues, but they, too, deserve practical thinking and careful prioritization. Fish and rain forests, like other resources subject to political control, tend to be overused. By contrast, when resources are controlled by individuals and private groups, their owners are forced to weigh long-term sustainability.

Indeed, Beinecke's response reflects the most unfortunate legacy of *The Limits to Growth*: because of its persistent belief that the planet is in crisis, the environmental movement suggests tackling all environmental problems at once. This is impossible, of course, so society ends up focusing mainly on what catches the public's attention. Beinecke acknowledges that campaigns to enact environmental policy "emerged from what people saw with their own eyes: raw sewage in the Great Lakes, smog so thick that it obscured the George Washington Bridge, oil despoiling Santa Barbara's pristine beaches." Yet the smog killed more than 300,000 Americans annually, whereas the effects of the oil spills, although serious, were of a much lower order of magnitude.

She claims that the U.S. Clean Air Act somehow contradicts my argument, when I in fact emphasized that society should have focused much more on cleaner air. Today, roughly 135,000 Americans still die from outdoor air pollution each year, and two million people, mostly in the developing world, die from indoor air pollution. Instead of focusing on the many negligible environmental problems that catch the public's attention, as the U.S. Environmental Protection Agency did when it focused so heavily on pesticides in the 1970s and 1980s, government should tackle the most important environmental problems, air quality chief among them. Beinecke misses this tradeoff entirely.

Harte and Harte demonstrate a similar lack of proportion and priority. In response to my claim that a slightly larger portion of the world's arable land—roughly five percent—will need to be tapped in order to feed humanity, they offer an unsubstantiated fear that such an expansion would undermine "giant planetary ecosystems." Yet when they fret about pesticides, they seem impervious to the fact that eschewing them would require society to increase the acreage of land it farms by more than ten times that amount.

COOL DOWN

If *The Limits to Growth* erred in some of its quantitative projections, then perhaps, as Harte and Harte put it, its "qualitative insights [are] still valid today." Randers cites global warming as the new reason the book was right. Discussing his predictions for high carbon dioxide emissions, Randers writes, "This future is unpleasantly similar to the 'persistent pollution scenario' from *The Limits to Growth*."

But the comparison is unfounded and leads to poor judgment. In *The Limits to Growth*'s original formulation, pollution led to civilizational decline and death. Although many environmentalists discuss global warming in similarly cataclysmic terms, the scenarios from the Intergovernmental Panel on Climate Change project instead a gradually worsening drag on development. Standard analyses show a reduction of zero to five percent of global GDP by 2100, in a world where the average person in the developing world will be 23 times as rich as he or she is today.

Moreover, although the responses to my essay invoke global warming as a new rallying cry for environmental activism, they fail to suggest specific actions to avert it. Harte and Harte claim that "the scientific community knows how to transition to renewable clean energy." Sure, developed countries have the technical know-how to adopt clean energy, but they have not done so because it would still be phenomenally expensive. Policies aimed at stopping climate change have failed for the last two decades because much of the environmental movement, clutching dearly to *The Limits to Growth*'s alarmism and confident sense of purpose, has refused to weigh the costs and benefits and has demanded that countries immediately abandon all polluting sources of energy.

Many economists, including the 27 climate economists involved in the 2009 Copenhagen Consensus on Climate conference, have pointed out smarter ways forward. The best means of tackling global warming would be to make substantial investments in green energy research and development, in order to find a way to produce clean energy at a lower cost than fossil fuels. As one of the leading advocates of this approach, I cannot comprehend how Harte and Harte could claim that I do not support clean-energy innovation.

Unfortunately, the world will be hard-pressed to focus on smarter environmental policies until it has expunged the dreadful doom of *The Limits to Growth*. And unless the environmental movement can overcome its fear of economic growth, it will also too easily forget the plight of the billions of poor people who require, above all, more and faster growth.

No Wars for Water

Why Climate Change
Has Not Led to Conflict

Shlomi Dinar, Lucia De Stefano,
James Duncan, Kerstin Stahl,

T he world economic downturn and upheaval in the Arab world might grab headlines, but another big problem looms: environmental change. Along with extreme weather patterns, rising sea levels, and other natural hazards, global warming disrupts freshwater resource availability—with immense social and political implications. Earlier this year, the Office of the Director of National Intelligence published a report, *Global Water Security*, assessing hydropolitics around the world. In it, the authors show that international water disputes will affect not only the security interests of riparian states, but also of the United States.

SHLOMI DINAR is associate professor in the Department of Politics and International Relations and associate director of the School of International and Public Affairs at Florida International University.

LUCIA DE STEFANO is associate professor at Complutense University of Madrid and researcher at the Water Observatory of the Botín Foundation.

JAMES DUNCAN is consultant on natural resource governance and geography with the World Bank.

KERSTIN STAHL is senior scientist at the Institute of Hydrology in the University of Freiburg.

KENNETH M. STRZEPEK is research scientist with the Massachusetts Institute of Technology Joint Program on the Science and Policy of Global Change.

AARON T. WOLF is a professor of geography in the College of Earth, Ocean, and Atmospheric Sciences at Oregon State University.

Shlomi Dinar, Lucia De Stefano, James Duncan, Kerstin Stahl,

In many parts of the world, freshwater is already a scarce resource. It constitutes only 2.5 percent of all available water on the planet. And only about .4 percent of that is easily accessible for human consumption. Of that tiny amount, a decreasing share is potable because of pollution and agricultural and industrial water use. All that would be bad enough, but many freshwater bodies are shared among two or more riparian states, complicating their management.

Of course, the policy community has long prophesied impending "water wars." In 2007, UN Secretary General Ban Ki Moon warned that "water scarcity . . . is a potent fuel for wars and conflict." Yet history has not witnessed many. In fact, the only official war over water took place about 4,500 years ago. It was a conflict between the city-states of Lagash and Umma in modern day Iraq over the Tigris river. More recently, there have been some close calls, especially in the arid Middle East. About two years before the 1967 War, Israel and Syria exchanged fire over the Jordan River Basin, which both said the other was overusing. The limited armed clashes petered out, but the political dispute over the countries' shared water sources continues. In 2002, Lebanon constructed water pumps on one of the river's tributaries, which caused concern for downstream Israel. The project never provoked any formal military action, but with peace in the region already precarious, verbal exchanges between the two countries prompted the United States to step in. Both parties eventually accepted a compromise that would allow Lebanon to withdraw a predetermined amount of water for its domestic needs.

In short, predictions of a Water World War are overwrought. However, tensions over water usage can still exacerbate other existing regional conflicts. Climate change is expected to intensify droughts, floods, and other extreme weather conditions that jeopardize freshwater quantity and quality and therefore act as a threat-multiplier, making shaky regions shakier.

So what river basins constitute the biggest risks today? In a World Bank report we published in 2010 (as well as a subsequent article in a special issue of the *Journal of Peace Research*) we analyzed the physical effects of climate change on international rivers. We modeled the variability in river annual runoff in the past and for future climate scenarios. We also considered the existence and nature of the institutional capacity around river basins, in the form of international water treaties, to potentially deal with the effects of climate change.

According to our research, 24 of the world's 276 international river basins are already experiencing increased water variability. These 24 basins, which collectively serve about 332 million people, are at high risk of water related political tensions. The majority of the basins are located in northern and sub-Saharan Africa. A few others are located in the Middle East, south-central Asia, and South America. They include the Tafna (Algeria and Morocco), the Dasht (Iran and Pakistan), the Congo (Central Africa), Lake Chad (Central Africa), the Niger (Western Africa), the Nile (Northeastern Africa), and the Chira (Ecuador and Peru). There are no strong treaties governing the use of these water reserves in tense territories. Should conflicts break out, there are no good mechanisms in place for dealing with them.

By 2050, an additional 37 river basins, serving 83 million people, will be at high risk for feeding into political tensions. As is the case currently, a large portion of these are in Africa. But, unlike today, river basins within Central Asia, Eastern Europe, Central Europe, and Central America will also be at high risk within 40 years. Some of these include the Kura-Araks (Iran, Turkey, and the Caucasus), the Neman (Eastern Europe) Asi-Orontes (Lebanon, Syria, Turkey), and the Catatumbo Basins (Colombia and Venezuela).

CROSSING THE NILE

Among the larger African basins, the Nile has the greatest implications for regional and global security. Tensions over access to the river already pit Ethiopia and Egypt, two important Western allies, against one another. Egypt has been a major player in the Middle

East Peace Process and Ethiopia is an important regional force in the Horn of Africa, currently aiding other African forces to battle Al-Shabbab in Somalia.

Over the years, a number of international water treaties have made rules for the basin, but they are largely limited to small stretches of it. In particular, only Egypt and Sudan are party to the 1959 Nile River Agreement, the principal treaty regarding the river. Egypt, which is the furthest downstream yet is one of the most powerful countries in the region, has been able to heavily influence the water-sharing regime. Upstream countries, such as Ethiopia and Burundi, have been left out, hard-pressed to harness the Nile for their own needs.

In 1999, with increasingly vitriolic rhetoric between Egypt and Ethiopia sidetracking regional development, the World Bank stepped up its involvement in the basin. It helped create a network of professional water managers as well as a set of investments in a number of sub-basins. Still, the drafting of a new agreement stalled: upstream countries would not compromise on their right to develop water infrastructure while downstream countries would not compromise on protecting their shares. In 2010, Ethiopia signed an agreement with a number of the other upstream countries hoping to balance against Egypt and Sudan. More recently, the country has also announced plans to construct a number of large upstream dams, which could affect the stability of the region.

By 2050, the environmental state of the Nile Basin will be even worse. That is why it is important to create a robust and equitable water treaty now. Such a treaty would focus on ways to harness the river's hydropower potential to satiate the energy needs of all the riparian states while maintaining ecosystem health. The construction of dams and reservoirs further upstream could likewise help even out water flows and facilitate agricultural growth. Projects such as these, mitigating damage to ecosystem health and local populations, would benefit all parties concerned and thus facilitate further basin-wide cooperation.

UP IN THE ARAL

Another water basin of concern is the Aral Sea, which is shared by Kazakhstan, Kyrgyzstan, Tajikistan, Turkmenistan, and Uzbekistan. The basin consists of two major rivers, the Syr Darya and Amu Darya. During the Soviet era, these two rivers were managed relatively effectively. The break-up of the Soviet Union, however, ended that. The major dispute now is between upstream Kyrgyzstan and downstream Uzbekistan over the Syr Darya. During the winter, Kyrgyzstan needs flowing water to produce hydroelectricity whereas Uzbekistan needs to store water to later irrigate cotton fields.

The countries have made several attempts to resolve the dispute. In particular, downstream Uzbekistan, which is rich in fuel and gas, has provided energy to Kyrgyzstan to compensate for keeping water in its large reservoirs until the cotton-growing season. Such barter agreements, however, have had limited success because they are easily manipulated. Downstream states might deliver less fuel during a rainy year, claiming they need less water from upstream reservoirs, and upstream states might deliver less water in retaliation. Kyrgyzstan, frustrated and desperate for energy in winter months, plans to build mega hydro-electric plants in its territory. And another upstream state, Tajikistan, is likewise considering hydro-electricity to satiate its own energy needs. Meanwhile, Uzbekistan is building large reservoirs.

Although these plans might make sense in the very near term, they are inefficient in the medium and long term because they don't solve the real needs of downstream states for large storage capacity to protect against water variability across time. In fact, both Kyrgyzstan and Uzbekistan, along with Kazakhstan, will see substantial increases in water variability between now and 2050. And so, the need to share the benefits of existing large-capacity upstream reservoirs and coordinate water uses through strong and more efficient inter-state agreements is unavoidable.

A stabilized Aral Sea basin would also benefit the United States. With its withdrawal from Afghanistan, Washington has been

Shlomi Dinar, Lucia De Stefano, James Duncan, Kerstin Stahl,

courting Uzbekistan as a potential alternative ally and provider of stability in the region. The Uzbek government seems willing to host U.S. military bases and work as a counter-weight to Russia. Kyrgyzstan is also an important regional player. The Manas Air Base, the U.S. military installation near Bishkek, is an important transit point. The country is also working with the United States to battle drug trafficking and infiltration of criminal and insurgent groups. Regional instability could disrupt any of these strategic relationships.

If the past is any indication, the world probably does not need to worry about impending water wars. But they must recognize how tensions over water can easily fuel larger conflicts and distract states from other important geopolitical and domestic priorities. Since formal inter-state institutions are key to alleviating tensions over shared resources, it would be wise, then, for the involved governments as well as the international community to negotiate sufficiently robust agreements to deal with impending environmental change. Otherwise, freshwater will only further frustrate stability efforts in the world's volatile regions.

The Devolution of the Seas

The Consequences of Oceanic Destruction

Alan B. Sielen

O f all the threats looming over the planet today, one of the most alarming is the seemingly inexorable descent of the world's oceans into ecological perdition. Over the last several decades, human activities have so altered the basic chemistry of the seas that they are now experiencing evolution in reverse: a return to the barren primeval waters of hundreds of millions of years ago.

A visitor to the oceans at the dawn of time would have found an underwater world that was mostly lifeless. Eventually, around 3.5 billion years ago, basic organisms began to emerge from the primordial ooze. This microbial soup of algae and bacteria needed little oxygen to survive. Worms, jellyfish, and toxic fireweed ruled the deep. In time, these simple organisms began to evolve into higher life forms, resulting in the wondrously rich diversity of fish, corals, whales, and other sea life one associates with the oceans today.

Yet that sea life is now in peril. Over the last 50 years—a mere blink in geologic time—humanity has come perilously close to

ALAN B. SIELEN is Senior Fellow for International Environmental Policy at the Center for Marine Biodiversity and Conservation at the Scripps Institution of Oceanography. He was Deputy Assistant Administrator for International Activities at the U.S. Environmental Protection Agency from 1995 to 2001.

reversing the almost miraculous biological abundance of the deep. Pollution, overfishing, the destruction of habitats, and climate change are emptying the oceans and enabling the lowest forms of life to regain their dominance. The oceanographer Jeremy Jackson calls it "the rise of slime": the transformation of once complex oceanic ecosystems featuring intricate food webs with large animals into simplistic systems dominated by microbes, jellyfish, and disease. In effect, humans are eliminating the lions and tigers of the seas to make room for the cockroaches and rats.

The prospect of vanishing whales, polar bears, bluefin tuna, sea turtles, and wild coasts should be worrying enough on its own. But the disruption of entire ecosystems threatens our very survival, since it is the healthy functioning of these diverse systems that sustains life on earth. Destruction on this level will cost humans dearly in terms of food, jobs, health, and quality of life. It also violates the unspoken promise passed from one generation to the next of a better future.

LAYING WASTE

The oceans' problems start with pollution, the most visible forms of which are the catastrophic spills from offshore oil and gas drilling or from tanker accidents. Yet as devastating as these events can be, especially locally, their overall contribution to marine pollution pales in comparison to the much less spectacular waste that finds its way to the seas through rivers, pipes, runoff, and the air. For example, trash—plastic bags, bottles, cans, tiny plastic pellets used in manufacturing—washes into coastal waters or gets discarded by ships large and small. This debris drifts out to sea, where it forms epic gyres of floating waste, such as the infamous Great Pacific Garbage Patch, which spans hundreds of miles across the North Pacific Ocean.

The most dangerous pollutants are chemicals. The seas are being poisoned by substances that are toxic, remain in the environment for a long time, travel great distances, accumulate in marine life, and move up the food chain. Among the worst culprits are heavy metals such as mercury, which is released into the atmosphere by the burning of coal and then rains down on the oceans, rivers, and lakes; mercury can also be found in medical waste.

Hundreds of new industrial chemicals enter the market each year, most of them untested. Of special concern are those known as persistent organic pollutants, which are commonly found in streams, rivers, coastal waters, and, increasingly, the open ocean. These chemicals build up slowly in the tissues of fish and shellfish and are transferred to the larger creatures that eat them. Studies by the U.S. Environmental Protection Agency have linked exposure to persistent organic pollutants to death, disease, and abnormalities in fish and other wildlife. These pervasive chemicals can also adversely affect the development of the brain, the neurologic system, and the reproductive system in humans.

Then there are the nutrients, which increasingly show up in coastal waters after being used as chemical fertilizers on farms, often far inland. All living things require nutrients; excessive amounts, however, wreak havoc on the natural environment. Fertilizer that makes its way into the water causes the explosive growth of algae. When these algae die and sink to the sea floor, their decomposition robs the water of the oxygen needed to support complex marine life. Some algal blooms also produce toxins that can kill fish and poison humans who consume seafood.

The result has been the emergence of what marine scientists call "dead zones"—areas devoid of the ocean life people value most. The high concentration of nutrients flowing down the Mississippi River and emptying into the Gulf of Mexico has created a seasonal offshore dead zone larger than the state of New Jersey. An even larger dead zone—the world's biggest—can be found in the Baltic Sea, which is comparable in size to California. The estuaries of China's two greatest rivers, the Yangtze and the Yellow, have similarly lost their complex marine life. Since 2004, the total number of such aquatic wastelands worldwide has more than quadrupled, from 146 to over 600 today.

TEACH A MAN TO FISH—THEN WHAT?

Another cause of the oceans' decline is that humans are simply killing and eating too many fish. A frequently cited 2003 study in the journal *Nature* by the marine biologists Ransom Myers and Boris Worm found that the number of large fish—both open-ocean species, such as tuna, swordfish, and marlin, and large groundfish, such as cod, halibut, and flounder—had declined by 90 percent since 1950. The finding provoked controversy among some scientists and fishery managers. But subsequent studies have confirmed that fish populations have indeed fallen dramatically.

In fact, if one looks back further than 1950, the 90 percent figure turns out to be conservative. As historical ecologists have shown, we are far removed from the days when Christopher Columbus reported seeing large numbers of sea turtles migrating off the coast of the New World, when 15-foot sturgeon bursting with caviar leaped from the waters of the Chesapeake Bay, when George Washington's Continental army could avoid starvation by feasting on swarms of shad swimming upriver to spawn, when dense oyster beds nearly blocked the mouth of the Hudson River, and when the early-twentieth-century American adventure writer Zane Grey marveled at the enormous swordfish, tuna, wahoo, and grouper he found in the Gulf of California.

Today, the human appetite has nearly wiped those populations out. It's no wonder that stocks of large predator fish are rapidly dwindling when one considers the fact that one bluefin tuna can go for hundreds of thousands of dollars at market in Japan. High prices—in January 2013, a 489-pound Pacific bluefin tuna sold for $1.7 million at auction in Tokyo—make it profitable to employ airplanes and helicopters to scan the ocean for the fish that remain; against such technologies, marine animals don't stand a chance.

Nor are big fish the only ones that are threatened. In area after area, once the long-lived predatory species, such as tuna and swordfish, disappear, fishing fleets move on to smaller, plankton-eating fish, such as sardines, anchovy, and herring. The overexploitation of smaller fish deprives the larger wild fish that remain of their food; aquatic mammals and sea birds, such as ospreys and eagles, also go hungry. Marine scientists refer to this sequential process as fishing down the food chain.

The problem is not just that we eat too much seafood; it's also how we catch it. Modern industrial fishing fleets drag lines with thousands of hooks miles behind a vessel, and industrial trawlers on the high seas drop nets thousands of feet below the sea's surface. In the process, many untargeted species, including sea turtles, dolphins, whales, and large sea birds (such as albatross) get accidentally captured or entangled. Millions of tons of unwanted sea life is killed or injured in commercial fishing operations each year; indeed, as much as a third of what fishermen pull out of the waters was never meant to be harvested. Some of the most destructive fisheries discard 80 to 90 percent of what they bring in. In the Gulf of Mexico, for example, for every pound of shrimp caught by a trawler, over three pounds of marine life is thrown away.

As the oceans decline and the demand for their products rises, marine and freshwater aquaculture may look like a tempting solution. After all, since we raise livestock on land for food, why not farm fish at sea? Fish farming is growing faster than any other form of food production, and today, the majority of commercially sold fish in the world and half of U.S. seafood imports come from aquaculture. Done right, fish farming can be environmentally acceptable. But the impact of aquaculture varies widely depending on the species raised, methods used, and location, and several factors make healthy and sustainable production difficult. Many farmed fish rely heavily on processed wild fish for food, which eliminates the fish-conservation benefits of aquaculture. Farmed fish can also escape into rivers and oceans and endanger wild populations by transmitting diseases or parasites or by competing with native species for feeding and spawning grounds. Open-net pens also pollute, sending fish waste, pesticides, antibiotics, uneaten food, diseases, and parasites flowing directly into the surrounding waters.

Tangled up in blue: an Antarctic fur seal caught in a fishing net, South Georgia Island.

DESTROYING THE EARTH'S FINAL FRONTIER

Yet another factor driving the decline of the oceans is the destruction of the habitats that have allowed spectacular marine life to thrive for millennia. Residential and commercial development have laid waste to once-wild coastal areas. In particular, humans are eliminating coastal marshes, which serve as feeding grounds and nurseries for fish and other wildlife, filter out pollutants, and fortify coasts against storms and erosion.

Hidden from view but no less worrying is the wholesale destruction of deep-ocean habitats. For fishermen seeking ever more elusive prey, the depths of the seas have become the earth's final frontier. There, submerged mountain chains called seamounts—numbering in the tens of thousands and mostly uncharted—have proved especially desirable targets. Some rise from the sea floor to heights approaching that of Mount Rainier, in Washington State. The steep slopes, ridges, and tops of seamounts in the South Pacific and elsewhere are home to a rich variety of marine life, including large pools of undiscovered species.

Today, fishing vessels drag huge nets outfitted with steel plates and heavy rollers across the sea floor and over underwater mountains, more than a mile deep, destroying everything in their path. As industrial trawlers bulldoze their way along, the surfaces of seamounts are reduced to sand, bare rock, and rubble. Deep cold-water corals, some older than the California redwoods, are being obliterated. In the process, an unknown number of species from these unique islands of biological diversity—which might harbor new medicines or other important information—are being driven extinct before humans even get a chance to study them.

Relatively new problems present additional challenges. Invasive species, such as lionfish, zebra mussels, and Pacific jellyfish, are disrupting coastal ecosystems and in some cases have caused the collapse of entire fisheries. Noise from sonar used by military systems and other sources can have devastating effects on whales, dolphins, and other marine life. Large vessels speeding through busy shipping lanes are also killing whales. Finally, melting Arctic ice creates new environmental hazards, as wildlife habitats disappear, mining becomes easier, and shipping routes expand.

IN HOT WATER

As if all this were not enough, scientists estimate that man-made climate change will drive the planet's temperature up by between four and seven degrees Fahrenheit over the course of this century, making the oceans hotter. Sea levels are rising, storms are getting stronger, and the life cycles of plants and animals are being up-ended, changing migration patterns and causing other serious disruptions.

Global warming has already devastated coral reefs, and marine scientists now foresee the collapse of entire reef systems in the next few decades. Warmer waters drive out the tiny plants that corals feed on and depend on for their vivid coloration. Deprived of food, the corals starve to death, a process known as "bleaching." At the same time, rising ocean temperatures promote disease in corals and other marine life. Nowhere are these complex interrelationships contributing to dying seas more than in fragile coral ecosystems.

The oceans have also become more acidic as carbon dioxide emitted into the atmosphere dissolves in the world's water. The buildup of acid in ocean waters reduces the availability of calcium carbonate, a key building block for the skeletons and shells of corals, plankton, shellfish, and many other marine organisms. Just as trees make wood to grow tall and reach light, many sea creatures need hard shells to grow and also to guard against predators.

On top of all these problems, the most severe impact of the damage being done to the oceans by climate change and ocean acidification may be impossible to predict. The world's seas support processes essential to life on earth. These include complex biological and physical systems, such as the nitrogen and carbon cycles; photosynthesis, which creates half of the oxygen that humans breathe and forms the base of the ocean's biological productivity; and ocean circulation. Much of this activity takes place in the open ocean, where the sea and the atmosphere interact. Despite flashes of terror, such as the Indian Ocean earthquake and tsunami of 2004, the delicate balance of nature that sustains these systems has remained remarkably stable since well before the advent of human civilization.

But these complex processes both influence and respond to the earth's climate, and scientists see certain recent developments as red flags possibly heralding an impending catastrophe. To take one example, tropical fish are increasingly migrating to the cooler waters of the Arctic and Southern oceans. Such changes may result in extinctions of fish species, threatening a critical food source especially in developing countries in the tropics. Or consider that satellite data show that warm surface waters are mixing less with cooler, deeper waters. This reduction in vertical mixing separates near-surface marine life from the nutrients below, ultimately driving down the population of phytoplankton, which is the foundation of the ocean's food chain. Transformations in the open ocean could dramatically affect the earth's climate and the complex processes that support life both on land and at sea. Scientists do not yet fully understand how all these processes work, but disregarding the warning signs could result in grave consequences.

A WAY FORWARD

Governments and societies have come to expect much less from the sea. The base lines of environmental quality, good governance, and personal responsibility have plummeted. This passive acceptance of the ongoing destruction of the seas is all the more shameful given how avoidable the process is. Many solutions exist, and some are relatively simple. For example, governments could create and expand protected marine areas, adopt and enforce stronger international rules to conserve biological diversity in the open ocean, and place a moratorium on the fishing of dwindling fish species, such as Pacific bluefin tuna. But solutions will also require broader changes in how societies approach energy, agriculture, and the management of natural resources. Countries will have to make substantial reductions in greenhouse gas emissions, transition to clean energy, eliminate the worst toxic chemicals, and end the massive nutrient pollution in watersheds.

These challenges may seem daunting, especially for countries focused on basic survival. But governments, international institutions, nongovernmental organizations, scholars, and businesses have the necessary experience and capacity to find answers to the oceans' problems. And they have succeeded in the past, through innovative local initiatives on every continent, impressive scientific advances, tough environmental regulation and enforcement, and important international measures, such as the global ban on the dumping of nuclear waste in the oceans.

So long as pollution, overfishing, and ocean acidification remain concerns only for scientists, however, little will change for the good. Diplomats and national security experts, who understand the potential for conflict in an overheated world, should realize that climate change might soon become a matter of war and peace. Business leaders should understand better than most the direct links between healthy seas and healthy economies. And government officials, who are entrusted with the public's well-being, must surely see the importance of clean air, land, and water.

The world faces a choice. We do not have to return to an oceanic Stone Age. Whether we can summon the political will and moral courage to restore the seas to health before it is too late is an open question. The challenge and the opportunity are there.

How Yemen Chewed Itself Dry

Farming Qat, Wasting Water

Adam Heffez

In a little over a decade, Sana'a, Yemen, may become the world's first capital to run out of water. Failed governance and environmental mismanagement share some of the blame for drying up the city. But there is also a more surprising culprit: a national addiction to qat, a narcotic that is incredibly water-intensive to cultivate.

If current trends continue, by 2025 the city's projected 4.2 million inhabitants will become water refugees, forced to flee their barren home for wetter lands. In preparation, some officials have already considered relocating the capital to the coast. Others have proposed focusing on desalination and conservation to buy time.

As policymakers butt heads over the best course for Yemen, the dwindling water supply is already leading to instability: according to *Al-Thawra*, one of the country's leading newspapers, 70 to 80 percent of conflicts in Yemen's rural regions are water-related. And across the country, Yemen's Interior Ministry estimates, water- and land-related disputes result in about 4,000 deaths each year—35 times the number of casualties in the deadliest al Qaeda attack in the country's history.

ADAM HEFFEZ is a research assistant in the Program on Arab Politics at the Washington Institute for Near East Policy.

Adam Heffez

THE QAT CAME BACK

The cultivation of qat, a mild narcotic plant that releases a stimulant when chewed, accounts for up to 40 percent of the water drawn from the Sana'a Basin each year, and that figure is rising. That is both because qat takes a lot of water to farm (much more than coffee, another plant that does well in Yemen's fertile soil) and because cultivation of it increases by around 12 percent each year, according to Yemen's Ministry of Agriculture and Water Resources. Not only is the crop drying the Sana'a Basin, it has displaced over tens of thousands of hectares of vital crops—fruits, vegetables, and coffee—which has sent food prices soaring. According to the World Bank, rising food prices, in turn, pushed an additional six percent of the country into poverty in 2008 alone.

Why the increasing reliance on qat production? Farmers are willing to put up with the plant's high demand for water because it has a more regular yield than other crops and because the market for it is virtually guaranteed. Every cubic meter of water used for qat cultivation returns a profit five times as great as that for the next most lucrative crop, grapes. No wonder: according to the World Health Organization, up to 90 percent of adult men in Yemen chew qat for three to four hours daily, and women literally sing its praises. (A popular song goes: "Long live qat, which . . . makes us stay peacefully at home with our friends.") At weddings and special events, a family's social standing is gauged by the value of qat served to guests. One might think that such a popular drug would have deep roots in a culture, but its widespread use is actually relatively new: in the 1970s, when Yemen had few paved roads, qat, which has a shelf life of only 24 to 48 hours, often could not reach its markets in time, so fewer people had access to it.

Yemen cannot continue using water this way. In 2011, the rate of water consumption from the Sana'a Basin exceeded the rate of natural recharge by a factor of five. And, even understanding this, Yemenis have placed little value on conservation: much of the country's 68 billion cubic meters of annual rainwater is wasted due to mismanagement and inadequate dams.

Part of the problem is that farmers, for whom the physical labor exerted in agriculture is a source of pride, are attached to wasteful practices, such as flood irrigation (the uncontrolled distribution of water over soil). Drip irrigation—a practice that is about 35 percent more efficient and widely available at low cost—could easily increase returns on water. But when asked about drip irrigation, one farmer told me that "flood irrigation is more honorable . . . all [drip irrigation] requires is pumping water up into the tank."

Making things worse, the country's decaying dams seep water that could otherwise be used productively. May 2010 saw flooding—the worst to hit Sana'a in decades—but very little of the water was captured for later use. Moreover, the country's well system is a disaster. By law, only the government is allowed to dig and maintain wells. But according to some interpretations of sharia, which Yemen's constitution specifies as the sole legal framework, a well drilled on privately owned land is the property of the landlord, not of the state. So drilling continues. Today, Yemen's National Water and Sanitation Authority, which is tasked with urban water administration, supplies water to only 36 percent of Sana'a's households. The other two-thirds get their supplies from groundwater wells.

The wells are a public health nightmare—the country's groundwater is increasingly contaminated by sewage effluent. Beyond that, the wells prevent the National Water and Resource Authority, which is responsible for managing the country's water resources in a sustainable way, from enforcing conservation measures, such as improving irrigation efficiency.

DON'T GO CHASING WATERFALLS

Of course, those officials know that Sana'a is facing an arid future. Moving the capital city, as some have proposed, would cost over $40 billion, according to some estimates. Securing the funds would be nearly impossible: approximately 75 percent of the government's revenue is derived from rapidly depleting oil reserves, and the World Bank predicts that oil will stop generating income for the Yemeni government by 2017. Foreign aid is similarly scant.

Even if it were possible to raise the funds, moving an entire city of over two million people would surely lead to internal strife. The tribal concept of *juwarah* (rights of neighbors) often inhibits the sale of land to members of other tribes. The transfer of land to Sana'a's two million displaced residents could thus lead to chaos.

Another idea, which the Ministry of Agriculture and Water Resources (MAWR) has discussed, is to transfer water to Sana'a from other sources. Unfortunately for Yemen, all the rest of the country's fresh water is currently in use. Therefore, transferring water to Sana'a would essentially involve siphoning it away from others, also inviting conflict.

Policymakers have also toyed with the idea of alleviating the strain on the Sana'a Basin by decreasing agriculture in the region. But that would only kick the can down the road, because, even without agriculture, and given all of Yemen's other poor water practices, the growing population would eventually dry out the basin anyway. In addition, decreasing agriculture would push up food prices even further.

LIQUID ASSET

Instead, the government should do three things to secure its water future: push farmers and the public away from qat, shore up Yemen's existing water infrastructure, and manufacture new potable water through desalinization.

First, the government should encourage farmers to switch to less water-intensive crops, such as cactus fruits. For now, the government subsidizes diesel—the main fuel used to extract groundwater—which accounts for 80 percent of the cost of qat cultivation. The low cost of extraction gives farmers little reason to switch to other crops or use sustainable farming practices. Attempts to lift a portion of the subsidy several times between 1995 and the present raised the price of diesel and dragged water up closer to its true economic price. Those changes were not enough to discourage qat production altogether, but at least obliged farmers to start thinking about more efficient irrigation techniques. Should the government opt to decrease the subsidy again, the farmers could be pushed even further.

On the supply side of the equation, the government should also launch a public campaign against qat use. Although qat is not deadly, the health risks associated with it are many—they include hyperactivity, increased blood pressure, liver complications, ulcers, and impotence—and the societal costs are nothing to sneeze at. Across the country, around 30 percent of household income, on average, is used for buying qat, despite the fact that 45 percent of Yemenis live below the poverty line. Qat has also been linked to diminished productivity at work.

In its campaign against qat use, the Yemeni government has a good model to follow: its own water conservation campaign from 2007, for which it developed a character named Rowyan (meaning "to have quenched one's thirst"). Rowyan's face appeared on wheel covers and in storefronts throughout Sana'a, and the campaign managed to at least convince some Yemenis that water scarcity was a problem A similar campaign against qat could help gradually wean some chewers away from the habit.

Second, the government needs to encourage improved irrigation techniques in all agricultural areas—ones that grow the narcotic as well as other crops. It should obligate more farmers to opt for rain irrigation instead of groundwater use, which wouldn't run counter to their desire to do things by hand. More than one million acres of arable land that used to be irrigated by rainfall (as of the 1970s) are now doused with water drawn from nonrenewable sources. There is no reason that those acres can't be reclaimed.

The National Water and Resource Authority also needs to cooperate with Yemen's local leadership, which, because it makes money off private wells and other water sources, has a vested interest in inefficient use. The NWRA can do so by taking advantage of the political transition in Yemen that accompanied the Arab Spring. For one, the ongoing national dialogue conference, which brings together 565 Yemenis from all segments of society to collaborate on forming a new government, might ease distrust of state institutions. A relationship of cooperation, rather than antagonism, will help the NWRA gain legitimacy in the eyes of local leadership, which will aid with the implementation of conservation measures in places that are outside of the government's reach.

The government should also take care of Yemen's leaky water pipes, which waste up to 60 percent of the water they contain. Money for that, too, will be hard to find. But it could court more investment from countries such as Saudi Arabia, whose security interests are inseparable from its southern neighbor's. Finally, the government must limit the drilling of wells for domestic purposes.

Conserving the water that Yemen has now will only go so far. The depletion of nonrenewable groundwater might leave Yemen with no real option other than to manufacture new water through desalinization. Pumping desalinated water from plants near the sea to Sana'a would be costly, but the fixed startup costs would be distributed across time and would be far less than moving the capital. In the beginning, the government will have to temporarily subsidize desalinated water so that it would be within reach for most consumers. The government would likely need foreign aid to implement this subsidy and to develop the desalination infrastructure.

In ancient times, Yemen was a world leader in agricultural production and water efficiency practices. Between 750 and 700 BC, in what is today northern Yemen, the Kingdom of Saba'a (Sheba) built the Marib Dam, which captured irrigation from rainfall for roughly a millennium. If it improves management of existing water resources and builds up infrastructure for conservation and desalination, Yemen, once a model of water conservation, may yet have hope for reviving its capital.

Suicide By Drought

How China is Destroying Its Own Water Supply

Sulmaan Khan

O n the grasslands of the Tibetan plateau, one sometimes hears a strange chattering—an excited buzz that seems to emanate from the earth itself. Anyone who stops to look for the source will quickly realize that the ground is marked by a series of holes, from which small, shy creatures are likely to be watching.

The labyrinthine burrows made by these mammals, called pikas, provide them security. But they provide China and much of Asia security as well. By digging holes in the ground, pikas allow rainwater to percolate into the earth and replenish the water table. Without the humble pika, the water simply runs along the surface, triggering floods and soil erosion. So it is no coincidence that, when the pikas became the target of a state-led poisoning campaign beginning in the mid-twentieth century, waters began, slowly, to dry up across the country. The pika was accused of being a pest that destroyed grasslands. Scientists have pointed out that the pika prefers long grass and that its visibility is a symptom, not a cause, of grassland degradation. But policy is slow to catch up with science; pika killings continue today.

The pikas' plight illustrates China's difficulties in confronting its water crisis. The economic development on which Beijing

SULMAAN KHAN is Assistant Professor of Chinese Foreign Relations at the Fletcher School, Tufts University, where he also directs the Water and Oceans Program at the Center for International Environment and Resource Policy.

depends to keep the population in check poses a dire threat to the fragile ecosystems that the country and the continent depend on for water. It might thus seem politically impossible for China to enact any of the far-reaching environmental reforms that it needs. In the long term, though, absent any policy changes, China is likely on the path to serious civil strife, and perhaps even civil war.

THE WILD WEST

Most of China's most important rivers originate in the plateaus of Tibet and the surrounding mountain ranges, an area known by scholars as the Third Pole because of its plentiful ice. The rivers flowing from the Third Pole—among them, the Mekong, the Yangtze, and the Yellow River—traditionally satisfied the majority of China's water needs. But those waters, along with China's other supplies, have been steadily disappearing. Since the 1950s, 27,000 rivers have vanished from China. China has only seven percent of the world's freshwater to meet the needs of about one-fifth of the world's population. Of that water, only 23 percent is located in northern China, which, as home to most of the country's major industries, uses much more water than China's south. Meanwhile, much of the country's available water supply has been rendered unusable by pollution.

The rapid economic development of western China in the last decade and a half has put even more pressure on China's water supply. Beijing has supported this economic development in spite of its pernicious ecological consequences, though, because it believes that economic growth is the key to calming the restive minorities in the west. (If Kazakhs, Tibetans, and Uighurs have plenty of employment opportunities, the theory holds, they will be less likely to rebel against Communist Party rule.) But Beijing's control over what goes on in western China is limited. Grand engineering projects designed in Beijing and implemented in distant provinces do exist: think of the railway to Tibet or the Three Gorges Dam. But lately, the process of development in western China has mostly been ground-up—cities have mushroomed out of nowhere, almost entirely unnoticed by the central government.

These cities are a byproduct of increasing unemployment in the country's east, sharpened in the aftermath of the global financial crisis that began in 2008. Out of work even in the larger cities such as Beijing, Shanghai, and Guangzhou, many young Chinese moved to existing cities in western China, such as Lanzhou, Xining, and Urumqi. When those cities grew too crowded, they ventured into what had once been virtually untouched land. Some of them went in search of caterpillar fungus, which serves as an aphrodisiac in Chinese medicine; those who were adept at finding the fungus in the wilds of western China could afford to live in small towns by working only a few weeks a year. Others believed that they would be part of a new tourism industry; wealthy tour groups from eastern China pay considerable money to see the snowy peaks of Tibet, even if the tourism infrastructure that has been built to accommodate them considerably diminishes their beauty.

With these new residents has come haphazard new infrastructure. In Qinghai province, the government is building a barrage of new roadways from the capital of Xining to the southern city of Yushu. In the Tibet Autonomous Region, Beijing is planning to build additional railways linking Lhasa and Shigatse, and extending to the border of Nepal.

The problem is that this development is taking place in ecosystems that hold the headwaters for China's water supply. And the pressures that urbanization puts on the headwaters—through overuse, grassland degradation, pollution, and threats to species that have a role to play in maintaining the health of the river ecosystem—is already having consequences downstream. On the Tibetan plateau, streambeds are dry and glaciers have melted into dead rock.

Similar threats confront China's other water sources. The Pearl River in Southern China is drying. In China's northeast, burgeoning construction projects are swallowing the wetlands that replenish the region's groundwater. As a result, water shortages have plagued the country in recent years, and experts predict that water demand will exceed supply by 2030. Given the unreliability of Chinese statistics and how swiftly ecosystems can shift course, that crunch could arrive even sooner than anticipated.

THE CHAIRMAN'S DELUSIONS

Rather than trying to conserve water, the Chinese government has endorsed a massive project inspired by China's first communist leader, Mao Zedong. The south had plentiful water, Mao reasoned in 1952, whereas the north did not; therefore, water should be diverted from the south to the north. In 2002, the Communist Party initiated a massive engineering project in order to realize this vision: a series of canals that will draw approximately 45 billion cubic meters of water from the south to the north. The first canal has already opened in eastern China. Two more—including a western route that will cut across the Himalayas—are underway.

It is true that water resources are distributed unevenly, with the south home to 77 percent of the country's total water resources. Of the total water resources available in northern China, about 45 percent get used; the south needs to use only about 20 percent of its water resources. It is also true that as the north continues to grow, so will its demand for water. But there are several problems with Beijing's water diversion policy. First, the ecological risks are immense. It is quite possible that the project will disrupt the river systems and exacerbate water shortages, rather than solve them, by triggering soil erosion and eliminating species responsible for maintaining a healthy river. The Three Gorges Dam provides a cautionary tale about tampering with natural forces: research shows that the dam caused an increase in seismic activity and landslides. Downstream of the infamous project, water shortages disrupted irrigation.

Second—and more important—the project solves nothing in the long term. If northern China's inefficient water use continues unchecked, the 45 billion cubic meters piped in from the south will eventually be too little—especially with the rivers' sources drying out. As Beijing diverts more and more water to the north, it will expose a long-standing political rift. In its long history, China has often split along north-south lines. Already, in southern places like Chongqing and Yunnan, one hears a growing complaint: Why should we southerners go thirsty so that the northerners can grow rich? As southern crops fail and people there feel the burden of water shortages, such complaints will only increase.

More generally, Beijing has yet to confront the many historical examples that suggest that water shortages can be a grave threat to national security. Persistent drought led to the collapse of Mayan civilization between 760 and 930 AD. In China, the Ming dynasty collapsed in the seventeenth century largely due to years of successive droughts. More recently, in the Middle East and South Asia, water shortages have led to political unrest. The recent swell of environmental protests in China indicates that it will not be immune to the trend.

A historian looking back in 2040 might well tell a story in which Beijing, unable to curb the state's relentless water use, condemned it to growing water shortages. As the south grew parched, political grievances flared into violent opposition, which became increasingly difficult to put down as angered military commanders joined in and residents of the desiccated third pole—Tibetans, Uighurs, Kazakhs—went into revolt. Like the Ming dynasty before it, the historian would conclude, China had collapsed because thirst spawns violence.

WAR ON DROUGHT

To avoid serious ecological and political calamity, China's central government will have to curtail its economic goals. Fortunately, Beijing's recent climate change policies suggest that it may be prepared to make such a compromise. Ahead of the United Nations climate change talks to be held in Paris in 2015, the Chinese government has talked of initiating a "war on pollution" and reducing its carbon emissions. There are plenty of signs, from the investment in renewable energy to discussing emissions with the US in the Strategic Economic Dialogue, that at least some in the Chinese government are serious.

But cutting carbon emissions without a plan to address water issues—and other problems like soil contaminated with toxins—is futile. Beijing needs to develop a plan that addresses the entirety of its environmental woes. For one, it has to mandate sustainable development, which will require strengthening the central government against the local governments. Cities can no longer be allowed to spring up in western China without Beijing's knowledge—the effects on water supply are simply too great. The government will also have to bring locally administered industries, which emit more pollutants and use more water than they report, under control. To aid these efforts, the Chinese government should also try to rally popular support around sustainable development. The Chinese public is tired of the water shortages, unsafe drinking water, and soil contamination caused by haphazard urban development. Xi Jinping could present environmental reform as the next chapter of China's glorious history and as part of the new model of great power relations that he has touted.

Once it has popular support in place, China could make other major changes. First, it would be worth putting a halt to the south-to-north water diversion project—perhaps even going so far as to undo the existing canal in eastern China—and insisting on water and energy efficiency in the north instead. As experts have pointed out, simple measures like water recycling and water price increases could help immensely. This would likely lead to vociferous complaints from provincial officials and industrial barons, but that should be preferable to steadily alienating the southern swath of the country and allowing the root causes of the problem to persist.

Second—and this too would lead to some political backlash—Beijing should move to curb, and perhaps even stop, development in the country's most ecologically sensitive areas. The Chinese government needs to treat the protection of the Tibetan plateau as a key to national security, not an impediment to economic growth, even if that means finding other ways of easing social tensions in western China.

One possibility would be to stanch the flow of Han migrants, which feeds the resentment that ethnic minorities often feel.

Beijing should also consult the platoon of conservation biologists, both Chinese and foreign, who have long been warning of looming ecological catastrophe. China's water security depends on a complex and subtle balance—the forests that enrich the watersheds, the alpine grasslands that limit soil erosion, the relationships between myriad organisms which maintain healthy waterways—that is extremely difficult to understand. The Chinese state may need to swallow its pride in reaching out to foreign experts, but that shouldn't be an impediment. China desperately needs to comprehend its environment in all its intricacy, and the country's officials should be open to reaching out to anyone who might be able to help. Even the diminutive pika, after all, has a critical role to play.

A Light in the Forest

Brazil's Fight to Save the Amazon and Climate-Change Diplomacy

Jeff Tollefson

Across the world, complex social and market forces are driving the conversion of vast swaths of rain forests into pastureland, plantations, and cropland. Rain forests are disappearing in Indonesia and Madagascar and are increasingly threatened in Africa's Congo basin. But the most extreme deforestation has taken place in Brazil. Since 1988, Brazilians have cleared more than 153,000 square miles of Amazonian rain forest, an area larger than Germany. With the resulting increase in arable land, Brazil has helped feed the growing global demand for commodities, such as soybeans and beef.

But the environmental price has been steep. In addition to providing habitats for untold numbers of plant and animal species and discharging around 20 percent of the world's fresh water, the Amazon basin plays a crucial role in regulating the earth's climate, storing huge quantities of carbon dioxide that would otherwise contribute to global warming. Slashing and burning the Amazon rain forest releases the carbon locked up in plants and soils; from a climate perspective, clearing the rain forest is no different from burning fossil fuels, such as oil and gas. Recent estimates suggest that deforestation and associated activities account for 10-15 percent of global carbon dioxide emissions.

JEFF TOLLEFSON is a U.S. correspondent for Nature, where he covers energy, climate, and environmental issues.

But in recent years, good news has emerged from the Amazon. Brazil has dramatically slowed the destruction of its rain forests, reducing the rate of deforestation by 83 percent since 2004, primarily by enforcing land-use regulations, creating new protected areas, and working to maintain the rule of law in the Amazon. At the same time, Brazil has become a test case for a controversial international climate-change prevention strategy known as REDD, short for "reducing emissions from deforestation and forest degradation," which places a monetary value on the carbon stored in forests. Under such a system, developed countries can pay developing countries to protect their own forests, thereby offsetting the developed countries' emissions at home. Brazil's preliminary experience with REDD suggests that, in addition to offering multiple benefits to forest dwellers (human and otherwise), the model can be cheap and fast: Brazil has done more to reduce emissions than any other country in the world in recent years, without breaking the bank.

The REDD model remains a work in progress. In Brazil and other places where elements of REDD have been applied, the funding has yet to reach many of its intended beneficiaries, and institutional reforms have been slow to develop. This has contributed to a rural backlash against the new enforcement measures in the Brazilian Amazon—a backlash that the government is still struggling to contain. But if Brazil can consolidate its early gains, build consensus around a broader vision for development, and follow through with a program to overhaul the economies of its rainforest regions, it could pave the way for a new era of environmental governance across the tropics. For the first time, perhaps, it is possible to contemplate an end to the era of large-scale human deforestation.

LULA GETS TOUGH

The deforestation crisis in Brazil ramped up in the 1960s, when the country's military rulers, seeking to address the country's poverty crisis, encouraged poor Brazilians to move into the Amazon basin with promises of free land and generous government subsidies. In response, tens of thousands of Brazilians left dry scrublands in the northeast and other poor areas for the lush Amazon basin—a mass internal migration that only increased in size throughout the 1970s and beyond.

But the government did not properly plan for the effect of a population explosion in the Amazon basin. The result was a land rush, during which short-term profiteering from slash-and-burn agriculture prevented anything resembling sustainable development. Environmental and social movements arose in response to the chaotic development, but it was not until the 1980s, when scientists began systematically tracking Amazonian deforestation using satellite imagery, that the true scale of the environmental destruction under way in the Amazon became apparent. The end of military rule in 1985 and Brazil's transition to democracy did nothing to slow the devastation; the ecological damage only worsened as road-building projects and government subsidies for agriculture fueled a real estate boom that wiped out forests and threatened traditional rubber tappers and native peoples. Meanwhile, the total population of the Amazon basin increased from around six million in 1960 to 25 million in 2010 (including some 20 million in Brazil), and agricultural production in the Amazon region ramped up as global commodity markets expanded.

Things began to change in 2003, when Luiz Inácio Lula da Silva, the newly elected Brazilian president, known as Lula, chose Marina Silva as his environment minister. A social and environmental activist turned politician, Silva hailed from the remote Amazonian state of Acre and had worked alongside Chico Mendes, a union leader and environmentalist whose murder in 1988 at the hands of a rancher drew global attention to the issue of the Amazon's preservation. With

Lula's blessing, Silva immediately set about doing what no Brazilian government had previously attempted: enforcing Brazil's 1965 Forest Code, which had set forth strong protections for forests and established strict limits on how much land could be cleared. Doing so represented a major shift in domestic policy and was equally striking at the international level: Brazil chose to act at a time when most developing countries were resisting any significant steps to combat global warming absent the industrialized world's own more aggressive actions and provision of financial aid.

After peaking in 2004, when an area of rain forest roughly the size of Massachusetts was mowed down in a single year, Brazil's deforestation rate began to fall. Then, in late 2007, scientists at Brazil's National Institute for Space Research warned that the rate of deforestation had spiked once again. The increase coincided with a sudden rise in global food prices, which created an incentive for landowners in the Amazon to illegally clear more forest for pasture and crops. This suggested that the earlier decline in the rate of deforestation might have been driven by market forces as much as by government intervention, but Lula nevertheless doubled down on enforcement. The government deployed hundreds of Brazilian soldiers in early 2008 to crack down on illegal logging, issuing fines to those who broke the law and in some instances hauling lawbreakers to jail.

The following year, Brazil announced that its rate of deforestation had hit a historic low, and Lula pledged that by 2020 the country would reduce its deforestation to 20 percent of the country's long-term baseline, then defined as the average from 1996 to 2005. His plan to achieve that goal was based on one version of the REDD model, which had vaulted onto the international agenda several years earlier as scientists made advances in quantifying the impact of tropical deforestation on climate change.

GREEN-LIGHTING REDD

Politicians and commentators usually describe global warming as a long-term threat, but scientists also worry about transgressing invisible thresholds and thus provoking potentially rapid and irreversible near-term changes in the way environmental and biological systems function. During the past decade, based in part on the results of intensive climate modeling, some scientists began to grow concerned that the Amazon could represent one of the clearest examples of such tipping points.

Think of the rain forest not as a collection of trees but as a hydrologic system, a massive machine for transporting and recycling water in which trees act as pumps, pulling water out of the ground and then injecting it, through transpiration, into the air. This process ramps up as the sun rises over the Amazon each day; as the forest heats up, evaporation increases, and trees transpire water to stay cool, simultaneously increasing the amount of water they take up through their roots. By constantly replenishing the atmosphere with water vapor, the Amazon helps create its own weather on a grand scale.

Humans interfere with this process whenever they chop down rain forests, and at some point, the system will begin to shut down. And this is not the only threat. Studies suggest that the Amazon could also be susceptible to rising temperatures and shifting rainfall patterns due to global warming. The nightmare scenario is known as "Amazon dieback," wherein the rains decrease and open savannas encroach on an ever-shrinking rain forest. The resulting loss of fresh water could be catastrophic for communities, agriculture, and hydropower systems in the Amazon, and dieback would have drastic effects on biodiversity and the global carbon dioxide cycle. The Amazon stores some 100 billion metric tons of carbon, equivalent to roughly a decade of global emissions. Converting carbon-rich rain forests into open savannas would pump massive quantities of carbon dioxide into the atmosphere, making it even harder for humans to prevent further warming.

Roughly 20 percent of the Amazon has been cleared to date, and there is already evidence that precipitation and river-discharge patterns are changing where the deforestation has been most intense, notably in the southwestern portion of the basin. And some scientists fear that the shifting climate may already be exerting an influence. In the past seven years, the Amazon has suffered two extremely severe droughts; normally, such droughts would be expected to occur perhaps once a century. One of the most comprehensive modeling studies to date, conducted in 2010 under the auspices of the World Bank, suggests that even current levels of deforestation, when combined with the impacts of increasing forest fires and global warming, are making the Amazon susceptible to dieback.

Such projections have heightened the sense of urgency in climate policy circles and helped focus attention on the REDD model. The concept has been around in some form for more than 15 years, but it was first placed on the international agenda in 2005 by the Coalition for Rainforest Nations, a group of 41 developing countries that cooperates with the un and the World Bank on sustainability issues. At the core of the model is the belief that it is possible to calculate how much carbon is released into the atmosphere when a given chunk of forest is cut down. Fears that this would prove impossible helped keep deforestation off the agenda when climate diplomats signed the Kyoto Protocol in 1997. Scientists are steadily improving their methods for estimating how much carbon is stored in forests, however, and most experts agree that carbon dioxide can be tracked with enough accuracy to calculate baseline figures for every country.

Under various proposed versions of the REDD model, wealthy countries or businesses seeking to offset their own impact on the climate would pay tropical countries to reduce their emissions below their baseline levels. There is no consensus about the best way to design such a system of payments; since REDD was formally adopted as part of the agenda for climate negotiations at the un Climate Change Conference in Bali, Indonesia, in 2007, dozens of countries and nongovernmental organizations have put forward a range of ideas. Most of these call for the creation of a global market that, like the European carbon-trading system, would allow industrial polluters to purchase carbon offsets generated by rain-forest preservation. Some environmentalists and social activists worry about the validity and longevity of such credits, as well as the prospect of banks and traders entering the conservation business. One fear is that "carbon cowboys," a new class of entrepreneurs specializing in the development of carbon-offset projects, would sweep through forests, trampling the rights of indigenous and poor people by taking control of their lands and walking away with the profits. This concern is valid, as there is always a danger of bad actors. But civil-society groups and governments, including Brazil's, are aware of the problem and are working on safeguards.

Brazilian officials have also expressed worries that the ability to simply purchase unlimited offsets would allow wealthy countries to delay the work that needs to be done to reduce their own emissions. An alternative backed by Brazil's climate negotiators and others would be a state-based funding system, in which money would flow from governments in the developed world to governments in the developing world, which would guarantee emissions reductions in return.

NORWEGIAN WOOD

In 2008, Lula, perhaps hoping to preempt an interminable debate over how best to design a global REDD system, announced the establishment of the Amazon Fund, calling on wealthy countries to contribute some $21 billion to directly fund rain-forest-preservation measures. The proposal went against the market-based approach being pushed by the Coalition for Rainforest Nations. Based on a more conventional system of government donations, the Amazon Fund would allow Brazil to control the money and manage its forests as it saw fit. To the fund's backers, the resulting reductions in emissions would represent offsets of a sort.

Only one country decided to take up Lula's challenge: Norway, which stepped forward with a commitment of up to $1 billion. Coming well in advance of any formal carbon market and the international treaty that many hoped would be signed at the un climate summit in Copenhagen in 2009, Norway's pledge was largely an altruistic vote of confidence in Brazil's approach, with donations conditioned on measurable progress. Since 2010, when the funding began, the Brazilian Development Bank, which manages the fund, has undertaken 30 projects, costing nearly $152 million. These projects include direct payments to landowners in return for preserving forests and initiatives to sort out disputes over landownership, educate farmers and ranchers about sustainability, and combat forest fires.

Although environmentalists and scientists have criticized some delays in the program, Brazil's deforestation rate has continued to plunge. Each year from 2009 to 2012, the country registered a new record low for deforestation; in 2012, only 1,798 square miles of forest were cleared. That is 76 percent below the long-term baseline, leaving Brazil just four percent shy of its Copenhagen commitment with eight years to go. Recent calculations by Brazilian scientists suggest that the cumulative release of carbon dioxide expected as a result of deforestation in the Brazilian Amazon dropped from more than 1.1 billion metric tons in 2004 to 298 million in 2011—roughly equivalent to the effect of France and the United Kingdom eliminating their combined carbon dioxide emissions for 2011.

REDD remains a distant promise for most landowners and communities, and the precipitous drop in deforestation in Brazil is more a function of broader government policy than the result of any individual project. Still, the Amazon Fund is demonstrating the promise and practicality of the REDD model. Although the actual cost of preventing emissions remains unclear, Brazil is offering donors carbon offsets at a discounted price of $5 per metric ton of carbon dioxide, intentionally underestimating how much biomass its forests contain in order to avoid arguments over the price. Of course, implementing the REDD model could prove significantly more expensive elsewhere. But the price would nonetheless be significantly cheaper than for many other methods of cutting emissions, such as capturing carbon dioxide from a coal-fired power plant and pumping it underground, which could cost upward of $100 per metric ton in the initial stages.

ROUSSEFF AND THE RURALISTAS

Lula was succeeded by his protégé and former chief of staff, Dilma Rousseff, in 2011. Although environmentalists have been critical of her broader development agenda in the Amazon and beyond, Rousseff has upheld Lula's deforestation policies. And she has done so despite intense pressure from the so-called ruralista coalition of landowners and major agricultural interests, which currently exercises tremendous influence in Brasília.

In the spring of 2012, the Brazilian Congress passed a bill that would have eviscerated the country's vaunted Forest Code by scaling back basic protections for land alongside rivers and embankments and offering outright amnesty to companies and landowners who had broken the law. Rousseff fought back, and a prolonged tussle ensued. The final result was a law that is generally more favorable to agricultural interests but that nonetheless retains minimum requirements for forest protection and recovery on private land.

More troubling than the new law itself, perhaps, is the political polarization that accompanied its passage. Brasília now seems divided into rigid environmentalist and agricultural factions. Fierce opposition to Brazil's rain-forest-preservation efforts is sure to persist, and many observers fear that landowners, impatient with the slow pace of progress on REDD, will ultimately begin to test the limits of the newly revised Forest Code. As if on cue, last September, Brazilian scientists announced that deforestation was 220 percent higher in August than it had been in August of 2011. But it is too early to tell what this latest outbreak might mean. After all, prior spikes have incurred a government response, and each time the damage has been contained.

It is also worth noting that not only has Brazilian deforestation decreased overall, but the size of the average forest clearing has also decreased over time. The powerful landowners and corporate interests responsible for large-scale deforestation have apparently decided that they can no longer cut down rain forests with impunity. The upshot is that for the first time ever, in 2011, the amount of land cleared in the Brazilian Amazon dropped below the combined amount cleared in the surrounding Amazon countries, which make up 40 percent of the basin. In those countries, the trend is not so encouraging: deforestation in the non-Brazilian Amazon increased from an estimated annual average of 1,938 square miles in the 1990s to 2,782 square miles last year, according to an analysis published by the World Wildlife Fund.

MISSING THE FOREST FOR THE TREES?

There was very little progress on REDD at the most recent un climate summit, in Doha, Qatar, last November. Negotiators left the door open to a full suite of REDD-style models, from government-to-government financial transfers to a privatized carbon market, but failed to agree on the details. Regardless of which particular models are codified in a hypothetical future treaty on climate change, countries need to focus on making the money flow: some studies suggest that halving deforestation would cost $20-$25 billion annually by 2020. So far, governments have committed several billion dollars to forest protection through various bilateral and multilateral agreements. Through the un, the industrialized countries have also made impressive commitments to combating climate change in the developing world, promising to contribute up to $100 billion annually by 2020, a portion of which could fund forest protection.

But it is not at all clear that this money will materialize, due in part to the current weakness of the global economy. And there is a limit to government largess. Advocates of rain-forest preservation are now trying to convince governments to commit money from revenue streams that do not depend on annual appropriations, which are more vulnerable to political and economic pressure. But that, too, is an uphill battle. Indeed, forest-preservation advocates cannot rely on governments alone; they will ultimately need to attract private-sector investment.

In the meantime, the fight against deforestation will rely on a patchwork of international partnerships and initiatives. Most significant, perhaps, Norway has transferred the model it developed with Brazil to Indonesia, which now ranks as the largest emitter of carbon dioxide from tropical deforestation. Just as in Brazil, the promise of REDD helped inspire some bold political commitments by Indonesian authorities, who have agreed to reduce their greenhouse gas emissions—most of which come from deforestation—by up to 41 percent by 2020 if international aid materializes. But Indonesia has neither the monitoring technology nor the institutional wherewithal of Brazil, so Norway's $1 billion commitment is aimed at helping the country build up its scientific and institutional capacity. Progress has been slow, but the advantage of a results-based approach, such as REDD, is that these initiatives cost money only if they yield positive results.

Brazil's experience offers some lessons for other tropical countries. The first is that science and technology must be the foundation of any solution. Brazil's progress has been made possible by major investments in scientific and institutional infrastructure to monitor the country's rain forests. Nations seeking to follow suit must invest in tools that will help them not only monitor their forests but also estimate just how much carbon those forests store. Working with scientists at the Carnegie Institution for Science, the governments of Colombia and Peru are deploying advanced systems for tracking deforestation from readily available satellite data. Combined with laser-based aerial technology that can map vast swaths of forest in three dimensions, these systems will be able to more accurately calculate and monitor stored carbon across an entire landscape—a feat that could allow these countries to leapfrog Brazil.

Brazil's Amazon Fund also shows that it is possible to move forward despite lingering scientific uncertainty about how to quantify the carbon stored in forests. Some critics of the REDD model have worried that it could draw attention away from the enforcement of existing forestry laws, ultimately increasing the cost of conservation and rewarding wealthy lawbreakers. But Brazil's experience shows that the two approaches can go hand in hand. Indeed, most of Brazil's progress to date has come from simply enforcing existing rules.

The government has also created formal land reserves, outlawing development on nearly half its territory, and environmental groups have played a role by rallying public opinion and partnering with industry groups to improve agricultural practices. Still, enforcement can go only so far with the smaller landholders and subsistence farmers who are responsible for an increasingly large share of the remaining deforestation. Brazil must focus the Amazon Fund and other government initiatives on projects that will create more sustainable forms of agriculture for these small-scale farmers and ranchers.

The government also needs to look ahead. Cities in the Amazon are booming, and larger populations will translate into additional demands for natural resources and food. The Brazilian government has sought to increase agricultural productivity across the basin, recognizing that there is more than enough land available to expand production without clearing more of it. But Brazil should also encourage more forest recovery, which would bolster the Amazon's ability to produce rain and absorb carbon dioxide from the atmosphere. Globally, forests currently absorb roughly a quarter of the world's carbon emissions, thanks to the regrowth of forests cut down long ago in places such as the United States, and they could provide an even larger buffer going forward. Roughly 20 percent of the areas once cleared in the Amazon are already regrowing as so-called secondary forest. Scientists have calculated that if the government can increase that figure to 40 percent, the Brazilian Amazon will transition from a net source of carbon dioxide emissions to a "carbon sink" by 2015, taking in more carbon dioxide than it emits.

Deforestation is just one of many challenges buffeting the Amazon region, and improvements on this front should not obscure the ongoing problems of poverty, violence, and corruption. But at a time when expectations for progress on climate change are falling, Brazil has given the world a glimmer of hope. In many ways, the hard work is just beginning, but the results so far more than justify continuing the experiment.

The Reincarnation Machine

From Cars to Skyscrapers, Indiana to Shandong

Adam Minter

That scrapyard smell is strong, even when you're driving in an air-conditioned pickup. I'm seated next to Dave Stage, the affable manager of OmniSource's immense scrapyard in Fort Wayne, Indiana, and he's giving me a brief driving tour of the facility, along with my soon-to-be wife, Christine, in the jump seat. This is a first for me: I don't usually take anyone on reporting trips. But if we're going to marry, then Christine needs to know why I like all this scrap so much.

Dave slows to point out stacks of junked Coke and Pepsi vending machines. There must be hundreds. "Most of them still have fluorescent bulbs and refrigerator compressors that we have to pull out," he says. Both items contain hazardous materials that need to be recycled elsewhere. "After that, we shred them."

I look back at Christine. "In the automobile shredder."

She flashes me an annoyed look meant to convey that, yes, she knows.

But I know she doesn't: until you've seen your first auto shredder, you can't.

ADAM MINTER is an American writer and Shanghai correspondent for Bloomberg World View. His most recent book is *Junkyard Planet: Travels in the Billion Dollar Trash Trade,* from which this article is excerpted. Copyright (c) 2013 by Bloomsbury Press.

Dave parks the truck at the office, and we step into a hot, yellow brass sun. All around me I hear the groan and crunch of scrap-processing equipment at work, turning ordinary objects into raw materials. "You'll need these." Dave hands us hard hats, safety glasses, and orange vests.

There are two piles of scrap steel in front of us, both roughly two stories tall. The one on the left is rusty in color, made up mostly of unrecognizable pieces of metal cut into short lengths that can be managed—and melted—by a steel mill. In industry parlance, that's "prepared steel."

The pile to the right, meanwhile, is a multicolored crush of everything from fences to old machine tools, scaffolding, pipes, a few bicycles, at least one swing set, and lots of shelving. This is known as "unprepared steel," meaning that it needs to be cut down to size and cleaned of anything that isn't steel before it can be sent off to a mill. Some of that work is done by hand and tool, and some of that work is done by dinosaur-like cranes outfitted with giant beaklike pincers that cut thick pieces of pipe like it's pasta.

There is another way to handle that steel, and it rises three stories above the scrapyard, casting a long shadow. From here, we can't see much except the car-wide conveyor that's currently lifting a crushed auto body skyward. But from the side it looks like a contained carnival ride—it goes up, and then it goes down. At the top, steam rises, along with an otherworldly screech and groan—that's the sound of an automobile being reduced to fragments the size of my reporter's notebook.

We're walking beside a wall of cars, six cars high and perhaps fifty cars long. They're a sad, deflated sight, emptied of engines, radiators, transmissions, wheels, tires, and anything else worth the trouble of extracting by hand. As we draw closer to the machine, the sound drowns thoughts, and Dave's voice rises. "We do one hundred and thirty tons per hour in the shredder," he yells in my ear.

"How many cars is that?" I yell in return.

"Seven to nine thousand cars per month. Depends on time of year, market." OmniSource's shredder is really big, but what's most remarkable about it is that it's not remarkable at all. North America is home to more than 300 metal shredders. Another 500, at least, are located in dozens of other countries from Brazil to China. The shredder stands as the singularly most important piece of recycling equipment ever developed. It is, among other things, the best and really only solution to managing the biggest source of consumer waste in the world today: the roughly 14 million American automobiles that are junked annually.

AGED AUTOS

In 1969, upwards of 70,000 automobiles and trucks were abandoned by their owners on the streets of New York City. Some leaked gas and oil; some provided habitat for rats and mosquitos; most were unsightly. And the problem was not exclusive to gritty New York. Across the United States, experts estimated, between 17 and 30 million cars had been abandoned since 1955.

Abandoned automobiles were not a new problem. In the 1920s, just a couple of decades into the American automobile era, Americans were retiring as many as one million cars per year. World War II slowed down the growth in auto buying, and forced Americans to repair what they'd otherwise retire, but by the early 1950s they'd returned to their car-buying and -abandoning ways. In 1951, the United States was home to an estimated 25,000 auto junkyards, and every last one was necessary: that year, 3.7 million cars and 600,000 light trucks were sold to scrapyards.

In general, the scrapyards were able to recycle those vehicles, with much of the work accomplished by hand. Workers would use axes and other hand tools to rip out the copper, the aluminum, the fabric, and the wood. Steel was the major leftover, easily marketed to American steel mills eager for raw materials to power midcentury American growth.

Two blows hit the American autojunking business in the mid-1950s. First, the price of American labor began to rise, making it increasingly difficult for U.S. scrapyards to pay teams of workers to tear down cars. Meanwhile, American steel mills began to upgrade their technologies, and by the early 1950s many were no longer interested in melting down old automobile bodies procured from scrapyards, which were often contaminated with copper. As American steel mills stopped buying cars from scrapyards, those same scrapyards stopped buying cars from Americans, and Americans began abandoning their cars by the millions.

By 1960, the abandoned automobile problem was a massive environmental crisis. Across the Unted States, streams, creeks, and fields were polluted by cars and their leaking oil, gas, and other fluids; junkyards with stacks of old automobiles destroyed views of the country's once-pristine countryside. In 1970, President Richard Nixon told the U.S. Congress, "Few of America's eyesores are so unsightly as its millions of junked automobiles." More likely than not, he was unaware that a solution to the problem was starting to grind away. It would take decades to catch up on the backlog, but the problem—more or less—was being solved by the first automobile shredders. The principle is simple: obliterate a car into small enough pieces that large, strong magnets can pull the steel almost completely free of whatever copper and other materials are left in it. On a pound-for-pound basis, it's a far cheaper and quicker way to recycle a car.

The shredder booth, were I am standing with Dave and Christine, shakes. I lean to look out the window, but there's only steam. We follow Dave down the stairs and behind the shredder, where shiny pieces of steel crumpled like sheets of paper are speeding by on conveyors. You don't want to get too close, though: they're sharp and hot. Above us, a thin conveyor lifts the stream of crumpled steel twenty feet into the air until it falls into a ten-foot-high pile, the pieces ringing like a wind chime in a breeze. It doesn't remain there long: a crane outfitted with a kitchen-table-size magnet is transferring the shredded metal, dip by magnetic dip, into a trailer bound for a steel mill.

For those who don't want to obtain their steelmaking materials from expensive, environmentally destructive iron ore mines, this is a windfall. Conservatively estimated, each ton of shredded metal loaded into that trailer is equal to 2,500 pounds of iron ore that won't be mined in northern Minnesota (or elsewhere), and 1,400 pounds of coal that won't be dug up in Kentucky to power the steel furnace. In 2012, the U.S. scrap industry processed 75.19 million tons of iron and steel, roughly half of which was shredded. And that shredded scrap metal, when remelted, accounted for roughly 30 percent of the new steel manufactured in the United States.

BANGKOK SCRAP

The scrap does not all stay in the United States. Early summer 2008, the global economy is flush with cash but ready to collapse. At the direction of *Scrap* magazine, I travel to Bangkok to figure out why a small country like Thailand has become—in very short order—a major importer of American shredded scrap metal. In a sense, I already know before I get there: Southeast Asia, in the shadow of China, is undergoing a construction boom that requires more and more steel to build more and more buildings and cars, and Americans generate an excess of scrap metal.

Over the course of several days, I visit a handful of major steel mills in the Bangkok area. They are flush with scrap, much of it imported. At GJ Steel, one of Thailand's biggest steel companies, a manager tells me that they have 120,000 tons of steel just lying on the ground. Then, after a beat, he asks me:

"Is that a lot?"

It is, I assure him. That's equivalent to the weight of a very large oil tanker, or perhaps 15 percent of the total American steel scrap exported to Thailand that year. We are in the mill, watching as a stream of imported shredded scrap as wide as a creek flows into one of the largest furnaces in Asia. That furnace looks like a science fiction nightmare: a flying saucer covered in dust and piping and shooting sparks. The heat is unbearable—we can't draw too close—and I'm led instead into a control room where a group of technicians is looking at a monitor that displays the precise recipe for the steel that they'll be making over the next few minutes.

- 20 ton—PIG IRON (an iron ore product used in steelmaking)
- 30 ton—HMS MIX (iron and steel scrap)
- 20 ton—BUNDLE NO. 1 (steel sheets in a bundle)
- 60 ton—BUSHELING (free, clean steel scrap)
- 60 ton—SHREDDED IMP (IMP, as in imported)

Why imported? Because Americans and Europeans don't use their metal goods—like cars—long enough to let them rust, they generally produce higher-quality scrap metal, including shredded metal, that melts better than local scrap. But even if Thai shredded scrap were equal in quality to American shredded scrap, there simply isn't enough of it in the market to fully supply all of the steel mills rushing to meet these boom times.

I leave the control room and walk around a scaffolding to where new sheets of steel are flowing out of machines, silver and clean, until they're rolled up into giant shiny tubes and left to cool. In coming days they'll be shipped to manufacturers of cars, washing machines, and other makers of middle-class comforts across Thailand.

Later that night, I'm in the back seat of a taxi in Bangkok. Outside the car, there's a skinny man with a pushcart walking along the sidewalk, carrying what looks to me like pieces of spindly rebar pulled from a demolition site. I suspect that the peddler will make a nice profit. Earlier in the morning, several traders had told me that they expected steel prices to break through the once unthinkable $1,000-per-metric-ton barrier, and never turning back.

I forget about this taxi ride until three years later, the summer of 2012, when I find myself and Christine in the office of Dave Stage, Omni-Source's Fort Wayne scrapyard manager. We've just finished our shredder tour, and now we're chatting about how hot the scrap markets were—even for low-quality scrap—right before everything crashed in the fall of 2008. I tell Dave about Thailand.

He laughs. "Sure, the summer of 2008 we had a line to drop scrap at the shredder that stretched all the way to downtown Fort

Wayne. Two miles." He continued, "That's what happens when the prices get real high. People start pulling stuff out of the garage, out of the woods, out of the fields, that they wouldn't touch otherwise." As Dennis Ross, a senior vice president at Huron Valley Steel, noted, it wasn't until the early 1990s that the pent-up stockpile of abandoned automobiles began to be whittled down, and not until the 2008 that the U.S. scrap industry finally caught up and just recycled what was entering the junkyards.

Sitting across from Dave, I ask if he agrees. Was 2008 the year that the last of the scrap cars came out of the woods?

"Tell you what. One day in the summer of 2008 we had an old farm tractor come into the yard for the shredder. It had a tree sticking out of it, with a trunk with a circumference the size of a baseball. That's how long it'd been sitting there. So yeah, I think it probably was 2008."

I look at Christine, and she's laughing with Dave as he tells the story. It's funny, for sure. But it's also astonishing, when you think about it: eighty years after the first Model T rolled off Henry Ford's assembly line, Americans finally managed to clean up a backlog of junked vehicles—and they did so in part because steel mills in Bangkok needed raw materials to make new cars and refrigerators for people in Southeast Asia.

The end of the automobile backlog should've been occasion for a television documentary, a presidential speech, and perhaps a commemorative postage stamp. Instead, there were daily orders of pan pizzas and barbecues in the long shadow of one of North America's biggest shredders. I just wish I'd been invited.

THE SHREDDER

Instead, I was in China—the fastest-growing market in the world for shredders. It's after midnight, midwinter 2010, and I'm drunk in the back seat of a car headed to a new shredder on the outskirts of Lianyungang, 270 miles north of Shanghai, owned by Armco Renewable Metals. Joining us is Song Yanzhao, deputy general manager of the Shandong Yuxi Group, a big-time steel recycling company in Shandong Province. By the look of his baby face, he's maybe 22, but by the look in his eyes he's losing his youth to the cold cynicism characteristic of anyone who grows too close to China's politically sensitive state-run steel industry. Earlier, before the drinking, he told me that his family started out simply, cleaning metal using hand tools and torch cutters, then cutting it into sizes that could be accepted by China's steel mills. They were successful: by 2005, using hand tools, cutting torches, and large alligator-like shears, they were able to process between two and three thousand tons per month—roughly, the weight of ten to fifteen blue whales.

That was pretty good, but the company aimed higher. By 2005, China's economy was one of the fastest-growing in the world, and its people and companies were beginning to throw away steel— buildings, cars, signs—at a pace that simply couldn't be processed by manpower alone. A scrapping company needed horsepower— specifically, the very modest 1,000-horsepower Chinese-built metal shredder that Shandong Yuxi Group purchased. Now the firm scraps about 50 blue whales a month.

Still, Song knows there are much bigger opportunities in the company's future. In 2009 China surpassed the United States to become the world's largest automobile market, with 18 million vehicles sold. Already plenty of older vehicles are being retired, but the bigger wave is due at the end of the decade, when the Chinese start junking the decade-old cars that constituted this latest boom. That's why Song is in the car: his father has entrusted him with finding a high-quality foreign-made shredder to handle the coming wave. The fact that the price of steel crashed in 2008 is no matter. Like most successful Chinese scrap processors, the Songs are pathological optimists with an unerring belief that China's long-term demand for raw materials all but guarantees future profits. Even if the cars aren't available yet, they will be, and so will the cash flow.

Frank Huang, a Beijing-based sales representative for Metso Lindemann, a major Finnish supplier of equipment to the recycling industry, tells me, "They plan to import American cars and start shredding them, too."

"American cars?"

"There aren't enough Chinese cars yet." Walking together, we emerge from behind the piles, and the shredder looms above us, three stories high. Two orange cranes work beneath the sodium lights, grasping motorcycle frames in claw-like grapples and adding them to the mix moving up the conveyor.

Frank, who can clearly handle his liquor better than I can, is waving at me from the stairs, and I follow him into a stairwell that leads up to the control room atop the shredder. The exertion makes me want to vomit. But I can't, because now I'm in the tiny control room, and it's crowded up here.

A big window overlooks the tangled motorcycle frames as they drop into the shredder. Seated in front of it, on a raised platform that gives him a better view, is a man in his early thirties, perched in a chair that reminds me of the captain's seat on the deck of the Starship Enterprise. His hands hang loosely over two joysticks that he uses to control the flow of the scrap, while his eyes move between the conveyor and a computer monitor that gives him a detailed readout of what's happening inside the machine. In the darkness, it feels very sci-fi, as if I'm dropping in on the future.

The Great Leap Backward?

Elizabeth C. Economy

China's environmental problems are mounting. Water pollution and water scarcity are burdening the economy, rising levels of air pollution are endangering the health of millions of Chinese, and much of the country's land is rapidly turning into desert. China has become a world leader in air and water pollution and land degradation and a top contributor to some of the world's most vexing global environmental problems, such as the illegal timber trade, marine pollution, and climate change. As China's pollution woes increase, so, too, do the risks to its economy, public health, social stability, and international reputation. As Pan Yue, a vice minister of China's State Environmental Protection Administration (SEPA), warned in 2005, "The [economic] miracle will end soon because the environment can no longer keep pace."

With the 2008 Olympics around the corner, China's leaders have ratcheted up their rhetoric, setting ambitious environmental targets, announcing greater levels of environmental investment, and exhorting business leaders and local officials to clean up their backyards. The rest of the world seems to accept that Beijing has charted a new course: as China declares itself open for environmentally friendly business, officials in the United States, the European Union, and Japan are asking not whether to invest but how much.

ELIZABETH C. ECONOMY is C. V. Starr Senior Fellow and Director for Asia Studies at the Council on Foreign Relations and the author of *The River Runs Black: The Environmental Challenges to China's Future.*

Unfortunately, much of this enthusiasm stems from the widespread but misguided belief that what Beijing says goes. The central government sets the country's agenda, but it does not control all aspects of its implementation. In fact, local officials rarely heed Beijing's environmental mandates, preferring to concentrate their energies and resources on further advancing economic growth. The truth is that turning the environmental situation in China around will require something far more difficult than setting targets and spending money; it will require revolutionary bottom-up political and economic reforms.

For one thing, China's leaders need to make it easy for local officials and factory owners to do the right thing when it comes to the environment by giving them the right incentives. At the same time, they must loosen the political restrictions they have placed on the courts, nongovernmental organizations (NGOs), and the media in order to enable these groups to become independent enforcers of environmental protection. The international community, for its part, must focus more on assisting reform and less on transferring cutting-edge technologies and developing demonstration projects. Doing so will mean diving into the trenches to work with local Chinese officials, factory owners, and environmental NGOs; enlisting international NGOs to help with education and enforcement policies; and persuading multinational corporations (MNCs) to use their economic leverage to ensure that their Chinese partners adopt the best environmental practices.

Without such a clear-eyed understanding not only of what China wants but also of what it needs, China will continue to have one of the world's worst environmental records, and the Chinese people and the rest of the world will pay the price.

SINS OF EMISSION

China's rapid development, often touted as an economic miracle, has become an environmental disaster. Record growth necessarily requires the gargantuan consumption of resources, but in China energy use has been especially unclean and inefficient, with dire consequences for the country's air, land, and water.

The coal that has powered China's economic growth, for example, is also choking its people. Coal provides about 70 percent of China's energy needs: the country consumed some 2.4 billion tons in 2006—more than the United States, Japan, and the United Kingdom combined. In 2000, China anticipated doubling its coal consumption by 2020; it is now expected to have done so by the end of this year. Consumption in China is huge partly because it is inefficient: as one Chinese official told Der Spiegel in early 2006, "To produce goods worth $10,000 we need seven times the resources used by Japan, almost six times the resources used by the U.S. and—a particular source of embarrassment—almost three times the resources used by India."

Meanwhile, this reliance on coal is devastating China's environment. The country is home to 16 of the world's 20 most polluted cities, and four of the worst off among them are in the coal-rich province of Shanxi, in northeastern China. As much as 90 percent of China's sulfur dioxide emissions and 50 percent of its particulate emissions are the result of coal use. Particulates are responsible for respiratory problems among the population, and acid rain, which is caused by sulfur dioxide emissions, falls on one-quarter of China's territory and on one-third of its agricultural land, diminishing agricultural output and eroding buildings.

Yet coal use may soon be the least of China's air-quality problems. The transportation boom poses a growing challenge to China's air quality. Chinese developers are laying more than 52,700 miles of new highways throughout the country. Some 14,000 new cars hit China's roads each day. By 2020, China is expected to have 130 million cars, and by 2050—or perhaps as early as 2040—it is expected to have even more cars than the United States. Beijing already pays a high price for this boom. In a 2006 survey, Chinese respondents rated Beijing the 15th most livable city in China, down from the 4th in 2005, with the drop due largely to increased traffic and pollution. Levels of airborne particulates are now six times higher in Beijing than in New York City.

China's grand-scale urbanization plans will aggravate matters. China's leaders plan to relocate 400 million people—equivalent to well over the entire population of the United States—to newly developed urban centers between 2000 and 2030. In the process, they will erect half of all the buildings expected to be constructed in the world during that period. This is a troubling prospect considering that Chinese buildings are not energy efficient—in fact, they are roughly two and a half times less so than those in Germany. Furthermore, newly urbanized Chinese, who use air conditioners, televisions, and refrigerators, consume about three and a half times more energy than do their rural counterparts. And although China is one of the world's largest producer of solar cells, compact fluorescent lights, and energy-efficient windows, these are produced mostly for export. Unless more of these energy-saving goods stay at home, the building boom will result in skyrocketing energy consumption and pollution.

China's land has also suffered from unfettered development and environmental neglect. Centuries of deforestation, along with the overgrazing of grasslands and overcultivation of cropland, have left much of China's north and northwest seriously degraded. In the past half century, moreover, forests and farmland have had to make way for industry and sprawling cities, resulting in diminishing crop yields, a loss in biodiversity, and local climatic change. The Gobi Desert, which now engulfs much of western and northern China, is spreading by about 1,900 square miles annually; some reports say that despite Beijing's aggressive reforestation efforts, one-quarter of the entire country is now desert. China's State Forestry Administration estimates that desertification has hurt some 400 million Chinese, turning tens of millions of them into environmental refugees, in search of new homes and jobs. Meanwhile, much of China's arable soil is contaminated, raising concerns about food safety. As much as ten percent of China's farmland is believed to be polluted, and every year 12 million tons of grain are contaminated with heavy metals absorbed from the soil.

WATER HAZARD

And then there is the problem of access to clean water. Although China holds the fourth-largest freshwater resources in the world (after Brazil, Russia, and Canada), skyrocketing demand, overuse, inefficiencies, pollution, and unequal distribution have produced a situation in which two-thirds of China's approximately 660 cities have less water than they need and 110 of them suffer severe shortages. According to Ma Jun, a leading Chinese water expert, several cities near Beijing and Tianjin, in the northeastern region of the country, could run out of water in five to seven years.

Growing demand is part of the problem, of course, but so is enormous waste. The agricultural sector lays claim to 66 percent of the water China consumes, mostly for irrigation, and manages to waste more than half of that. Chinese industries are highly inefficient: they generally use 10-20 percent more water than do their counterparts in developed countries. Urban China is an especially huge squanderer: it loses up to 20 percent of the water it consumes through leaky pipes—a problem that China's Ministry of Construction has pledged to address in the next two to three years. As urbanization proceeds and incomes rise, the Chinese, much like people in Europe and the United States, have become larger consumers of water: they take lengthy showers, use washing machines and dishwashers, and purchase second homes with lawns that need to be watered. Water consumption in Chinese cities jumped by 6.6 percent during 2004-5. China's plundering of its ground-water reserves, which has created massive underground tunnels, is causing a corollary problem: some of China's wealthiest cities are sinking—in the case of Shanghai and Tianjin, by more than six feet during the past decade and a half. In Beijing, subsidence has destroyed factories, buildings, and underground pipelines and is threatening the city's main international airport.

Pollution is also endangering China's water supplies. China's ground water, which provides 70 percent of the country's total drinking water, is under threat from a variety of sources, such as polluted surface water, hazardous waste sites, and pesticides and fertilizers. According to one report by the government-run Xinhua News Agency, the aquifers in 90 percent of Chinese cities are polluted. More than 75 percent of the river water flowing through China's urban areas is considered unsuitable for drinking or fishing, and the Chinese government deems about 30 percent of the river water throughout the country to be unfit for use in agriculture or industry. As a result, nearly 700 million people drink water contaminated with animal and human waste. The World Bank has found that the failure to provide fully two-thirds of the rural population with piped water is a leading cause of death among children under the age of five and is responsible for as much as 11 percent of the cases of gastrointestinal cancer in China.

One of the problems is that although China has plenty of laws and regulations designed to ensure clean water, factory owners and local officials do not enforce them. A 2005 survey of 509 cities revealed that only 23 percent of factories properly treated sewage before disposing of it. According to another report, today one-third of all industrial wastewater in China and two-thirds of household sewage are released untreated. Recent Chinese studies of two of the country's most important sources of water—the Yangtze and Yellow rivers—illustrate the growing challenge. The Yangtze River, which stretches all the way from the Tibetan Plateau to Shanghai, receives 40 percent of the country's sewage, 80 percent of it untreated. In 2007, the Chinese government announced that it was delaying, in part because of pollution, the development of a $60 billion plan to divert the river in order to supply the water-starved cities of Beijing and Tianjin. The Yellow River supplies water to more than 150 million people and 15 percent of China's agricultural land, but two-thirds of its water is considered unsafe to drink and 10 percent of its water is classified as sewage. In early 2007, Chinese officials announced that over one-third of the fish species native to the Yellow River had become extinct due to damming or pollution.

China's leaders are also increasingly concerned about how climate change may exacerbate their domestic environmental situation. In the spring of 2007, Beijing released its first national assessment report on climate change, predicting a 30 percent drop in precipitation in three of China's seven major river regions—around the Huai, Liao, and Hai rivers—and a 37 percent decline in the country's wheat, rice, and corn yields in the second half of the century. It also predicted that the Yangtze and Yellow rivers, which derive much of their water from glaciers in Tibet, would overflow as the glaciers melted and then dry up. And both Chinese and international scientists now warn that due to rising sea levels, Shanghai could be submerged by 2050.

COLLATERAL DAMAGE

China's environmental problems are already affecting the rest of the world. Japan and South Korea have long suffered from the acid rain produced by China's coal-fired power plants and from the eastbound dust storms that sweep across the Gobi Desert in the spring and dump toxic yellow dust on their land. Researchers in the United States are tracking dust, sulfur, soot, and trace metals as these travel across the Pacific from China. The U.S. Environmental Protection Agency estimates that on some days, 25 percent of the particulates in the atmosphere in Los Angeles originated in China.[1] Scientists have also traced rising levels of mercury deposits on U.S. soil back to coal-fired power plants and cement factories in China. (When ingested in significant quantities, mercury can cause birth defects and developmental problems.) Reportedly, 25-40 percent of all mercury emissions in the world come from China.

What China dumps into its waters is also polluting the rest of the world. According to the international NGO the World Wildlife Fund, China is now the largest polluter of the Pacific Ocean. As Liu Quangfeng, an adviser to the National People's Congress, put it, "Almost no river that flows into the Bo Hai [a sea along China's

---

1 The original Associated Press story that was the source for the statement was mistaken and has been corrected. In fact, the EPA, citing a model saying that Asia contributes about 30 percent of the background sulfate particulate matter in the western United States, estimates that Asia contributes about one percent of all particulate matter in Los Angeles

northern coast] is clean." China releases about 2.8 billion tons of contaminated water into the Bo Hai annually, and the content of heavy metal in the mud at the bottom of it is now 2,000 times as high as China's own official safety standard. The prawn catch has dropped by 90 percent over the past 15 years. In 2006, in the heavily industrialized southeastern provinces of Guangdong and Fujian, almost 8.3 billion tons of sewage were discharged into the ocean without treatment, a 60 percent increase from 2001. More than 80 percent of the East China Sea, one of the world's largest fisheries, is now rated unsuitable for fishing, up from 53 percent in 2000.

Furthermore, China is already attracting international attention for its rapidly growing contribution to climate change. According to a 2007 report from the Netherlands Environmental Assessment Agency, it has already surpassed the United States as the world's largest contributor of carbon dioxide, a leading greenhouse gas, to the atmosphere. Unless China rethinks its use of various sources of energy and adopts cutting-edge environmentally friendly technologies, warned Fatih Birol, the chief economist of the International Energy Agency, last April, in 25 years China will emit twice as much carbon dioxide as all the countries of the Organization for Economic Cooperation and Development combined.

China's close economic partners in the developing world face additional environmental burdens from China's economic activities. Chinese multinationals, which are exploiting natural resources in Africa, Latin America, and Southeast Asia in order to fuel China's continued economic rise, are devastating these regions' habitats in the process. China's hunger for timber has exploded over the past decade and a half, and particularly since 1998, when devastating floods led Beijing to crack down on domestic logging. China's timber imports more than tripled between 1993 and 2005. According to the World Wildlife Fund, China's demand for timber, paper, and pulp will likely increase by 33 percent between 2005 and 2010.

China is already the largest importer of illegally logged timber in the world: an estimated 50 percent of its timber imports are reportedly illegal. Illegal logging is especially damaging to the environment because it often targets rare old-growth forests, endangers biodiversity, and ignores sustainable forestry practices. In 2006, the government of Cambodia, for example, ignored its own laws and awarded China's Wuzhishan LS Group a 99-year concession that was 20 times as large as the size permitted by Cambodian law. The company's practices, including the spraying of large amounts of herbicides, have prompted repeated protests by local Cambodians. According to the international NGO Global Witness, Chinese companies have destroyed large parts of the forests along the Chinese-Myanmar border and are now moving deeper into Myanmar's forests in their search for timber. In many instances, illicit logging activity takes place with the active support of corrupt local officials. Central government officials in Myanmar and Indonesia, countries where China's loggers are active, have protested such arrangements to Beijing, but relief has been limited. These activities, along with those of Chinese mining and energy companies, raise serious environmental concerns for many local populations in the developing world.

SPOILING THE PARTY

In the view of China's leaders, however, damage to the environment itself is a secondary problem. Of greater concern to them are its indirect effects: the threat it poses to the continuation of the Chinese economic miracle and to public health, social stability, and the country's international reputation. Taken together, these challenges could undermine the authority of the Communist Party.

China's leaders are worried about the environment's impact on the economy. Several studies conducted both inside and outside China estimate that environmental degradation and pollution cost the Chinese economy between 8 percent and 12 percent of GDP annually. The Chinese media frequently publish the results of studies on the impact of pollution on agriculture, industrial output, or public health: water pollution costs of $35.8 billion one year, air pollution costs of $27.5 billion another, and on and on with weather disasters ($26.5 billion), acid rain ($13.3 billion), desertification

($6 billion), or crop damage from soil pollution ($2.5 billion). The city of Chongqing, which sits on the banks of the Yangtze River, estimates that dealing with the effects of water pollution on its agriculture and public health costs as much as 4.3 percent of the city's annual gross product. Shanxi Province has watched its coal resources fuel the rest of the country while it pays the price in withered trees, contaminated air and water, and land subsidence. Local authorities there estimate the costs of environmental degradation and pollution at 10.9 percent of the province's annual gross product and have called on Beijing to compensate the province for its "contribution and sacrifice."

China's Ministry of Public Health is also sounding the alarm with increasing urgency. In a survey of 30 cities and 78 counties released in the spring, the ministry blamed worsening air and water pollution for dramatic increases in the incidence of cancer throughout the country: a 19 percent rise in urban areas and a 23 percent rise in rural areas since 2005. One research institute affiliated with SEPA has put the total number of premature deaths in China caused by respiratory diseases related to air pollution at 400,000 a year. But this may be a conservative estimate: according to a joint research project by the World Bank and the Chinese government released this year, the total number of such deaths is 750,000 a year. (Beijing is said not to have wanted to release the latter figure for fear of inciting social unrest.) Less well documented but potentially even more devastating is the health impact of China's polluted water. Today, fully 190 million Chinese are sick from drinking contaminated water. All along China's major rivers, villages report skyrocketing rates of diarrheal diseases, cancer, tumors, leukemia, and stunted growth.

Social unrest over these issues is rising. In the spring of 2006, China's top environmental official, Zhou Shengxian, announced that there had been 51,000 pollution-related protests in 2005, which amounts to almost 1,000 protests each week. Citizen complaints about the environment, expressed on official hotlines and in letters to local officials, are increasing at a rate of 30 percent a year;

they will likely top 450,000 in 2007. But few of them are resolved satisfactorily, and so people throughout the country are increasingly taking to the streets. For several months in 2006, for example, the residents of six neighboring villages in Gansu Province held repeated protests against zinc and iron smelters that they believed were poisoning them. Fully half of the 4,000-5,000 villagers exhibited lead-related illnesses, ranging from vitamin D deficiency to neurological problems.

Many pollution-related marches are relatively small and peaceful. But when such demonstrations fail, the protesters sometimes resort to violence. After trying for two years to get redress by petitioning local, provincial, and even central government officials for spoiled crops and poisoned air, in the spring of 2005, 30,000-40,000 villagers from Zhejiang Province swarmed 13 chemical plants, broke windows and overturned buses, attacked government officials, and torched police cars. The government sent in 10,000 members of the People's Armed Police in response. The plants were ordered to close down, and several environmental activists who attempted to monitor the plants' compliance with these orders were later arrested. China's leaders have generally managed to prevent— if sometimes violently—discontent over environmental issues from spreading across provincial boundaries or morphing into calls for broader political reform.

In the face of such problems, China's leaders have recently injected a new urgency into their rhetoric concerning the need to protect the country's environment. On paper, this has translated into an aggressive strategy to increase investment in environmental protection, set ambitious targets for the reduction of pollution and energy intensity (the amount of energy used to produce a unit of GDP), and introduce new environmentally friendly technologies. In 2005, Beijing set out a number of impressive targets for its next five-year plan: by 2010, it wants 10 percent of the nation's power to come from renewable energy sources, energy intensity to have been reduced by 20 percent and key pollutants such as sulfur dioxide by 10 percent, water consumption to have decreased by

30 percent, and investment in environmental protection to have increased from 1.3 percent to 1.6 percent of GDP. Premier Wen Jiabao has issued a stern warning to local officials to shut down some of the plants in the most energy-intensive industries—power generation and aluminum, copper, steel, coke and coal, and cement production—and to slow the growth of other industries by denying them tax breaks and other production incentives.

These goals are laudable—even breathtaking in some respects—but history suggests that only limited optimism is warranted; achieving such targets has proved elusive in the past. In 2001, the Chinese government pledged to cut sulfur dioxide emissions by 10 percent between 2002 and 2005. Instead, emissions rose by 27 percent. Beijing is already encountering difficulties reaching its latest goals: for instance, it has failed to meet its first target for reducing energy intensity and pollution. Despite warnings from Premier Wen, the six industries that were slated to slow down posted a 20.6 percent increase in output during the first quarter of 2007—a 6.6 percent jump from the same period last year. According to one senior executive with the Indian wind-power firm Suzlon Energy, only 37 percent of the wind-power projects the Chinese government approved in 2004 have been built. Perhaps worried that yet another target would fall by the wayside, in early 2007, Beijing revised its announced goal of reducing the country's water consumption by 30 percent by 2010 to just 20 percent.

Even the Olympics are proving to be a challenge. Since Beijing promised in 2001 to hold a "green Olympics" in 2008, the International Olympic Committee has pulled out all the stops. Beijing is now ringed with rows of newly planted trees, hybrid taxis and buses are roaming its streets (some of which are soon to be lined with solar-powered lamps), the most heavily polluting factories have been pushed outside the city limits, and the Olympic dormitories are models of energy efficiency. Yet in key respects, Beijing has failed to deliver. City officials are backtracking from their pledge to provide safe tap water to all of Beijing for the Olympics; they now say that they will provide it only for residents of the

Olympic Village. They have announced drastic stopgap measures for the duration of the games, such as banning one million of the city's three million cars from the city's streets and halting production at factories in and around Beijing (some of them are resisting). Whatever progress city authorities have managed over the past six years—such as increasing the number of days per year that the city's air is deemed to be clean—is not enough to ensure that the air will be clean for the Olympic Games. Preparing for the Olympics has come to symbolize the intractability of China's environmental challenges and the limits of Beijing's approach to addressing them.

PROBLEMS WITH THE LOCALS

Clearly, something has got to give. The costs of inaction to China's economy, public health, and international reputation are growing. And perhaps more important, social discontent is rising. The Chinese people have clearly run out of patience with the government's inability or unwillingness to turn the environmental situation around. And the government is well aware of the increasing potential for environmental protest to ignite broader social unrest.

One event this spring particularly alarmed China's leaders. For several days in May in the coastal city of Xiamen, after months of mounting opposition to the planned construction of a $1.4 billion petrochemical plant nearby, students and professors at Xiamen University, among others, are said to have sent out a million mobile-phone text messages calling on their fellow citizens to take to the streets on June 1. That day, and the following, protesters reportedly numbering between 7,000 and 20,000 marched peacefully through the city, some defying threats of expulsion from school or from the Communist Party. The protest was captured on video and uploaded to YouTube. One video featured a haunting voice-over that linked the Xiamen demonstration to an ongoing environmental crisis near Tai Hu, a lake some 400 miles away (a large bloom of blue-green algae caused by industrial wastewater and sewage dumped in the lake had contaminated the water supply of the city of Wuxi). It also referred to the Tiananmen Square protest of 1989. The Xiamen march, the narrator said, was perhaps "the first genuine parade since Tiananmen."

In response, city authorities did stay the construction of the plant, but they also launched an all-out campaign to discredit the protesters and their videos. Still, more comments about the protest and calls not to forget Tiananmen appeared on various Web sites. Such messages, posted openly and accessible to all Chinese, represent the Chinese leadership's greatest fear, namely, that its failure to protect the environment may someday serve as the catalyst for broad-based demands for political change.

Such public demonstrations are also evidence that China's environmental challenges cannot be met with only impressive targets and more investment. They must be tackled with a fundamental reform of how the country does business and protects the environment. So far, Beijing has structured its environmental protection efforts in much the same way that it has pursued economic growth: by granting local authorities and factory owners wide decision-making power and by actively courting the international community and Chinese NGOs for their expertise while carefully monitoring their activities.

Consider, for example, China's most important environmental authority, SEPA, in Beijing. SEPA has become a wellspring of China's most innovative environmental policies: it has promoted an environmental impact assessment law; a law requiring local officials to release information about environmental disasters, pollution statistics, and the names of known polluters to the public; an experiment to calculate the costs of environmental degradation and pollution to the country's GDP; and an all-out effort to halt over 100 large-scale infrastructure projects that had proceeded without proper environmental impact assessments. But SEPA operates with barely 300 full-time professional staff in the capital and only a few hundred employees spread throughout the country. (The U.S. Environmental Protection Agency has a staff of almost 9,000 in Washington, D.C., alone.) And authority for enforcing SEPA's mandates rests overwhelmingly with local officials and the local environmental protection officials they oversee. In some cases, this has allowed for exciting experimentation. In the eastern province of Jiangsu, for instance, the World Bank and the Natural Resources Defense Council have launched the Greenwatch program, which grades 12,000 factories according to their compliance with standards for industrial wastewater treatment and discloses both the ratings and the reasons for them. More often, however, China's highly decentralized system has meant limited progress: only seven to ten percent of China's more than 660 cities meet the standards required to receive the designation of National Model Environmental City from SEPA. According to Wang Canfa, one of China's top environmental lawyers, barely ten percent of China's environmental laws and regulations are actually enforced.

One of the problems is that local officials have few incentives to place a priority on environmental protection. Even as Beijing touts the need to protect the environment, Premier Wen has called for quadrupling the Chinese economy by 2020. The price of water is rising in some cities, such as Beijing, but in many others it remains as low as 20 percent of the replacement cost. That ensures that factories and municipalities have little reason to invest in wastewater treatment or other water-conservation efforts. Fines for polluting are so low that factory managers often prefer to pay them rather than adopt costlier pollution-control technologies. One manager of a coal-fired power plant explained to a Chinese reporter in 2005 that he was ignoring a recent edict mandating that all new power plants use desulfurization equipment because the technology cost as much as would 15 years' worth of fines.

Local governments also turn a blind eye to serious pollution problems out of self-interest. Officials sometimes have a direct financial stake in factories or personal relationships with their owners. And the local environmental protection bureaus tasked with guarding against such corruption must report to the local governments, making them easy targets for political pressure. In recent years, the Chinese media have uncovered cases in which local officials have put pressure on the courts, the press, or even hospitals to prevent the wrongdoings of factories from coming to light. (Just this year, in the province of Zhejiang, officials reportedly promised factories with an output of $1.2 million or more that they would not be subjected to government inspections without the factories' prior approval.)

Moreover, local officials frequently divert environmental protection funds and spend them on unrelated or ancillary endeavors. The Chinese Academy for Environmental Planning, which reports to SEPA, disclosed this year that only half of the 1.3 percent of the country's annual GDP dedicated to environmental protection between 2001 and 2005 had found its way to legitimate projects. According to the study, about 60 percent of the environmental protection funds spent in urban areas during that period went into the creation of, among other things, parks, factory production lines, gas stations, and sewage-treatment plants rather than into waste- or wastewater-treatment facilities.

Many local officials also thwart efforts to hold them accountable for their failure to protect the environment. In 2005, SEPA launched the "Green GDP" campaign, a project designed to calculate the costs of environmental degradation and pollution to local economies and provide a basis for evaluating the performance of local officials both according to their economic stewardship and according to how well they protect the environment. Several provinces balked, however, worried that the numbers would reveal the extent of the damage suffered by the environment. SEPA's partner in the campaign, the National Bureau of Statistics of China, also undermined the effort by announcing that it did not possess the tools to do Green GDP accounting accurately and that in any case it did not believe officials should be evaluated on such a basis. After releasing a partial report in September 2006, the NBS has refused to release this year's findings to the public.

Another problem is that many Chinese companies see little direct value in ratcheting up their environmental protection efforts. The computer manufacturer Lenovo and the appliance manufacturer

Haier have received high marks for taking creative environmental measures, and the solar energy company Suntech has become a leading exporter of solar cells. But a recent poll found that only 18 percent of Chinese companies believed that they could thrive economically while doing the right thing environmentally. Another poll of business executives found that an overwhelming proportion of them do not understand the benefits of responsible corporate behavior, such as environmental protection, or consider the requirements too burdensome.

NOT GOOD ENOUGH

The limitations of the formal authorities tasked with environmental protection in China have led the country's leaders to seek assistance from others outside the bureaucracy. Over the past 15 years or so, China's NGOs, the Chinese media, and the international community have become central actors in the country's bid to rescue its environment. But the Chinese government remains wary of them.

China's homegrown environmental activists and their allies in the media have become the most potent—and potentially explosive—force for environmental change in China. From four or five NGOs devoted primarily to environmental education and biodiversity protection in the mid-1990s, the Chinese environmental movement has grown to include thousands of NGOs, run primarily by dynamic Chinese in their 30s and 40s. These groups now routinely expose polluting factories to the central government, sue for the rights of villagers poisoned by contaminated water or air, give seed money to small newer NGOs throughout the country, and go undercover to expose multinationals that ignore international environmental standards. They often protest via letters to the government, campaigns on the Internet, and editorials in Chinese newspapers. The media are an important ally in this fight: they shame polluters, uncover environmental abuse, and highlight environmental protection successes.

Beijing has come to tolerate NGOs and media outlets that play environmental watchdog at the local level, but it remains vigilant in making sure that certain limits are not crossed, and especially that the central government is not directly criticized. The penalties for misjudging these boundaries can be severe. Wu Lihong worked for 16 years to address the pollution in Tai Hu (which recently spawned blue-green algae), gathering evidence that has forced almost 200 factories to close. Although in 2005 Beijing honored Wu as one of the country's top environmentalists, he was beaten by local thugs several times during the course of his investigations, and in 2006 the government of the town of Yixing arrested him on dubious charges of blackmail. And Yu Xiaogang, the 2006 winner of the prestigious Goldman Environmental Prize, honoring grassroots environmentalists, was forbidden to travel abroad in retaliation for educating villagers about the potential downsides of a proposed dam relocation in Yunnan Province.

The Chinese government's openness to environmental cooperation with the international community is also fraught. Beijing has welcomed bilateral agreements for technology development or financial assistance for demonstration projects, but it is concerned about other endeavors. On the one hand, it lauds international environmental NGOs for their contributions to China's environmental protection efforts. On the other hand, it fears that some of them will become advocates for democratization.

The government also subjects MNCs to an uncertain operating environment. Many corporations have responded to the government's calls that they assume a leading role in the country's environmental protection efforts by deploying top-of-the-line environmental technologies, financing environmental education in Chinese schools, undertaking community-based efforts, and raising operating standards in their industries. Coca-Cola, for example, recently pledged to become a net-zero consumer of water, and Wal-Mart is set to launch a nationwide education and sales initiative to promote the use of energy-efficient compact fluorescent bulbs. Sometimes, MNCs have been rewarded with awards or significant publicity. But in the past two years, Chinese officials (as well as local NGOs) have adopted a much tougher stance toward them, arguing at times that MNCs have turned China into the pollution capital of the world. On issues such as electronic waste, the detractors have a point. But China's attacks, with Internet postings accusing MNCs of practicing "eco-colonialism," have become unjustifiably broad. Such antiforeign sentiment spiked in late 2006, after the release of a pollution map listing more than 3,000 factories that were violating water pollution standards. The 33 among them that supplied MNCs were immediately targeted in the media, while the other few thousand Chinese factories cited somehow escaped the frenzy. A few Chinese officials and activists privately acknowledge that domestic Chinese companies pollute far more than foreign companies, but it seems unlikely that the spotlight will move off MNCs in the near future. For now, it is simply more expedient to let international corporations bear the bulk of the blame.

FROM RED TO GREEN

Why is China unable to get its environmental house in order? Its top officials want what the United States, Europe, and Japan have: thriving economies with manageable environmental problems. But they are unwilling to pay the political and economic price to get there. Beijing's message to local officials continues to be that economic growth cannot be sacrificed to environmental protection—that the two objectives must go hand in hand.

This, however, only works sometimes. Greater energy efficiency can bring economic benefits, and investments to reduce pollution, such as in building wastewater-treatment plants, are expenses that can be balanced against the costs of losing crops to contaminated soil and having a sickly work force. Yet much of the time, charting a new environmental course comes with serious economic costs up front. Growth slows down in some industries or some regions. Some businesses are forced to close down. Developing pollution-treatment and pollution-prevention technologies requires serious investment. In fact, it is because they recognize these costs that local officials in China pursue their short-term economic interests first and for the most part ignore Beijing's directives to change their ways.

This is not an unusual problem. All countries suffer internal tugs of war over how to balance the short-term costs of improving environmental protection with the long-term costs of failing to do so. But China faces an additional burden. Its environmental problems stem as much from China's corrupt and undemocratic political system as from Beijing's continued focus on economic growth. Local officials and business leaders routinely—and with impunity—ignore environmental laws and regulations, abscond with environmental protection funds, and silence those who challenge them. Thus, improving the environment in China is not simply a matter of mandating pollution-control technologies; it is also a matter of reforming the country's political culture. Effective environmental protection requires transparent information, official accountability, and an independent legal system. But these features are the building blocks of a political system fundamentally different from that of China today, and so far there is little indication that China's leaders will risk the authority of the Communist Party on charting a new environmental course. Until the party is willing to open the door to such reform, it will not have the wherewithal to meet its ambitious environmental targets and lead a growing economy with manageable environmental problems.

Given this reality, the United States—and the rest of the world—will have to get much smarter about how to cooperate with China in order to assist its environmental protection efforts. Above all, the United States must devise a limited and coherent set of priorities. China's needs are vast, but its capacity is poor; therefore, launching one or two significant initiatives over the next five to ten years would do more good than a vast array of uncoordinated projects. These endeavors could focus on discrete issues, such as climate change or the illegal timber trade; institutional changes, such as strengthening the legal system in regard to China's environmental protection efforts; or broad reforms, such as promoting energy efficiency throughout the Chinese economy. Another key to an effective U.S.-Chinese partnership is U.S. leadership. Although U.S. NGOs and U.S.-based MNCs are often at the forefront of environmental policy and technological innovation, the U.S. government itself is not a world leader on key environmental concerns. Unless the United States improves its own policies and practices on, for example, climate change, the illegal timber trade, and energy efficiency, it will have little credibility or leverage to push China.

China, for its part, will undoubtedly continue to place a priority on gaining easy access to financial and technological assistance. Granting this, however, would be the wrong way to go. Joint efforts between the United States and China, such as the recently announced project to capture methane from 15 Chinese coal mines, are important, of course. But the systemic changes needed to set China on a new environmental trajectory necessitate a bottom-up overhaul. One way to start would be to promote energy efficiency in Chinese factories and buildings. Simply bringing these up to world standards would bring vast gains. International and Chinese NGOs, Chinese environmental protection bureaus, and MNCs could audit and rate Chinese factories based on how well their manufacturing processes and building standards met a set of energy-efficiency targets. Their scores (and the factors that determined them) could then be disclosed to the public via the Internet and the print media, and factories with subpar performances could be given the means to improve their practices.

A pilot program in Guangdong Province, which is run under the auspices of the U.S. consulate in Hong Kong, provides just such a mechanism. Factories that apply for energy audits can take out loans from participating banks to pay for efficiency upgrades, with the expectation that they will pay the loans back over time out of the savings they will realize from using fewer materials or conserving energy. Such programs should be encouraged and could be reinforced by requiring, for example, that the U.S.-based MNCs that worked with the participating factories rewarded those that met or exceeded the standards and penalized those that did not (the MNCs could either expand or reduce their orders, for example). NGOs and the media in China could also publicize the names of the factories that refused to cooperate. These initiatives would have the advantages of operating within the realities of China's environmental protection system, providing both incentives and disincentives to encourage factories to comply; strengthening the role of key actors such as NGOs, the media, and local environmental protection bureaus; and engaging new actors such as Chinese banks. It is likely that as with the Greenwatch program, factory owners and local officials not used to transparency would oppose such efforts, but if they were persuaded that full participation would bring more sales to MNCs and grow local economies, many of them would be more open to public disclosure.

Of course, much of the burden and the opportunity for China to revolutionize the way it reconciles environmental protection and economic development rests with the Chinese government itself. No amount of international assistance can transform China's domestic environment or its contribution to global environmental challenges. Real change will arise only from strong central leadership and the development of a system of incentives that make it easier for local officials and the Chinese people to embrace environmental protection. This will sometimes mean making tough economic choices.

Improvements to energy efficiency, of the type promoted by the program in Guangdong, are reforms of the low-hanging-fruit variety: they promise both economic gains and benefits to the environment. It will be more difficult to implement reforms that are economically costly (such as reforms that raise the costs of manufacturing in order to encourage conservation and recycling and those that impose higher fines against polluters), are likely to be unpopular (such as reforms that hike the price of water), or could undermine the Communist Party's authority (such as reforms that open up the media or give freer rein to civil society). But such measures are also necessary. And their high up-front costs must be weighed against the long-term costs to economic growth, public health, and social stability in which the Chinese government's continued inaction would result. The government must ensure greater accountability among local officials by promoting greater grass-roots oversight, greater transparency via the media or other outlets, and greater independence in the legal system.

China's leaders have shown themselves capable of bold reform in the past. Two and half decades ago, Deng Xiaoping and his supporters launched a set of ambitious reforms despite stiff political resistance and set the current economic miracle in motion. In order to continue on its extraordinary trajectory, China needs leaders with the vision to introduce a new set of economic and political initiatives that will transform the way the country does business. Without such measures, China will not return to global preeminence in the twenty-first century. Instead, it will suffer stagnation or regression—and all because leaders who recognized the challenge before them were unwilling to do what was necessary to surmount it.

Pollution Without Revolution

Why China's Environmental Crisis Won't Bring Down the Regime

Scott M. Moore

O
n a smoggy day this past February, Chinese President Xi
Jinping did a remarkable thing: he went for a stroll outside without the face mask that Beijingers often don to
protect themselves against the capital's air pollution. With Xi's grin
on full display, the political message was unmistakable. "In the
Midst of Smog, Xi Jinping Tours Beijing," a headline in state-run
media declared the next day. "He Breathes the Same Air and Shares
the Same Fate."

To many observers, Xi's stroll through the smog hinted at Beijing's concern that environmental issues could drive widespread
opposition to the regime. In recent decades, the idea that environmental crises can help drive democratic reforms has gained
popular credence. Perhaps most notably, some historians have
argued that the Soviet Union's bungled response to the Chernobyl nuclear disaster helped to hasten its demise. Others have
documented how environmental issues helped to galvanize new
opposition movements in eastern Europe, South Korea, and
Taiwan.

SCOTT M. MOORE is Giorgio Ruffolo Postdoctoral Research Fellow at the
Belfer Center for Science and International Affairs and a 2014–2015 International Affairs Fellow at the Council on Foreign Relations.

Xi is well aware of this history, and he has a plan to prevent it from playing out in the Middle Kingdom. By shifting blame for environmental failures to players outside the central government, he intends to use them to strengthen his own control.

That won't be easy, of course; China is facing an enormous environmental crisis. According to official reports (which likely underrepresent the problem), pesticides and heavy metals contaminate a fifth of China's farmland, and a quarter of the country's water is so polluted that it can't even be used for industrial purposes. Other challenges will likely prove even more overwhelming in coming years. Parts of central and southern China are experiencing unprecedented droughts, which are thought to be brought on by climate change. Add to these problems declining groundwater tables in the country's north-central breadbasket region, rapid warming on the Tibetan plateau, and a severe loss of biodiversity nationwide, and it's clear that environmental issues constitute one of the greatest threats to China's future development.

This threat is reflected in the growing focus on the environment in domestic politics. The number of nongovernmental organizations focused on the environment is growing, and, according to a 2013 survey, 80 percent of Chinese citizens believe that environmental protection should be a higher priority than economic development. Of particular concern to China's leadership, the number of pollution-related protests appears to be increasing, and they are occasionally turning violent. During one recent rally in Hangzhou, a major city near Shanghai, dozens of residents and police were reportedly hurt in a scuffle over the planned construction of a waste incinerator.

To be sure, for Beijing, discontent is dangerous, and the growing degree of ambition and sophistication in China's environmental policy partly reflects that. But outside observers, including the policy and business community in the United States, would be mistaken to believe that popular discontent over the environment will lead to major political or policy changes in China. Beijing is pursuing a deliberate and largely successful strategy of protecting the central government from environmental fallout by skillfully deflecting blame toward protectionist local officials and state-owned enterprises. In the process, the central government is enhancing its own power.

BLAME GAME

China's environmental protection system resembles a pyramid, in which top leaders and officials in central government ministries develop policies for implementation at provincial and local levels. This division of power is meant to ensure that centrally formulated policies are appropriately applied according to local circumstances. The fact that local officials operate at arm's length from the central government also helps insulate Beijing from being blamed for local environmental disasters.

Local governments do deserve much of the criticism, but there are so many problems precisely because Beijing encourages such lapses. The party generally evaluates and promotes lower-level officials based on their ability to meet short-term economic growth and development targets, which are often at odds with long-term goals such as decreasing pollution and addressing other environmental concerns. Moreover, the latitude that local officials have to promote economic development in their jurisdictions has incentivized them to maintain incestuous ties to local business interests—ties that encourage them to shield favored companies from compliance with environmental regulations. In 2009, for example, a chemical company released several tons of industrial acids into a major waterway, disrupting water supplies to some 200,000 people in southern China for days. A government investigation later revealed that the company had been reprimanded several times for illegally discharging waste. But thanks to patrons in the local government, the company had gotten off each time with little more than a warning.

As China's environmental crisis worsens, Beijing appears to rely on the blame game more and more. One favored tactic has been the use of "name-and-shame" lists, which feature highly polluting cities and municipalities that fail to meet Beijing's environmental protection benchmarks. More recently, the central government has begun to target state-owned enterprises for environmental policy failures. A 2013 editorial in the government-run *China Daily*, for example, lauded a fine that a provincial government levied on the state-owned Sinopec oil company for polluting a city in the eastern province of Anhui. At fault, the editorial argued, was a "combination of power and money." China's local governments, the article concluded, must therefore "perform their duties better and consider long-term development instead of short-term interests." There's no question that addressing environmental concerns in China requires curbing the excesses of powerful state-owned enterprises. But doing so also serves another purpose for Beijing: it increases the regime's leverage over increasingly powerful segments of the economy and of society.

GREEN POWER GRAB

Since the liberalization of the Chinese economy in the late 1970s, Beijing's development model has emphasized economic decentralization. In this context, local governments and enterprises have been given greater leeway to pursue growth. From Beijing's point of view, an unwelcome side effect of this approach has been the rise of players that are independent of the central government. Local officials routinely approve large real-estate deals that accumulate massive debt and raise the ire of displaced residents. In some mining regions, so-called coal bosses effectively run their own government. And due to their sheer size, state-owned companies have become increasingly difficult for the central government to control. (In 2012, Sinopec, a state-owned oil firm, employed over 370,000 people across China.) Many of Beijing's proposed environmental reforms, such as the strengthening of local environmental performance targets and the phasing out of ageing, inefficient power stations, could rein in such players—and thereby help contain any threat they might pose to the central government.

The most recent reforms seem to do just that, prioritizing central control over other environmental goals. In 2011, for example, China's Ministry of Environmental Protection, historically weak and ineffectual, advocated revising the country's environmental protection law that would allow citizens' groups to help monitor polluting enterprises and raise fines on noncompliant local governments. When the measure finally passed this year, however, the participation provisions had been stripped out but the fines had been left alone, centralizing power but depriving the ministry of the power to leverage growing public concern to increase its monitoring and enforcement capabilities. Subsequent reforms have taken a similar tack, providing for closer monitoring of local officials' environmental performance and giving environmental groups in some areas standing to sue state-run enterprises.

Beijing's South-North Water Transfer Project, which aims to correct a regional imbalance in water availability, provides another striking example of this dynamic. The project consists of three canals, including one that crosses the Tibetan Plateau, and will eventually pump some 45 billion cubic meters of water from southern to northern China each year. Construction has already displaced over 300,000 people, and Chinese scientists have raised grave concerns about the project's effect on the region's fragile ecosystems. Moreover, water pollution has been so acute during the project's first phase that Beijing has had to construct over 400 sewage treatment plants along the route to meet and maintain minimum water quality standards. Despite the scale of the damage, the central government has pushed ahead, claiming that the canals will ultimately serve the environment by providing much-needed water to the parched Yellow River. In reality, one of the project's primary goals is to strengthen support for the central government in areas that have fallen behind in China's headlong economic expansion. According to one Chinese expert on the project, it's "a good incentive tool for the central government to encourage local governments" to closely follow Beijing's marching orders.

OUT OF THE HAZE

China's leaders increasingly portray themselves as guardians of the country's environment, promising a greener future courtesy of a strong central government committed to environmental protection. At the 2010 Shanghai Exposition, a propaganda-laced tour of Chinese history ended in an exhibition promising a low-carbon future. Recent statements have served to further reinforce the idea that Chinese leaders are devoted to environmental protection. Last year, in his final major address as premier, Wen Jiabao vowed to "construct an ecological civilization." More recently, current Premier Li Keqiang pledged to wage a "war on pollution" as part of the next phase of the country's economic development strategy, which emphasizes a cleaner, higher-value-added growth model.

Although it's difficult to gauge public opinion on the matter, China's green activists and other concerned citizens appear to support the central government's increasing power over environmental regulations and enforcement. In 2012, Reuters quoted the resident of a heavily polluted city as saying, "If [former Premier] Wen Jiabao or Xi Jinping were to come here now I would certainly tell them what's going on. But I wouldn't trust anyone else." China's environmental NGOs take a similar tack, issuing unsparing criticism of local governments for permitting pollution, while merely calling for a stronger central role in protecting the environment. These calls are not disingenuous; most environmental activists, along with scholars and analysts, believe that pollution stems largely from weaknesses in local-level enforcement. But the fact is that this approach suits Beijing just fine.

It's too early to say how far Beijing's environmental protection efforts will go toward effectively addressing China's environmental ills. Given the country's rapidly growing resource demands, the strain on its environment is unlikely to ebb anytime soon. And given the scale of contamination, water scarcity and soil pollution will likely remain vexing challenges in the years to come. What's more, Western countries' historical experiences suggest that real environmental reforms come through genuine political opposition, something that Beijing will seek to thwart at all costs. But out of this hazy picture emerges a new set of challenges and opportunities for those both within China and abroad who are affected by Beijing's environmental policy.

At the broadest level, the central government's tight embrace of the environmental agenda is likely to complicate the ways in which U.S. companies and nonprofits engage with China. For the business community, access to China's environmental protection industry is and will continue to be a rich prize—government investment in clean technology has continually risen, and the green sector is expected to be worth several hundred billion U.S. dollars by 2015. Yet, for now, foreign enterprises have been largely shut out of this market, and expanding access should be a focus of Washington's economic diplomacy in Beijing. It may also become more difficult for international environmental NGOs to work in China. U.S.-based organizations have had considerable influence in important areas of environmental policy, such as air pollution control, but Beijing's expanding role could crowd out these players going forward. International environmental NGOs should therefore be careful about maintaining their relationships with the Chinese policy community.

Given Beijing's new emphasis on the environment, an even bigger challenge will be addressing the global dimensions of its pollution, the effects of which don't stop at the water's edge. China is by far the largest source of air pollution among all Asian countries, including India, and Chinese emissions negatively affect air quality in a host of neighboring countries, particularly Japan. Chinese air pollution is even degrading air quality in the United States. According to a study recently published in *Proceedings of the National Academy of Sciences*, Chinese air pollution accounts for somewhere between 12 and 24 percent of sulfate pollution in the western United States.

The international community's challenge going forward will be to use Beijing's strong domestic political interest in alleviating pollution to prod it to take substantive steps to reduce the burdens of such pollution on other countries. Looking ahead, one of the more promising areas of cooperation is regional initiatives to combat air pollution, which remains China's largest environmental liability.

This past May, environment ministers from China, Japan, and South Korea met to discuss air pollution. Given poor relations among the three countries involved, it was notable that the ministers pledged to "continue cooperating in the fight against cross-border air pollution, despite strained relations." There is already a wide range of existing intergovernmental agreements among northeast Asian countries concerning air pollution, but most are severely limited in scope. The long-term aim should therefore be to win Asian participation in the UN's Convention on Long-Range Transboundary Air Pollution, which commits parties to reducing air pollutants but, for now, includes only European and North American countries. Such a goal is ambitious; it would require an unprecedented political commitment on Beijing's part to reduce pollutants—not just for its own sake but for the sake of regional cooperation, as well.

In the meantime, China's environmental crisis, severe as it is, won't bring down the Chinese regime—its leaders are too clever to let that happen. Instead, they have carefully co-opted China's growing environmental movement as their own. But there's another side to this dark picture: if Beijing plays its strong hand deftly, it can also achieve some real progress in clearing the haze that hangs over its cities—and the region as a whole.

Harder to Breathe

India's Pollution Crisis—
And What To Do About It

Ira Trivedi

Just a few days before U.S. President Barack Obama arrived in India in January this year, the U.S. embassy in New Delhi recorded an Air Quality Index reading of 222, a level that the U.S. Environmental Protection Agency describes as "very unhealthy," nearly "hazardous." In fact, the pollution level was so bad that the embassy purchased 1,800 Swedish air purifiers ahead of the president's arrival.

A year before Obama's visit, New Delhi surpassed Beijing as the most polluted city in the world. As a whole, India's air quality lags far behind that of the other BRIC countries. The country has 13 of the 20 most polluted cities in the world and, along with China, the highest average exposure to cancerous fine particles, which, because of their small size, can lodge deeply into human lungs. In 2010, India's Central Pollution Control Board found that the particulate matter in 180 Indian cities was six times higher than World Health Organization standards.

Air pollution is an urgent public health crisis. More people in India die of chronic respiratory diseases and asthma than in any other nation in the world. According to a 2015 study conducted by Michael Greenstone, an economist at the University of Chicago, the 660 million people who live in India's most polluted cities will

IRA TRIVEDI is a writer and novelist. Her most recent book is India in Love: Sexuality and Marriage in the 21st Century.

lose an average of 3.2 years of life because of toxic air; all together, that is 2.1 billion lost years.

And dirty air is just one of India's many environmental problems. In addition to poor air quality, groundwater pollution, river contamination, indiscriminate mining, and the destruction of forests have severely comprised the health of the country and its citizens. If India does not change course—and soon—the country will be facing disaster.

A FAMILIAR STORY

India's environmental crisis is not just endangering human lives, but is also holding back the country's economy, which relies heavily on agriculture. Over the last four decades, air pollution, degraded lands, depleted forests, and declining biodiversity have cut agricultural yields in India by almost half. According to the World Bank, each year, environmental degradation costs India $80 billion, or 5.7 percent of GDP.

Meanwhile, nearly 63 percent of India's energy needs are met by coal, the nation's top source of carbon dioxide emissions. India has been reluctant to increase regulations on emissions, which are due to rise by 60 percent between 2020 and 2040, even though the country has one of the worst power plant emission standards in the world. (Its plants are allowed to emit three times the maximum carbon dioxide allowed in Japan and twice that in China.)

The country's ruling Bharatiya Janata Party has even dismantled a number of environmental protections—including the Forest Rights Act and the Forest Conservation Act—to make it easier to raze forests for coal mines and other industrial projects. According to the Indian Ministry of Power, the nationally owned coal producer Coal India Limited will double its annual production target to one billion tons over the next five years.

For Narendra Modi, India's prime minister, this story isn't new. During his 15-year tenure as chief minister of the Western Indian state of Gujarat, the Central Pollution Control Board of India declared Gujarat the most polluted state in the country; in those days, it accounted for a whopping 29 percent of the country's total hazardous waste. Gujarat is also home to India's three most polluted rivers: Sabarmati, Amlakhadi, and Khari. In response, Modi set up what was touted as Asia's first government department for climate change and supported the development of renewable energy.

Environmental challenges will become all the more pressing in the coming years as Modi embarks on his "Make in India" campaign, which aims to transform the country from an agrarian society to a global manufacturing hub. This transformation has already begun in the Gujarati city, Vapi. Due to industrial and chemical waste, it has become one of the most polluted cities in the world. The level of mercury in the city's groundwater is 96 times higher than the safety levels set by the WHO.

TOO HIGH A PRICE

The author and geostrategist Brahma Chellaney have argued that environmental damage is the price that India will have to pay to develop and transform its economy, just as China has done in the recent past, and as Japan and Western Europe did after World War II. But India need not fall into the same trap. The country can still greatly improve the lives of its citizens by focusing on environmental sustainability and greener growth.

India should begin by setting firm targets to reduce emissions. According to a study by the World Bank, although a low-emissions strategy may be more expensive in the short-run, it could deliver significant benefits in the long run. Reducing hazardous particulate matter by 30 percent would cut average annual GDP growth by 0.04 percent, but it would also cut carbon dioxide emissions by 30 to 60 percent and save a total of $47–$105 billion from reduced damage to human health.

India should also work to make its cities green. Building reliable public transportation systems and introducing mandatory vehicular fuel efficiency standards are two important steps toward reducing toxic air. The country has pledged to increase support for solar and wind energy, another positive step.

Beyond cleaning up its air, India must also develop a comprehensive approach to sanitation and waste treatment. The federal government has drafted a new National Urban Sanitation Policy that proposes innovative and cost-effective methods to manage waste in cities, which it must ensure that state governments implement. The federal government often enacts environmental policies, but local officials rarely prioritize implementing them. India should thus stress a bottom-up rather than a top-down approach. A better sanitation system would lead to long-term health benefits and also prevent costs associated with environmental cleanup. According to Chellaney, it is more cost-effective to invest in systems that will prevent degradation now than to clean up later.

But corruption may be the ultimate pollutant. In 2011, the Indian government levied a tax on coal, which was supposed to go into a National Clean Energy Fund that bankrolls research regarding green technologies. Although $6.4 billion has been collected for the fund, only $250,000 has been spent. A ministry official, speaking to The Economic Times in June 2014, blamed "lack of inter-ministerial coordination and delay in allocation."

In the end, it comes down to Modi. India is poised for change under the leadership of a determined prime minister hungry for growth. But commercial development should not come at the cost of the natural environment and public health, risking irreversible consequences for generations to come.

The only remaining question is whether Modi and his fellow politicians care enough to act. In the recently concluded Delhi state elections, air pollution did not feature on any party manifesto. The media has also largely ignored the issue. India's late entry into the manufacturing sector gives it the unique advantage of learning from China's mistakes—if only it so chooses.

Why We Still Need Nuclear Power

Making Clean Energy Safe and Affordable

Ernest Moniz

In the years following the major accidents at Three Mile Island in 1979 and Chernobyl in 1986, nuclear power fell out of favor, and some countries applied the brakes to their nuclear programs. In the last decade, however, it began experiencing something of a renaissance. Concerns about climate change and air pollution, as well as growing demand for electricity, led many governments to reconsider their aversion to nuclear power, which emits little carbon dioxide and had built up an impressive safety and reliability record. Some countries reversed their phaseouts of nuclear power, some extended the lifetimes of existing reactors, and many developed plans for new ones. Today, roughly 60 nuclear plants are under construction worldwide, which will add about 60,000 megawatts of generating capacity—equivalent to a sixth of the world's current nuclear power capacity.

But the movement lost momentum in March, when a 9.0-magnitude earthquake and the massive tsunami it triggered devastated Japan's Fukushima nuclear power plant. Three reactors were severely damaged, suffering at least partial fuel meltdowns

ERNEST MONIZ is Cecil and Ida Green Distinguished Professor of Physics and Engineering Systems and Director of the Energy Initiative at MIT. He served as Undersecretary of the U.S. Department of Energy in 1997–2001.

and releasing radiation at a level only a few times less than Chernobyl. The event caused widespread public doubts about the safety of nuclear power to resurface. Germany announced an accelerated shutdown of its nuclear reactors, with broad public support, and Japan made a similar declaration, perhaps with less conviction. Their decisions were made easier thanks to the fact that electricity demand has flagged during the worldwide economic slowdown and the fact that global regulation to limit climate change seems less imminent now than it did a decade ago. In the United States, an already slow approach to new nuclear plants slowed even further in the face of an unanticipated abundance of natural gas.

It would be a mistake, however, to let Fukushima cause governments to abandon nuclear power and its benefits. Electricity generation emits more carbon dioxide in the United States than does transportation or industry, and nuclear power is the largest source of carbon-free electricity in the country. Nuclear power generation is also relatively cheap, costing less than two cents per kilowatt-hour for operations, maintenance, and fuel. Even after the Fukushima disaster, China, which accounts for about 40 percent of current nuclear power plant construction, and India, Russia, and South Korea, which together account for another 40 percent, show no signs of backing away from their pushes for nuclear power.

Nuclear power's track record of providing clean and reliable electricity compares favorably with other energy sources. Low natural gas prices, mostly the result of newly accessible shale gas, have brightened the prospects that efficient gas-burning power plants could cut emissions of carbon dioxide and other pollutants relatively quickly by displacing old, inefficient coal plants, but the historical volatility of natural gas prices has made utility companies wary of putting all their eggs in that basket. Besides, in the long run, burning natural gas would still release too much carbon dioxide. Wind and solar power are becoming increasingly widespread, but their intermittent and variable supply make them poorly suited for large-scale use in the absence of an affordable way to store electricity. Hydropower, meanwhile, has very limited prospects for expansion in the United States because of environmental concerns and the small number of potential sites.

Still, nuclear power faces a number of challenges in terms of safety, construction costs, waste management, and weapons proliferation. After Fukushima, the U.S. Nuclear Regulatory Commission, an independent federal agency that licenses nuclear reactors, reviewed the industry's regulatory requirements, operating procedures, emergency response plans, safety design requirements, and spent-fuel management. The NRC will almost certainly implement a number of the resulting recommendations, and the cost of doing business with nuclear energy in the United States will inevitably go up. Those plants that are approaching the end of their initial 40-year license period, and that lack certain modern safety features, will face additional scrutiny in having their licenses extended.

At the same time, new reactors under construction in Finland and France have gone billions of dollars over budget, casting doubt on the affordability of nuclear power plants. Public concern about radioactive waste is also hindering nuclear power, and no country yet has a functioning system for disposing of it. In fact, the U.S. government is paying billions of dollars in damages to utility companies for failing to meet its obligations to remove spent fuel from reactor sites. Some observers are also concerned that the spread of civilian nuclear energy infrastructure could lead to the proliferation of nuclear weapons—a problem exemplified by Iran's uranium-enrichment program.

If the benefits of nuclear power are to be realized in the United States, each of these hurdles must be overcome. When it comes to safety, the design requirements for nuclear reactors must be reexamined in light of up-to-date analyses of plausible accidents. As for cost, the government and the private sector need to advance new designs that lower the financial risk of constructing nuclear power plants. The country must also replace its broken nuclear waste management system with a more adaptive one that safely disposes of waste and stores it for centuries. Only then can the public's trust be earned.

SAFER AND CHEAPER

The tsunami that hit Japan in March marked the first time that an external event led to a major release of radioactivity from a nuclear power plant. The 14-meter-high wave was more than twice the height that Fukushima was designed to withstand, and it left the flooded plant cut off from external logistical support and from its power supply, which is needed to cool the reactor and pools of spent fuel. Such natural disasters, although infrequent, should have been planned for in the reactor's design: the Pacific Ring of Fire has seen a dozen earthquakes in the 8.5 to 9.5 range in the last hundred years, and Japan has the most recorded tsunamis in the world, with waves sometimes reaching 30 meters high. Just four years ago, the world's largest nuclear generating station, Kashiwazaki-Kariwa, was shut down by an earthquake that shook the plant beyond what it was designed to handle, and three of the seven reactors there remain idle today.

The Fukushima disaster will cause nuclear regulators every-where to reconsider safety requirements—in particular, those specifying which accidents plants must be designed to withstand. In the 40 years since the first Fukushima reactor was commissioned, seismology and the science of flood hazards have made tremendous progress, drawing on advances in sensors, modeling, and other new capabilities. This new knowledge needs to be brought to bear not only when designing new power plants but also when revisiting the requirements at older plants, as was happening at Fukushima before the tsunami. Outdated safety requirements should not be kept in place. In the United States, the NRC's review led to a recommendation that nuclear power plant operators reevaluate seismic and flood hazards every ten years and alter the design of the plants and their operating procedures as appropriate. With few exceptions, the needed upgrades are likely to be modest, but such a step would help ensure that the designs of plants reflect up-to-date information.

The NRC also proposed regulations that would require nuclear power stations to have systems in place to allow them to remain safe if cut off from outside power and access for up to three days. It issued other recommendations addressing issues such as the removal of combustible gas and the monitoring of spent-fuel storage pools. These proposals do not mean that the NRC lacks confidence in the safety of U.S. nuclear reactors; their track record of running 90 percent of the time is an indicator of good safety performance and extraordinary when compared with other methods of electricity generation. Nevertheless, the incident at Fukushima clearly calls for additional regulatory requirements, and the NRC's recommendations should be put in place as soon as is feasible.

New regulations will inevitably increase the costs of nuclear power, and nuclear power plants, with a price tag of around $6-$10 billion each, are already much more expensive to build than are plants powered by fossil fuels. Not only are their capital costs inherently high; their longer construction times mean that utility companies accumulate substantial financing charges before they can sell any electricity. In an attempt to realize economies of scale, some utilities have turned to building even larger reactors, building ones that produce as much as 1,600 megawatts, instead of the typical 1,000 megawatts. This pushes up the projects' cost and amplifies the consequences of mistakes during construction.

All this can make nuclear power plants seem like risky investments, which in turn raises investors' demands on return and the cost of borrowing money to finance the projects. Yet nuclear power enjoys low operating costs, which can make it competitive on the basis of the electricity price needed to recover the capital investment over a plant's lifetime. And if governments eventually cap carbon dioxide emissions through either an emissions charge or a regulatory requirement, as they are likely to do in the next decade or so, then nuclear energy will be more attractive relative to fossil fuels.

In the United States, there is still a great deal of uncertainty over the cost of new nuclear power plants. It has been almost 40 years since the last new nuclear power plant was ordered. The Tennessee Valley Authority, a federally owned corporation, is currently finishing construction of the Watts Bar Unit 2 reactor, in eastern Tennessee, which was started long ago, and it has plans to complete another, Bellefonte Unit 1, in Hollywood, Alabama. The first new nuclear plants of next-generation design are likely to be built in Georgia by the Southern Company, pending the NRC's approval. Scheduled for completion in 2016, the proposed project entails two reactors totaling 2,200 megawatts at an estimated cost of $14 billion. It will take advantage of substantial subsidies (loan guarantees, production tax credits, and the reimbursement of costs caused by regulatory delay) that were put forward in the 2005 Energy Policy Act to kick-start the construction of new nuclear plants. Even after Fukushima, Congress and the White House appear to still be committed to this assistance program. The success or failure of these construction projects in avoiding delays and cost overruns will help determine the future of nuclear power in the United States.

A SMALLER SOLUTION

The safety and capital cost challenges involved with traditional nuclear power plants may be considerable, but a new class of reactors in the development stage holds promise for addressing them. These reactors, called small modular reactors (SMRs), produce anywhere from ten to 300 megawatts, rather than the 1,000 megawatts produced by a typical reactor. An entire reactor, or at least most of it, can be built in a factory and shipped to a site for assembly, where several reactors can be installed together to compose a larger nuclear power station. SMRs have attractive safety features, too. Their design often incorporates natural cooling features that can continue to function in the absence of external power, and the underground placement of the reactors and the spent-fuel storage pools is more secure.

Since SMRs are smaller than conventional nuclear plants, the construction costs for individual projects are more manageable, and thus the financing terms may be more favorable. And because they are factory-assembled, the on-site construction time is shorter. The utility company can build up its nuclear power capacity step by step, adding additional reactors as needed, which means that it can generate revenue from electricity sales sooner. This helps not only the plant owner but also customers, who are increasingly being asked to pay higher rates today to fund tomorrow's plants.

The assembly-line-like production of SMRs should lower their cost, too. Rather than chasing elusive economies of scale by building larger projects, SMR vendors can take advantage of the economies of manufacturing: a skilled permanent work force, quality control, and continuous improvement in reactors' design and manufacturing. Even though the intrinsic price per megawatt for SMRs may be higher than that for a large-scale reactor, the final cost per megawatt might be lower thanks to more favorable financing terms and shorter construction times—a proposition that will have to be tested. The feasibility of SMRs needs to be demonstrated, and the government will almost certainly need to share some of the risk to get this done.

No SMR design has yet been licensed by the NRC. This is a time-consuming process for any new nuclear technology, and it will be especially so for those SMR designs that represent significant departures from the NRC's experience. Only after SMRs are licensed and built will their true cost be clear. The catch, however, is that the economies of manufacturing can be realized and understood only if there is a reliable stream of orders to keep the manufacturing lines busy turning out the same design. In order for that to happen, the U.S. government will have to figure out how to incubate early movers while not locking in one technology prematurely.

With the U.S. federal budget under tremendous pressure, it is hard to imagine taxpayers funding demonstrations of a new nuclear technology. But if the United States takes a hiatus from creating new clean-energy options—be it SMRs, renewable energy, advanced batteries, or carbon capture and sequestration—Americans will look back in ten years with regret. There will be fewer economically viable options for meeting the United States' energy and environmental needs, and the country will be less competitive in the global technology market.

WASTE BASKET CASE

If nuclear energy is to enjoy a sustained renaissance, the challenge of managing nuclear waste for thousands of years must be met. Nuclear energy is generated by splitting uranium, leaving behind dangerous radioactive products, such as cesium and strontium, that must be isolated for centuries. The process also produces transuranic elements, such as plutonium, which are heavier than uranium, do not occur in nature, and must be isolated for millennia. There is an alternative to disposing of transuranic elements: they can be separated from the reactor fuel every few years and then recycled into new nuclear reactor fuel as an additional energy source. The downside, however, is that this process is complex and expensive, and it poses a proliferation risk since plutonium can be used in nuclear weapons. The debate over the merits of recycling transuranic elements has yet to be resolved.

What is not disputed is that most nuclear waste needs to be isolated deep underground. The scientific community has supported this method for decades, but finding sites for the needed facilities has proved difficult. In the United States, Congress adopted a prescriptive approach, legislating both a single site, at Yucca Mountain, in Nevada, and a specific schedule for burying spent fuel underground. The massive project was to be paid for by a nuclear waste fund into which nuclear power utilities contribute about $750 million each year. But the strategy backfired, and the program is in a shambles. Nevada pushed back, and the schedule slipped by two decades, which meant that the government had to pay court-ordered damages to the utility companies. In 2009, the Obama administration announced that it was canceling the Yucca Mountain project altogether, leaving no alternative in place for the disposal of radioactive waste from nuclear power plants. The Nuclear Waste Fund has reached $25 billion but has no disposal program to support.

Fukushima awakened the American public and members of Congress to the problem of the accumulation of radioactive spent fuel in cooling pools at reactor sites. The original plan had been to allow the spent fuel to cool for about five years, after which it would be either disposed of underground or partly recycled. Now, the spent nuclear fuel has nowhere to go. Many utilities have moved some of the spent fuel out of the pools and into dry storage facilities built on site, which the NRC has judged safe for a century or so. The dry storage facilities at Fukushima were not compromised by the earthquake and tsunami, a sharp contrast to the problems that arose with the spent-fuel pools when cooling could not be maintained. To deal with the immediate problem of waste building up in reactor pools, Congress should allow the Nuclear Waste Fund to be used for moving the spent fuel accumulating in pools into dry-cask storage units nearby. But such an incremental step should not substitute for a comprehensive approach to waste management.

Instead of being stored near reactors, spent fuel should eventually be kept in dry casks at a small number of consolidated sites set up by the government where the fuel could stay for a century. This approach has several advantages. The additional cooling time would provide the Department of Energy, or some other organization, with more flexibility in designing a geological repository. The government would no longer have to pay utilities for not meeting the mandated schedule, and communities near reactors would be reassured that spent fuel has a place to go. At each site, the aging fuel would be monitored, so that any problems that arose could be addressed. The storage facilities would keep Washington's options open as the debate over whether spent fuel is waste or a resource works itself out. These sites should be paid for by the Nuclear Waste Fund, a change that would require congressional approval.

At the same time, Washington must find an alternative to Yucca Mountain for storing nuclear waste in the long run. As it does so, it must adopt a more adaptive and flexible approach than it did last time, holding early negotiations with local communities, Native American tribes, and states. Sweden upgraded its waste disposal program with just such a consensus-based process, and for a dozen years the U.S. Department of Energy has operated a geological repository for transuranic waste near Carlsbad, New Mexico, with strong community support. The government should also investigate new approaches to disposal. For example, it might make sense to separate out the long-living transuranic elements in nuclear reactor waste, which constitute a nasty but very small package, and dispose of them in a miles-deep borehole, while placing the shorter-living materials in repositories closer to the surface. Given the sustained challenge of waste management, an overhaul to the existing program should include the establishment of a new federally chartered organization that is a step or two removed from the short-term political calculus.

Another break from the past would be to manage civilian nuclear waste separately from military nuclear waste. In 1985, the government elected to comingle defense and civilian waste in a single geological repository. This made sense at the time, since the planners assumed that Yucca Mountain would be available for storing both types. But now, it looks as though it will be many years before a large-scale repository opens. Today, it makes more sense to put plans for storing military waste on a separate, faster track, since that process is less daunting than coming up with a solution to civilian waste. To begin with, there is simply much less military waste, and the volume will hardly grow in the future. Moreover, most of the military waste already has the uranium and plutonium separated out from the spent fuel, since the aim was to produce nuclear weapons material. Thus, what is left is definitely waste, not a resource.

Fast-tracking a defense waste program would allow the federal government to meet its obligations to states that host nuclear weapons facilities, from which it has agreed to remove radioactive waste. It would also make the finances of waste storage much clearer, since the nuclear utility companies pay for their waste management, whereas Congress has to approve payments for defense waste. And assuming a defense waste repository were established first, the experience gained operating it would be highly valuable when it comes time to establish a civilian one.

The United States' dysfunctional nuclear waste management system has an unfortunate international side effect: it limits the options for preventing other countries from using nuclear power infrastructure to produce nuclear weapons. If countries such as Iran are able to enrich uranium to make new reactor fuel and separate out the plutonium to recover its energy value, they then have access to the relevant technology and material for a weapons program. Safeguards agreements with the International Atomic Energy Agency are intended to make sure that civilian programs do not spill over into military ones, but the agency has only a limited ability to address clandestine programs.

Developing enrichment or separation facilities is expensive and unlikely to make economic sense for countries with small nuclear power programs. What these countries care about most is an assured supply of reactor fuel and a way to alleviate the burden of waste management. One promising scheme to keep fissile material out of the hands of would-be proliferators involves returning nuclear waste to the fuel-supplying country (or a third country). In effect, nuclear fuel could be leased to produce electricity. The country supplying the fuel would treat the returned spent fuel as it does its own, disposing of it directly or reprocessing it. In most cases, the amount of additional waste would be small in comparison to what that country is already handling. In return for giving up the possibility of reprocessing fuel and thus separating out weapons-grade material, the country using the fuel would free itself from the challenges of managing nuclear waste.

The United States already runs a similar program on a smaller scale, having provided fuel, often highly enriched uranium, to about 30 countries for small research reactors. But with no functioning commercial waste management system in place, the program cannot be extended to accommodate waste from commercial reactors. Instead, Washington is trying to use diplomacy to impose constraints on a country-by-country basis, in the futile hope that countries will agree to give up enrichment and reprocessing in exchange for nuclear cooperation with the United States. This ad hoc approach might have worked when the United States was the dominant supplier of nuclear technology and fuel, but it no longer is, and other major suppliers, such as France and Russia, appear uninterested in imposing such restrictions on commercial transactions. Putting together a coherent waste management program would give the United States a leg to stand on when it comes to setting up a proliferation-resistant international fuel-cycle program.

NOW OR NEVER

As greenhouse gases accumulate in the atmosphere, finding ways to generate power cleanly, affordably, and reliably is becoming an even more pressing imperative. Nuclear power is not a silver bullet, but it is a partial solution that has proved workable on a large scale. Countries will need to pursue a combination of strategies to cut emissions, including reining in energy demand, replacing coal power plants with cleaner natural gas plants, and investing in new technologies such as renewable energy and carbon capture and sequestration. The government's role should be to help provide the private sector with a well-understood set of options, including nuclear power—not to prescribe a desired market share for any specific technology.

The United States must take a number of decisions to maintain and advance the option of nuclear energy. The NRC's initial reaction to the safety lessons of Fukushima must be translated into action; the public needs to be convinced that nuclear power is safe. Washington should stick to its plan of offering limited assistance for building several new nuclear reactors in this decade, sharing the lessons learned across the industry. It should step up its support for new technology, such as SMRs and advanced computer-modeling tools. And when it comes to waste management, the government needs to overhaul the current system and get serious about long-term storage. Local concerns about nuclear waste facilities are not going to magically disappear; they need to be addressed with a more adaptive, collaborative, and transparent waste program.

These are not easy steps, and none of them will happen overnight. But each is needed to reduce uncertainty for the public, the energy companies, and investors. A more productive approach to developing nuclear power—and confronting the mounting risks of climate change—is long overdue. Further delay will only raise the stakes.

Tough Love for Renewable Energy

Making Wind and Solar Power Affordable

Jeffrey Ball

O ver the past decade, governments around the world threw money at renewable power. Private investors followed, hoping to cash in on what looked like an imminent epic shift in the way the world produced electricity. It all seemed intoxicating and revolutionary: a way to boost jobs, temper fossil-fuel prices, and curb global warming, while minting new fortunes in the process.

Much of that enthusiasm has now fizzled. Natural gas prices have plummeted in the United States, the result of technology that has unlocked vast supplies of a fuel that is cleaner than coal. The global recession has nudged global warming far down the political agenda and led cash-strapped countries to yank back renewable-energy subsidies. And some big government bets on renewable power have gone bad, most spectacularly the bet on Solyndra, the California solar-panel maker that received a $535 million loan guarantee from the U.S. Department of Energy before going bankrupt last fall.

JEFFREY BALL is Scholar in Residence at Stanford University's Steyer-Taylor Center for Energy Policy and Finance. Previously, he wrote about energy and the environment for The Wall Street Journal, where he spent 14 years as a reporter, columnist, and editor, serving most recently as Environment Editor.

Critics of taxpayer-sponsored investment in renewable energy point to Solyndra as an example of how misguided the push for solar and wind power has become. Indeed, the drive has been sloppy, failing to derive the most bang for the buck. In the United States, the government has schizophrenically ramped up and down support for renewable power, confusing investors and inhibiting the technologies' development; it has also structured its subsidies in inefficient ways. In Europe, where support for renewable power has been more sustained, governments have often been too generous, doling out subsidies so juicy they have proved unaffordable. And in China, the new epicenter of the global renewable-power push, a national drive to build up indigenous wind and solar companies has spurred U.S. allegations of trade violations and has done little to curb China's reliance on fossil fuels.

But these challenges don't justify ending the pursuit of renewable power; they justify reforming it. It is time to push harder for renewable power, but to push in a smarter way. Recent advances have made wind and solar power more competitive than ever. Now, for renewable power to reach its potential, the world's approach to it will have to grow up, too. Governments will have to redesign their renewable-power policies to focus ruthlessly on slashing costs. Renewable-power producers will also have to act more strategically, picking the technologies they deploy, and the locations where they place them, in ways that make more economic sense. As renewable power comes of age, it needs some tough love.

This rigor will be crucial, because today's energy challenge is fundamentally harder than those of past decades. Historically, countries have made big energy shifts only when confronted with acute fossil-fuel crises: oil embargoes, debilitating pollution, or wars. That is why in the wake of the 1970s oil shocks, France embraced nuclear power, Denmark ramped up its energy efficiency and then its development of wind power, and Brazil began fueling some of its auto fleet with ethanol. But today's threats—climate change, fluctuating energy prices, and the prospect that other countries might dominate a still-nascent clean-energy industry—are more chronic and less immediate. Thus, they are unlikely to sustain the generous spending that has nurtured renewable energy so far.

SO FRESH AND SO CLEAN

The first step to adopting a more mature approach to renewable power is to understand how the various technologies work and what challenges they face. Historically, most renewable electricity has come from hydroelectric dams, which now provide about 16 percent of the world's electricity. Today, the sources growing the fastest and receiving the most investor attention are wind and solar power.

Wind power, which generates about 1.4 percent of the world's electricity, is produced as pinwheel-style turbines spin atop towers that rise hundreds of feet above the ground. Solar power provides an even smaller share of global electricity: just 0.1 percent. Techniques for generating it vary; the most popular uses panels containing wafers of silicon thinner than a fingernail to convert sunlight into electrical current. A few of these photovoltaic panels, as they are known, can be mounted directly on a building's roof, letting the occupants produce at least some of their own power. Or hundreds of panels can be grouped together on the ground in vast arrays that funnel power into the electrical grid—sprawling, centralized power plants of a new sort, some of which have been built in the American Southwest.

Although wind power is more widespread today, solar power is theoretically more attractive. The sun emits a nearly limitless supply of energy, and it does so during the daytime, when people use the most electricity. (Wind tends to blow most strongly at night.) Solar power also is easily distributed—panels can be placed on a streetlight or a soldier's backpack—whereas wind power is mostly a centralized energy source, requiring clumps of turbines to generate sizable amounts of power. But both wind and solar energy offer big advantages over fossil fuels. Wind and sunshine are clean, emitting neither the pollutants that cause smog nor the carbon dioxide that contributes to climate change. They are ubiquitous, providing a domestic energy source even in places with no indigenous fossil fuels. And they are essentially never-ending.

There are huge caveats to this rosy assessment, and they come down mostly to money. In most places, producing electricity from new wind and solar projects is more expensive than making it in new conventional power plants. Wind and solar power are younger technologies, with much work left to be done to wring out cost. The downsides of fossil fuels, notably their geopolitical and environmental risks, are not fully reflected in their market prices. And everything about the modern electrical system is predicated on the use of fossil fuels: the coal mines and gas fields that produce them; the railroads, pipelines, and ships that transport them; and the power plants that burn them. That system has been built up and its costs largely paid down over decades.

Wind and solar power enjoy no such entrenched infrastructure. The challenge of making and installing the wind turbines and solar panels is just the start. Massive new transmission lines must be built to move large amounts of renewable electricity from the out-of-the-way places where it is generated to the metropolitan areas where it is consumed. This new equipment costs money, and it often stokes opposition from people who are not used to living near industrial-scale energy infrastructure of any sort. Along with other opponents, a group of landowners in Cape Cod, Massachusetts, for instance, has managed to delay the construction of an offshore wind farm that was proposed back in 2001. Even environmental activists often fight large renewable-energy projects, out of concern for local landscapes or animals. Last spring, the Obama administration temporarily halted construction on part of a solar project in the Mojave Desert because of concerns that it would harm endangered tortoises; the government later let the construction resume.

Taking wind and solar power mainstream will also require better ways to get it to consumers when they need it, since the times when wind turbines and solar panels generate the most electricity are not necessarily the times when people use electricity most. Power plants fired by natural gas can be dialed up or down to meet changing electricity demand, but the sun shines and the wind blows only at certain times. One potential solution is to stockpile renew-able power—either in large-scale storage equipment, such as mas-sive batteries, or in smaller-scale devices, such as people's plug-in hybrid cars. Other approaches include better technologies to pre-dict gusts and rays and "smart" electrical-transmission grids that could tie together far-flung renewable-power projects. Both could help compensate in one place for doldrums or gray skies some-where else. Scientists are working to bring down the cost of all these ideas. For now, in some places with dense concentrations of wind turbines, some of the power they could produce is wasted; the turbines are shut off when the wind is blowing so hard that the turbines would produce more power than the grid could handle.

Wind and solar power will not replace fossil fuels anytime soon—not by a long shot. The International Energy Agency proj-ects that by 2035, wind and solar could be producing ten percent of global electricity, up from 1.5 percent now, and that renewables of all sorts could be generating 31 percent of the world's electricity, up from about 19 percent now. But even that expansion would require an increase in subsidies—"support that in some cases," the IEA notes, "cannot be taken for granted in this age of fiscal austerity." Some countries with particularly generous subsidies and high elec-tricity prices have made wind and solar power big enough to mat-ter. Denmark gets 18 percent of its electricity from wind, and Spain gets two percent from the sun—the world's leaders by share, ac-cording to the IEA's latest figures. But even that renewable elec-tricity is backed up by fossil-fuel power plants. Last year, fully one-third of the new electricity-generating capacity brought on line in the United States came from wind and solar projects. Even so, given the vastness of the conventional energy system, wind and solar power remained relatively tiny, accounting for just three per-cent of the electricity the country actually produced. For the fore-seeable future, renewable power is likely to supplement, not supplant, conventional energy.

That is why two other shifts will be at least as important as re-newable power in addressing the energy problem. One is cleaning up the burning of coal and natural gas, fuels that are cheap, plentiful, and, according to most estimates, likely to continue to generate the lion's share of the world's electricity for a long time. The other is wasting less of the power the world produces from all sources. That means making buildings, appliances, and industrial processes more energy efficient, a complicated but potentially profitable shift that policymakers and entrepreneurs are working on. According to IEA estimates, between now and 2035, improving the efficiency of fossil-fuel power plants would likely cut global carbon emissions more than 1.5 times as much as would rolling out more wind and solar power.

Considering what renewable power is up against, the drive for it might seem a folly. But giving up now would be a mistake. As a result of recent technological improvements, the prospect of renewable power as an economically competitive part of the energy mix is no longer a pipe dream. Wind turbines and solar panels have gotten more efficient and less expensive. According to government and Wall Street analyses, in some particularly windy places, the long-term cost to investors of producing power from new wind projects can now be less than the cost of producing it from new coal- or gas-fired power plants. Solar power remains more expensive than conventional power (except in a few sunny places with high power prices, such as Hawaii), but its costs, too, are falling rapidly. Now more than ever, sustained but strategic support could produce blockbuster innovations with the potential to meaningfully change the energy mix.

PAYING FOR POWER

Wind and solar power would be nowhere near as viable without the subsidies they get from governments. To be sure, all energy sources, including fossil fuels, receive state support. But as the energy world's upstarts, wind and solar power will have to be especially scrappy to gain ground. So far, governments worldwide have tended to promote renewable power in ham-fisted ways, spending money inefficiently.

The modern renewable-power push dates to the 1973 Arab oil embargo. At the time, the West generated much of its power from petroleum, so the embargo threatened not just transportation but also the electricity supply. Many countries decided to seek alternative sources of power. The United States made a particular push into wind. In 1978, it rolled out a subsidy called the investment tax credit. It gave wind-farm developers a tax break for every dollar they spent on wind projects, regardless of how many megawatts those projects produced. The goal was wind turbines, not efficient wind turbines, and the result was predictable: by the early 1990s, many of those subsidized machines were breaking down.

In 1992, the U.S. government enacted a smarter wind subsidy, called the production tax credit. It pegged a wind-farm developer's tax break to the amount of electricity the project produced. Around the same time, states began passing laws requiring power companies to produce a given percentage of their electricity from renewable sources. Today, 29 states, plus Washington, D.C., and Puerto Rico, have such standards on their books.

The combination of the federal tax break and the state renewable-energy mandates transformed wind power from an inventor's dalliance into an investment banker's dream. Wind power became a nationwide industry with guaranteed buyers and an attractive rate of return. The tax break did not directly help the mom-and-pop wind developers; their tax liabilities were too small to exploit the full value of the credit. But it appealed to financial institutions, which, by buying into the developers' wind projects, could apply the federal tax break to their own bottom lines.

Propelled by the tax break, wind turbines have spread across the United States, particularly in the so-called wind alley running from North Dakota down to Texas. But the tax-break strategy has made the campaign for renewable power more expensive than it might have been. Whereas tax breaks for the fossil-fuel industry are long term, those for wind power have come in only one- or two-year bursts, a sign that the country has viewed renewable power as an afterthought. The consequence has been an inefficient, boom-bust cycle of wind-farm development. Companies race to get wind projects built before the current subsidy expires, often installing more turbines than the grid can handle. In some parts of windswept Texas, so many turbines are competing to shove power into the transmission grid that wind farms have had to hold back on windy days.

The tax break, moreover, is not just paying for the construction of wind turbines; it is also lining bankers' pockets. The financial institutions investing in wind farms in exchange for the tax break exact a profit. That's capitalism, of course, and energy is hardly the only industry in the United States that relies on financing from tax breaks. Yet according to some estimates, about 30 percent of the value of renewable-power tax credits ends up benefiting financiers rather than funding renewable-energy production.

The United States is not alone in spending inefficiently on renewable power. Some western European countries have spent even more money than the United States for each unit of renewable power that they have produced. Their solar-panel push, in particular, illustrates how poorly designed subsidies can stymie the development of renewable power.

Germany, hardly a sunny place, was Europe's first big solar power enthusiast. It began promoting the sector in earnest in the early 1990s, largely in response to two crises: the 1986 Chernobyl nuclear accident, which soured many Germans on nuclear power as a fossil-fuel alternative, and the 1990 reunification of poor East Germany and rich West Germany, which launched a national push for job-creation programs, such as solar-industry subsidies. By the late 1990s, Germany had rolled out a subsidy more generous than the United States' renewable-power tax credit. Called a feed-in tariff, it lets solar-project developers sell power to the German electrical grid at a premium price guaranteed by the government. By the middle years of the last decade, the country had become the world's biggest solar market. Investors, from big banks to small entrepreneurs, profited handsomely.

Other countries in Europe eyed Germany's solar stampede with envy. By 2007, with the global economy roaring and popular concern about climate change cresting, Spain enacted its own solar feed-in tariff, which guaranteed a similarly high electricity price. Sure enough, solar developers raced to build projects in Spain (a sunnier place than Germany), and the Spanish government found itself paying out more in subsidies than it had anticipated. Then, the global recession hit, and Spain decided its solar power extravaganza was a luxury it could no longer afford.

Several European countries are now dialing back their subsidies. Germany and Italy have slashed the guaranteed prices they offer new solar projects. The Czech Republic and Spain are going further, retroactively pulling back subsidies they already gave to existing projects. That retrenchment has slammed the brakes on the development of solar power in Europe. And it has had a ripple effect worldwide, eroding the stock prices of solar-panel makers from California to China that had ramped up their production to supply the European market.

CHINA'S RENEWABLES PUSH

As Western governments have scaled back their support for renewable power, China has been pushing full steam ahead. Probably more than any other country today, China feels an imperative to develop renewable power—to boost jobs and exports, to consume cash and counter inflationary pressure, to ease the country's rising fossil-fuel demand, and to help clean up its polluted air. In China, the global leader, renewable-energy investment, excluding spending on research and development, surged to about $50 billion in 2010, according to Bloomberg New Energy Finance. Next came Germany, at $41 billion, and then the United States, at about $30 billion.

The scale of China's push, although massive, should not be overstated. China still generates about 80 percent of its electricity from coal. It is building dozens of new coal-fired power plants each year and is laying a massive network of pipelines to import more natural gas. According to IEA figures, wind and solar in China, as worldwide, together provided about 1.5 percent of electricity in 2009, and that share might rise to ten percent by 2035.

China's push has produced some of the biggest wind-turbine makers in the world. Bigger, however, does not necessarily mean more efficient. China's early wind power subsidies, like those in the United States, rewarded installing wind turbines, not producing wind power. That subsidy structure, combined at the time with rules requiring that a certain percentage of the material for each turbine to be produced domestically, gave Chinese wind power companies a powerful leg up on foreign competitors. (In the past two years, the Chinese company Sinovel displaced General Electric as the world's second-biggest wind-turbine manufacturer by market share, behind Denmark's Vestas.) But the Chinese system also led to overkill. In the region of Inner Mongolia, Chinese companies installed more turbines than the grid could handle, and about 25 percent of those turbines have yet to be connected to transmission lines. China is racing to beef up the grid, but for now, the excess turbines amount to very tall white elephants.

China's solar power industry has grown even faster than its wind power sector. More than any other factor, the torrid expansion of low-cost Chinese manufacturing to feed the heavily subsidized European solar power market is what has slashed the price of silicon, and of solar panels, over the past two years. Indirectly, the Chinese solar power juggernaut killed Solyndra. The company's product, a novel system of photovoltaic tubes that used less silicon than traditional flat panels, was not competitive in a world where silicon was suddenly cheap. Last fall, a handful of Western solar-panel makers filed a trade complaint against their Chinese counterparts, alleging that China's solar power subsidies violate trade laws, allowing Chinese companies to dump solar panels on the U.S. market at prices below the cost of production. Beijing has denied the charge, saying in return that it will investigate the fairness of U.S. renewable-power subsidies.

U.S. officials are expected to issue a final decision later this year about whether to impose unfair-trade duties on imported Chinese panels. But beyond this legal dispute lies a larger lesson: if the goal of the renewable-power push is a cleaner, more diversified power supply, then low-cost solar equipment, from China or anywhere else, is a good thing. That, in turn, suggests a bedrock principle for a smart U.S. renewable-power strategy: exploit globalization rather than fight it.

POWER PLAY

A sensible push for renewable power in the United States would start with a broader effort to make the nation's energy system cleaner and more secure. The Obama administration's stimulus plan sought to compensate for the lack of a comprehensive energy strategy by picking a portfolio of short-term winners, such as Solyndra. Even if some of those bets pay off—and many still might—those sorts of wagers are insufficient. A better approach would be to set a broad direction for the energy system and then let that newly defined market determine which technologies and companies rise to the top. One worthwhile move would be for the government to boost funding for advanced energy research, just as it raised funding for space research when it wanted to send a man to the moon and ratcheted up spending on defense research when it wanted to win the Cold War. Another would be to aggressively prioritize improvements in energy efficiency, because it makes no sense to pay for wind and solar power that then will be frittered away in inefficient buildings and machines. Yet another reasonable step would be to slap a price on carbon emissions, although its effectiveness would depend on the details. Many corporations and investors have been advocating a carbon price, but they disagree mightily over how to structure it. And the structure would determine how the policy affected U.S. consumers, various industries, and, indeed, the planet.

An essential part of any shift to a cleaner and more secure energy system would be rationalizing the patchwork of conflicting energy subsidies that has been stitched together over decades. According to the IEA, renewable energy worldwide receives less money in annual subsidies than fossil fuels do. Renewable energy, including fuels for transportation and electricity, got $66 billion in subsidies globally in 2010, the IEA says, a fraction of just one sub-set of subsidies for fossil fuels: the $409 billion to defray their cost to consumers. But the flip side, some studies conclude, is that re-newable sources in their early years have been more heavily subsi-dized than fossil fuels for every unit of electricity they actually produce. An apples-to-apples comparison of energy subsidies, and an open debate about which ones most effectively promote the kind of energy system the United States wants, should appeal to honest partisans of all stripes.

Once the United States sets out a sensible overall energy ap-proach, it should tailor its wind and solar strategies to play to the country's strengths. That means focusing on the higher end of the market, developing next-generation technologies and business models that have the potential to make wind and solar power truly cost competitive with fossil fuels. Despite much hype about the potential for "green jobs," the United States should be selective about the kinds of green jobs it pursues: not run-of-the-mill assembly-line positions that can be easily outsourced, but jobs in engineering, high-value manufacturing, and renewable-power in-stallation, financing, and servicing. Studies of the solar power in-dustry suggest that the bulk of the jobs are not in making the panels. They lie upstream, in producing the raw materials and the machinery that are used to make the panels, and downstream, in installing and servicing the panels. Indeed, much of the machinery used in Chinese solar-panel factories today is made in America. Similarly, some of the most innovative business models for deploy-ing solar panels on rooftops—such as that in which companies in-stall the equipment for property owners at no up-front cost and then charge the consumers a favorable electricity price—come from U.S. firms.

To the extent that the United States installs today's renewable-energy equipment, it should relentlessly squeeze out cost. One way to do that would be to auction renewable-power subsidies to com-panies that agree to produce the largest amount of electricity at the lowest price. Another would be to expand the box of tools used to finance wind and solar power—moving beyond today's tax credits to instruments that broaden the pool of investors and thus lower the cost of capital. A third would be to clear away the thicket of regulatory barriers that impede innovation and distort the renewable-energy market.

In the United States, regulators at the federal, state, and local levels should simplify the permit process for wind and solar projects, including the installation of transmission lines, even in the face of opposition from landowners and environmentalists. Some studies suggest that upward of 20 percent of the cost of installing solar-panel systems in the United States comes not from the panels themselves but from administrative red tape. Balancing the desire for renewable power with property rights and local environmental concerns is crucial. But prioritizing certain areas of the country for renewable-energy development, and then streamlining the process of breaking ground on projects, would accelerate those ventures that make the most economic sense.

Globally, policymakers should resist the urge to slap tariffs and local-content requirements on renewable-energy equipment. All countries, including China, should be forced to comply with international trade rules. If they play fair, however, they should be allowed to play hard. In renewable power as in other industries, tough competition will produce the most cost-effective products. The most enduring way for the United States to snag a profitable piece of the global renewable-power market is to do certain things better than other countries, not to try to deny American consumers commodities that other countries can make legally at a lower cost.

If the United States followed this strategic approach, far from ceding its ambitions as a global renewable-power leader, it would harness its strengths as a technological innovator to make wind and solar power more competitive as a complement to coal and natural gas. On the one hand, such a strategy would recognize that renewable power has benefits over fossil fuels that, in this early stage of its development, are worth paying extra for. On the other hand, it would seek to ensure that subsidies for renewable power, as well as subsidies for conventional energy, gradually shrink and eventually even stop.

The energy debate has been too ideological for too long. Wind and solar power will never reach the scale necessary to make a difference to national security or the environment unless they can be produced economically. That is why the United States needs to be clear about its goals. The objective is not wind turbines or solar panels. It is an affordable, convenient, secure, and sustainable stream of electrons. Wind and solar power may well provide much of that electricity, but only if they can be produced in a way that doesn't break the bank.

Cleaning Up Coal

From Climate Culprit to Solution

Richard K. Morse

oal, the rock that fueled the industrial age, is once again remaking the global energy landscape. Over the past decade, while most of the world stood transfixed by the gyrations of the oil markets, the promise of alternative energy, and the boom in cheap natural gas, coal left all other forms of energy in its dust, contributing nearly as much total energy to the global economy as every other source combined.

That explosive increase in coal use came not from the developed world, where demand is plateauing, but from the developing world, where the fuel remains the cheapest, most reliable source of electricity. This year, the market in globally traded coal used to generate electricity is expected to reach 850 megatons—twice the total in 2000. If current trends continue, according to the International Energy Agency (IEA), China and India alone will drive 75 percent of the growth in coal demand before 2035, and coal will become the world's single largest source of energy before 2030.

But just as coal is remaking energy markets, it is also remaking the climate. Coal combustion is the world's largest source of carbon dioxide emissions, responsible for almost 13 billion tons per year. (By comparison, oil and natural gas account for 11 billion tons and 6 billion tons, respectively.) With demand for coal ballooning in Asia, between 2010 and 2035, fully half the total increase in global

---

RICHARD K. MORSE is Director of Research on Coal and Carbon Markets at Stanford University's Program on Energy and Sustainable Development.

carbon dioxide emissions from fossil-fuel use will come from coal use in the region. The climate problem, in other words, is a coal problem.

For the last two decades, economists and diplomats have tended to favor one solution to that problem: putting a price on carbon dioxide emissions, which would allow markets to find the cheapest route to a cooler climate. But so far, doing what may be economically optimal has proved politically infeasible in most economies. Another strategy, promoting renewable power, is a necessary part of solving the climate problem but will not be enough on its own. Developing economies are adding new coal plants on a scale that still dwarfs the contribution of renewable energy, and those plants will continue churning out more and more emissions for decades to come.

Coal, despite the proliferation of clean-energy policies, is not going away anytime soon. As of 2010 (the most recent year with available data), 30 percent of the energy used in the world came from coal, second only to oil, at 34 percent. Most of this coal is used in the power sector, where it accounts for more than 40 percent of global generation capacity—a larger share than any other form of energy.

Given how dominant coal is, one of the most promising ways to fight global warming is to make it emit less carbon dioxide, a solution that is less elusive than commonly thought. Merely installing the best available technologies in coal plants in the developing world could slash the volume of carbon dioxide released by billions of tons per year, doing more to reduce emissions on an annual basis than all the world's wind, solar, and geothermal power combined do today. And advanced technologies now in the works could someday allow coal to be burned without releasing any carbon dioxide into the atmosphere.

In order for these innovations to materialize, multilateral banks will have to offer financing, and individual governments will have to fund research and encourage private investment. Efforts to clean up coal should not replace a more comprehensive climate policy that includes putting a price on carbon and promoting renewable energy. But absent the unlikely event of a sudden global consensus on pricing carbon dioxide, they are one of the most practical ways to make immediate progress in the fight against global warming.

COAL FEVER

In order to confront the coal problem, it is important to understand how the fuel became so popular in the first place. Although coal is often cast as an environmental villain today, just four decades ago, it seemed the obvious answer to some of the developed world's most pressing political and economic challenges. The oil crises of the 1970s showed industrialized countries that disruptions in the supply of petroleum could send shockwaves not only through their transportation systems but, because much electricity was generated by burning oil products, through their power sectors, too. So they rushed to replace cartel-controlled oil with abundant, cheap coal.

Between 1980 and 2000, countries that were members of the Organization for Economic Cooperation and Development (OECD) increased the use of coal in electricity generation by 61 percent and reduced the use of oil in that sector by 41 percent. Formerly dispersed in niche regional markets, the international trade in coal grew into a sophisticated global commodities exchange and quadrupled in size. Stable, diversified networks of suppliers offered coal-importing countries low energy costs and enhanced energy security. No longer were electricity prices vulnerable to instability in the Middle East. Swapping oil for coal paid handsome dividends.

By the 1990s, however, natural gas had emerged as a competitive alternative for generating electricity in the developed world, and the coal fever that had been gripping Western capitals started cooling off. Between 2000 and 2008, the use of coal for power generation in OECD countries grew by only four percent, while the use of natural gas increased by 55 percent. Coal's future in the developed world looks bleaker every year. Today, experts predict that coal demand in the OECD countries will remain flat, and may even shrink, from now until 2035. In the United States, coal is losing market share thanks to newly cheap natural gas (a consequence of the shale gas boom) and tighter federal pollution regulations. In Europe, the main threat to coal comes from environmental policies. The capstone of the EU's climate policy, the EU Emissions Trading System, which was launched in 2005, has caused countries to shift to cleaner natural gas. Renewable-energy mandates, meanwhile, have also started pushing coal out of the market.

The rest of the world is racing in the opposite direction. Whereas industrialized countries once embraced coal to diversify their energy supplies, by the 1990s, the developing world was turning to it to answer a different problem: poverty. Rapidly growing economies needed more and more electricity, and coal was the cheapest and most practical way to get it. It was not the cleanest energy source, to be sure, but developing countries saw pollution as a cost worth incurring in order to obtain the benefits of a modern economy. As the Indian economist Rajendra Pachauri, chair of the Intergovernmental Panel on Climate Change, has asked, "Can you imagine 400 million people who do not have a light bulb in their homes?" He continued, "You cannot, in a democracy, ignore some of these realities. . . . We really don't have any choice but to use coal."

As the developing world keeps growing, coal will remain its fuel of choice. The IEA expects coal demand in non-OECD countries to nearly double by 2035 if current policies continue, with Chinese and Indian demand alone accounting for more than 80 percent of that growth. Indonesia, Vietnam, and much of the rest of Asia are also rapidly building new coal plants. The coal markets of Asia are thus at the heart of the global-warming problem.

The case of China, the world's biggest carbon emitter, demonstrates just how hard it is to give up the fuel. The country's reliance on coal is becoming increasingly costly. Over the last five years, as demand for coal has risen while supply has struggled to keep up, Chinese coal prices have skyrocketed. Meanwhile, tightly regulated electricity prices have not been allowed to rise in parallel. Pricing has become so distorted that at many points, a ton of coal has cost more than the value of the electricity it could create. China's dependence on coal is not only an expensive habit but also an environmental hazard. In addition to emitting carbon dioxide and sulfur dioxide, coal combustion creates mountains of toxic ash that are swept up in storms and blanket cities with particulate poison. That pollution is increasingly drawing the ire of the Chinese public and has even sparked protests.

Beijing is making every effort to kick its coal habit. The government has set a target of deriving 15 percent of the country's energy from nonfossil fuels by 2020 (the current figure is eight percent), with nuclear and hydroelectric power likely to make up most of the difference in the electricity sector. It has given generous subsidies to wind and solar power, industries that have made strong gains in recent years. Beijing is also focusing on improving the efficiency of coal-fired power generation by funding state-of-the-art engineering research and shutting down older, dirtier coal plants. As a result, the average Chinese coal plant is already far more efficient than the average American one.

These policies have started to curb China's coal addiction, but they are fighting an uphill battle against ever-increasing energy demand. Coal's share of new electricity capacity in China dropped from 81 percent in 2007 to 64 percent in 2010, but the figure rose to 65 percent in 2011, proving that the march toward alternative sources of energy will not be linear. Last year, droughts reduced hydroelectric output and caused severe power shortages. China's central planners no doubt see coal plants as the only available way to maintain the stability of the electrical grid, especially as the country relies more on wind and solar power, the outputs of which are intermittent.

Moreover, new technologies that can convert coal into more valuable liquid fuels, natural gas, and chemicals could stymie progress toward a coal-free future. When oil prices have been high, China has flirted with large-scale investments in these technologies. Although the resulting fuels can be less environmentally friendly than gasoline, in a world of $100-a-barrel crude oil, the economics get more tempting every year.

If China keeps up its efforts at diversifying its energy supply, coal's share of total electricity capacity there might drop one to three percent each year before 2020. After that, it could fall faster as nuclear power and natural gas gain a stronger foothold. But even then, it will be difficult for China to get less than 50 percent of its electricity from coal by 2030. Like it or not, coal will remain the dominant fuel in China and the other emerging Asian economies for quite some time.

EFFICIENT ELECTRICITY

Fortunately, a coal-fired future can be made cleaner. In order to prevent emissions from rising as fast as the demand for coal, developing countries need to install advanced clean-coal technologies on a large scale. To do so, they will need help from the developed world. The countries of the OECD should work with international institutions such as the IEA and the World Bank to provide expertise on the latest clean-coal technologies and the financing to pay for them. In the short run, they should focus on helping the developing world upgrade its existing coal plants and build more efficient new ones.

The world's existing coal plants are the low-hanging fruit. Simply improving basic maintenance and replacing old turbine blades can make coal plants two percent more efficient and emit four to six percent less carbon dioxide. Those reductions can add up. If China were to make just its least-efficient coal plants two percent more efficient, the country would slash emissions by an estimated 120 megatons annually—nearly as much as the United Kingdom emits every year.

Opportunities for simple upgrades are ripe across most of Asia, and such improvements typically take little time to pay for themselves. To put them in place, all that developing countries need from the rest of the world is engineering know-how and modest financing. International organizations such as the IEA Clean Coal Center, a research institute that offers expertise on how to affordably reduce coal-plant emissions, ought to be expanded. Developed countries should consider such efforts part of their foreign aid strategy.

The next big opportunity is to change the type of new coal plants that get built. Much of the world is still constructing what the industry calls "subcritical" plants, which operate at low pressures and temperatures and are thus inefficient. As a result, the average efficiency of the world's coal plants is around 30 percent, meaning that 70 percent of the potential energy in the coal is lost as it gets converted into electricity. More efficient "supercritical" coal plants, which burn at higher temperatures, can achieve efficiency levels of around 40 to 41 percent; even hotter "ultra-supercritical" plants can reach levels of 42 to 44 percent. Within ten years, advanced plants that can operate at still higher temperatures will hit the market with efficiency levels approaching 50 percent. So, too, will new plants that boost efficiency by gasifying coal before burning it.

Replacing old coal plants with state-of-the-art ones would cut carbon dioxide emissions drastically, since every one percent gain in efficiency translates into a two to three percent reduction in carbon dioxide emissions. Given how much of the world's electricity is generated at outdated coal plants, collectively, those gains would be massive. If the average efficiency of all coal plants in the world were boosted to 50 percent, emissions from coal-fired power would fall by a whopping 40 percent. At current emission levels, that amounts to three billion fewer tons of carbon dioxide annually, equivalent to more than half of what the United States releases every year.

More efficient plants make long-term economic sense. Although a 750-megawatt ultra-supercritical plant costs around $200 million more to build than does a subcritical plant of the same size, by saving coal, power companies can recoup these expenses over the lifetime of the plant. The economics are such that the carbon dioxide reductions end up paying for themselves; if one were to calculate the abatement cost, it would come out to around -$10 per ton. As a point of comparison, under California's cap-and-trade system, companies have to pay around $15 to emit one ton of carbon dioxide.

The problem, however, is that cash-strapped utilities in the developing world don't have the funds on hand to realize these gains over the course of several decades. Multilateral development banks do, and so they should step in to finance the additional capital costs of building highly efficient coal plants. The increased revenues that result from wasting less coal could more than cover the loan payments.

If development banks are unwilling to finance new plants, utilities could turn to the market for help. Their additional revenue streams could be packaged into tradable "green" securities and sold to private investors, functioning like bonds. Investors would loan capital up-front to pay for more efficient plants that generate higher profit margins. In return, when long-term power sales agreements for the plant are structured, investors would receive a portion of that extra profit. In order to maximize the environmental gains, any loan program should not finance anything less efficient than ultra-supercritical plants.

Critics may argue that financing any kind of coal is bad environmental policy. The calculus, however, is more complicated, and it depends on counterfactuals. In places where financing coal power would crowd out cleaner sources of energy, development banks should refrain from doing so. But much of the developing world, constrained by tight budgets and limited alternatives for large-scale power generation, faces a choice not between coal and renewable energy but between inefficient coal plants and efficient ones. In those places, it makes sense to finance more efficient coal plants because they would reduce emissions substantially. In other cases, the reality will lie somewhere in between, and development banks should finance packages of renewable sources alongside cleaner coal. That is precisely the arrangement the World Bank reached in South Africa in 2010, when the country was experiencing crippling electricity shortages.

A push for efficiency can bring the economic and environmental interests of the developing world into alignment. Although China is already aggressively replacing its outdated plants with world-class ones, many other countries have been unable to overcome the scientific and financial hurdles to boosting efficiency. That lack of progress represents a massive opportunity to prevent billions of tons of carbon dioxide from polluting the atmosphere.

COAL WITHOUT CARBON

Eventually, as the world's coal plants reach the limits of efficiency and the economics of renewable energy grow more favorable, advanced coal plants will yield diminishing returns. But because coal is so cheap and plentiful, it will remain a major part of the world energy mix for some time to come. In the long run, then, the goal should be to develop the capability to produce electricity from coal without releasing any emissions at all. Technologies that offer that possibility are beginning to emerge. Yet in order to become commercially viable, they will need financial and regulatory support from governments.

One of the leading clean-coal technologies is carbon capture and sequestration (CCS), whereby carbon dioxide is siphoned off from a power plant's emissions and pumped underground. Right now, the process is prohibitively expensive, costing roughly $50 to $100 for every ton of carbon dioxide stored. But since carbon dioxide from coal plants is one of the largest sources of emissions, it is worth trying to bring these costs down. To do so, governments that already sponsor CCS research, including those of Australia, China, the European Union, and the United States, need to ramp up funding. (So far, the sum of global public support for CCS demonstration projects has reached only $23 billion.) Countries should coordinate their efforts more closely so as to accelerate innovation in CCS, planning demonstration efforts in places, such as China, that offer lower costs and fewer regulatory hurdles. Additionally, governments should fast-track regulatory approval for projects that use captured carbon dioxide to revive old oil reservoirs, a practice that would make the economics of CCS more attractive.

A more revolutionary clean-coal technology allows energy companies to capture coal's energy without ever bringing the coal itself aboveground. Underground coal gasification (UCG) involves igniting coal seams deep below the earth's surface, which transforms them into a gas that can then be piped aboveground to fuel electrical generators or create diesel substitutes. The technology is experiencing a wave of new investment thanks to new advances in drilling and computer modeling that are bringing down costs. UCG leaves most of the pollution associated with burning coal belowground, especially when the process is combined with CCS.

UCG technology is not yet widely commercially viable, but pilot projects across the globe are allowing engineers to perfect their drilling and combustion techniques so that the costs can eventually come down. The Lawrence Livermore National Laboratory estimates that the gas created by UCG could be environmentally equivalent to natural gas and cost around $6 to $8 per million BTUs. That range far exceeds current U.S. natural gas prices, which hover between $2 and $3, but it is roughly half of what China and India pay for natural gas on world markets. The gas from UCG would also be cheaper than oil per unit of energy and could be turned into transportation fuel to compete directly with it.

Governments should bankroll more research into this promising technology, which could yield huge environmental and energy security benefits. Companies in Australia and China are already pursuing advanced UCG projects. According to scientists at the Lawrence Livermore National Laboratory, if the U.S. government spent $122 million on a domestic UCG research program, the country would have a shot at developing commercially viable technology.

In a time of fiscal austerity, these worthy emissions-reducing innovations are unlikely to get much government funding, at least not enough for them to become commercially viable. So innovators will have to attract some of the $1 trillion managed by private equity groups and venture capital firms. Smart tax policies can make that task easier. In the United States, Congress should create a new tax category for private equity and venture capital funds that invest in energy innovation. Then it should offer investors, such as pensions and endowments, tax credits for funneling capital into these funds. The result would be the creation of an entire asset class that would allow markets to seek out the energy innovations that will deliver both the greatest environmental benefits and the greatest profits.

A CLEANER, COOLER FUTURE

The growth of demand for coal in the developing world is simply a replay of the developed world's own industrial past. Once-poor societies are now clamoring for the same opportunities and luxuries their richer counterparts have enjoyed for decades, and they are turning to coal, dirty as it may be, to fuel that expansion. As one Chinese energy official put it during an energy conference at Stanford University in 2011, the average man in Guangzhou "would rather choke than starve."

Cleaner alternative energy sources are beginning to sate the developing world's appetite for coal, but it will be decades before they can meaningfully displace coal's dominant share of the global electricity mix. Any energy and climate strategy for the future must accept that fact. Indulging in quixotic visions of a coal-free world is an incoherent and inadequate response to the problem of global warming.

No matter what one thinks about coal, this much is clear: cleaning it up has to be a central part of any climate strategy. If the governments, multilateral institutions, and financial markets of the industrialized world helped the developing world upgrade its existing coal plants and ensured that only the cleanest coal plants were built, the effect on the climate would be profound. All told, smarter policies could lower the volume of carbon dioxide emissions per megawatt of coal-fired electricity by more than 40 percent before 2050. And if CCS or UCG can be made commercially viable, that volume could be reduced even further.

Ultimately, these transformations will cost money, and most of it will have to be spent in the developing world, where emissions are rising the fastest. The best way to pay for that would be to assign a market-based price to carbon—through a cap-and-trade program, tax policies, or other alternatives—and then allow the market to finance the cheapest sources of carbon dioxide reductions. But as the aftermath of the Kyoto Protocol negotiations has demonstrated, getting countries to agree on that idea is immensely difficult. The good thing about a strategy to make coal cleaner is that it doesn't require a price on carbon or a global climate deal.

The lack of a price on carbon will make it harder to finance some clean-coal technologies, and it will affect which strategies hold the most near-term promise. In particular, the profitability of CCS technology depends on governments assigning a price to carbon dioxide; otherwise, there is little incentive to capture a gas with almost no value. But other strategies to deal with coal use in the developing world—namely, highly efficient coal plants and UCG technologies—can still be successful because they are aligned with developing countries' own incentives to deliver cheap and secure energy. Slashing emissions from coal doesn't require a price on carbon, and there is no reason to wait for one.

As demand for coal climbs to new heights and as global temperatures keep rising, the world cannot afford to pass up the opportunity to make the fuel cleaner. This strategy represents a pragmatic way to cut carbon dioxide emissions by billions of tons each year. Humanity has come a long way since the Industrial Revolution, when sooty skies signaled economic progress. As the developing world industrializes, it is time to reenvision coal, not just as the leading cause of climate change but also as a leading opportunity to fight it.

Don't Just Drill, Baby—Drill Carefully

How to Make Fracking Safer for the Environment

Fred Krupp

The energy business has a way of making smart people look dumb. Experts were blindsided by the shale revolution in the United States. For most of the last few decades, they had assumed that U.S. domestic energy supplies were dwindling. Then, advances in horizontal drilling and hydraulic fracturing, or "fracking"—the injection of high-pressure streams of sand, water, and chemicals into underground shale and other rock to unlock oil and natural gas trapped there—significantly boosted total U.S. natural gas production, by as much as 25 percent in recent years, forcing many experts to change their tune. Horizontal drilling and fracking are now having an even bigger impact on domestic oil production: five years ago, most new onshore rigs were drilling for shale gas, but today, most are drilling for oil in shale and so-called tight rock formations. Experts are confidently pointing to the benefits of abundant supplies of this unconventional oil and gas for the U.S. economy: lower energy costs, new jobs, and even a revival in some parts of the manufacturing sector. Politicians from both parties, meanwhile, are vying to be the most enthusiastic boosters of domestic natural gas.

FRED KRUPP is President of the Environmental Defense Fund. Follow him on Twitter @FredKrupp.

Yet these same experts and policymakers are in danger of being blindsided again, by failing to grasp the extent of the growing concern among Americans over the environmental costs of unconventional oil and gas production—a crisis of confidence that threatens to halt the boom in some states. From Pennsylvania to North Dakota, more and more people are expressing concern about the environmental problems associated with this production, including local air pollution from drilling sites known as "well pads," the contamination of drinking water from spills or leaky wells, and noise and dust from trucks serving drilling sites.

Some U.S. communities and states, and even entire foreign countries, have responded to these worries by choosing to press pause on the development of their unconventional oil and gas resources. New York State, which sits atop the Marcellus Shale, a rock formation that extends through Pennsylvania to West Virginia and holds an estimated 141 trillion cubic feet of recoverable natural gas, imposed a statewide moratorium on fracking in 2010. Last year, in Colorado, the cities of Boulder and Fort Collins voted to ban fracking for at least five years, and nearby Lafayette prohibited all new oil and gas wells. Similar efforts are under way in other states, including California. In 2011, France declared its own moratorium on fracking; after its 2013 election, the German government did the same, pending an environmental risk assessment. And although the British government appears eager to exploit the United Kingdom's vast shale gas reserves, public unease and protests could block development there from moving forward, as well.

Until recently, many people assumed that natural gas would, on balance, prove beneficial for the environment. After all, unlike coal-fired power plants, natural-gas-fired ones produce negligible amounts of mercury, sulfur dioxide (which causes acid rain), and other air pollutants. Moreover, when burned, natural gas produces much less carbon dioxide than coal. But producing natural gas can impact the environment in several ways, including by releasing methane, a highly potent greenhouse gas that has the potential to reduce or even erase any near-term climate advantage. So the best one can say is that natural gas has the potential to provide a net environmental benefit—if the serious problems associated with it can be resolved. And that remains a big if. Add the growing concern that cheap natural gas could crowd out investments in solar and wind power and other renewable sources of zero-carbon energy, and it's no wonder that so many Americans have turned against shale gas and fracking more generally.

DIRTY WATER

Opposition to shale gas is not irrational. Local concerns stem from real problems. Three years ago, while serving on a panel set up by then U.S. Energy Secretary Steven Chu to examine the risks and realities of shale gas, I visited rural Pennsylvania to see the industry's impact firsthand. There, I met a mother who told me that she had been forced to leave her family farm because of severe air pollution from shale gas wells. The pollution had made her young son ill. He was staying with friends so that he could attend school; she was living out of her car.

Things were even worse in Pinedale, Wyoming, a town that has just 2,000 residents but, due to its gas operations, smog rivaling that found in Los Angeles. Last year, the American Lung Association, which grades counties annually on their air quality, gave the county containing Pinedale an F for smog. In the last decade, Denver's once-notorious smog had dissipated, largely because of the introduction of cleaner vehicles. But now, it is back, thanks to the oil and gas industry. In fact, although smog levels are decreasing in cities across the United States, in Colorado, they have ticked upward since 2010. The state's 51,000 oil and gas wells, most of which were drilled in the past decade, are now its largest source of smog-producing volatile organic compounds—harmful air pollutants that escape from storage tanks, valves, and other equipment.

Shale gas exploitation may also be polluting the water. The gas industry insists that there is no scientific evidence that fracking, which usually takes place thousands of feet below the water table, can contaminate water. But fracking is only one part of unconventional gas operations, and scientists and observers contend that other parts of the process, when improperly executed, can in fact do so. In a 2011 study, the Ground Water Protection Council, an association of state regulators, concluded that the gas industry, through poor well construction and surface spills, had directly caused ground-water contamination in Ohio and Texas.

Despite the economic benefits of shale gas, the environmental risks have dragged public opinion of it to an all-time low. In a Pew poll conducted in September 2013, 49 percent of respondents opposed fracking, whereas just 44 percent favored it. In 2012, John Deutch, a former director of the CIA and the chair of Chu's natural gas panel, said that the group's report showed that "the environmental impacts here were real." If the gas industry wanted to get people behind shale gas, he said, it "had to have a method of measurement and continuous improvement."

The industry cannot spin the facts to gain public acceptance or brush aside the harmful local impacts of drilling. Nor can it ignore the prospect that leaks and other releases of natural gas, which is composed primarily of methane (methane is also released all along the natural gas supply chain and from oil wells), could accelerate climate change. Unburned methane is a particularly powerful greenhouse gas. According to the Intergovernmental Panel on Climate Change, during its first 20 years in the atmosphere, methane is 84 times as potent a greenhouse gas as carbon dioxide.

WHAT LIES BENEATH

To understand the dangers of methane leakage from oil and gas development, consider how it affects the balance between the energy the earth absorbs from the sun and the energy the earth radiates back into space—a concept known as "radiative forcing." The bigger the difference between the amount of energy coming to the earth and the amount leaving it, the greater the global warming. Climate pollutants, such as methane, soot, and the class of refrigerants called "hydrofluorocarbons," currently cause over one-third of radiative forcing—and methane accounts for most of that amount and is expected to continue to do so. So reducing methane emissions is essential to mitigating climate change.

Today, about one-third of methane emissions in the United States come from the oil and gas industry. For natural gas, the most recent scientific research suggests that the break-even point for methane emissions—when an emissions rate that was any higher would make the switch from coal to natural gas worse for the climate in the short run—is 2.7 percent of production. No one can say with certainty how much methane is actually leaking from wellheads, processing plants, pipelines, and other natural gas facilities. The Environmental Protection Agency estimated in 2012 that total methane emissions in the United States from the natural gas supply chain represented 1.5 percent of all U.S. natural gas produced, meaning that 1.5 percent of the gas was lost through emissions. But that number may understate the true level: a 2013 Harvard study found that total U.S. methane emissions could be 50 percent higher than the EPA's estimate.

The Environmental Defense Fund, the nongovernmental organization I have led for the past 29 years, has studied natural gas closely. Two years ago, it launched 16 scientific research projects designed to fill in the gaps in what is known about methane leakage across the natural gas supply chain. The projects involve about 100 universities, research institutions, and, crucially, oil and gas companies.

The first of the 16 studies, the results of which appeared last year in *PNAS (Proceedings of the National Academy of Sciences)*, measured methane emissions from 190 drilling sites in the United States. Although it found total emissions from the production of natural gas to be similar to the EPA's estimate, it discovered that emissions from certain sources were much higher than the EPA found. Valves and compressors located at well pads, for example, all leaked more methane than the EPA estimated. Emissions from chemical injection pumps, which are used at wellheads to keep pipelines flowing or to neutralize corrosive substances, were found to be twice as high as the EPA's estimate.

The study also pointed to the promise of new emissions controls mandated by the EPA during well completions—a technique for capturing methane released at the end of the fracking process. When companies conducted "reduced emissions completions," as the process is known, the amount of leakage was much lower than the EPA's estimate for wells not conducting them. The EPA will require all new natural gas wells to employ this technique beginning in January 2015, but it does not cover oil wells, many of which also produce considerable quantities of methane. Given how effective the process is, it should be required across the board.

There is little reason for the gas industry to balk at these requirements and other methods of reducing emissions, since many of them cost very little. A study commissioned by the Environmental Defense Fund and released this year by the consulting firm ICF International analyzed 11 ways to reduce methane from 19 emissions sources. Such measures include shifting to lower-emitting pneumatic valves and closely monitoring and repairing equipment to reduce unintended methane leaks. If the most cost-effective reductions were fully adopted, the gas industry would actually save roughly $164 million annually. Overall, ICF found that using currently available technologies alone, 40 percent of methane emissions could be eliminated over the next five years for less than a penny per thousand cubic feet of gas produced.

COLORADO RULES

Reducing the shale gas industry's methane emissions is important, but that alone will not restore the public's confidence in natural gas. The creation last year of the Center for Sustainable Shale Development, in Pittsburgh, however, could help. A collaboration among oil and gas companies, environmental groups, and philanthropic organizations, the center set 15 voluntary environmental standards to improve shale gas development practices in the Appalachian basin. Drilling companies can seek certificates of operational excellence in two categories—air and climate and water and waste management—through an independent auditor. Among the companies participating are Chevron, Shell, EQT, and CONSOL Energy. Although these voluntary efforts by industry leaders can help distinguish the best from the rest and raise the bar for all, only strong rules enforced by a system that demands compliance will fully protect public air, water, and health from hazardous oil and gas development.

States have the leading role in regulating the oil and gas industry. More than 20 of them have adopted rules requiring companies to disclose which chemicals they use in fracking; at least another seven have such requirements under consideration. But work must still be done to develop regulations that can get around the industry's claims of trade secrecy, which oil and gas companies invoke to resist public disclosure of the chemicals they use. Eighty-four percent of all fracking jobs use chemicals that the industry says are trade secrets. Competitive businesses rely, of course, on intellectual property protections to foster innovation, and trade secrecy could, in some cases, encourage the development of greener chemistry. But when it comes to chemicals that could threaten water tables, the public's interest should trump the industry's concerns, and strict disclosure rules should be put in place for these chemicals.

States are also getting better at monitoring the construction and maintenance of wells. Gas wells consist of steel pipes surrounded by cement, which isolates ground water from the gas and fluids that travel through the wells. But poorly constructed well casings and weak cement can increase the chances that the ground water will be contaminated. Texas recently overhauled its outdated well-construction requirements, incorporating several dozen improvements, such as enhanced testing of well integrity, more stringent criteria for cement jobs, and new safety procedures during fracking. Many of these improvements were part of the model regulations that the Environmental Defense Fund and the company

Southwestern Energy had drafted over the past several years. Environmental activists have hailed the new rules.

States are making progress on methane leakage, too. In February, Colorado adopted the first rules anywhere in the United States that directly regulate methane emissions, over the opposition of industry trade associations in the state. Taking a cue from the leadership of Governor John Hickenlooper, who declared last year his intention to eliminate methane emissions in Colorado, the Environmental Defense Fund and three of Colorado's largest oil and gas producers—Anadarko Petroleum, Encana, and Noble Energy—developed a proposal for regulations to reduce air pollution, which shaped the final rules. Now, companies must find leaks and fix them and use stronger emissions controls for storage tanks, dehydrators, and gas vents from wells. For that equipment, the regulations force companies to eliminate 95 percent of uncontrolled toxic pollutants and volatile organic compounds.

The Colorado rules are a major breakthrough and a bellwether for other states seeking to minimize the air pollution produced by the oil and gas industry. The process led by Hickenlooper could chart a path for the energy industry and environmentalists to work together to not only reduce emissions but address other environmental issues as well.

Other countries with large shale gas reserves are likely to follow the United States' lead in developing them, so the regulations in Colorado and elsewhere in the country will set the tone well beyond U.S. borders. China has the world's largest recoverable shale gas reserves, over 1,000 trillion cubic feet, more than the United States and Canada combined. Poland, with 148 trillion cubic feet, has the largest shale gas reserves in western Europe, and France isn't far behind. European countries currently import much of their natural gas from Russia, and many Europeans worry about the use of gas supplies as a political weapon, so tapping these reserves could reduce Russia's leverage.

Shale gas is not the solution to global climate change. But it can help reduce the use of high-carbon coal in the United States—and perhaps in China, Europe, and elsewhere. Reforming this growing segment of the gas industry must not overshadow another, bigger challenge: accelerating the transition to truly clean, renewable energy.

For the next 20 years, however, slowing the rate of climate change is critical in order to give communities and wildlife a better chance to adapt. Reducing emissions of climate pollutants such as methane can reduce the rate of warming over the next few decades. Scientists have long warned that the unprecedented current rate of climate change is the greatest threat to biodiversity. And the human cost is apparent in more frequent and more intense extreme weather, from hurricanes and heat waves to droughts.

Working to reduce the emissions of pollutants that accelerate climate change is a project that industry leaders and environmentalists in the United States should be able to agree on. By forging unlikely alliances based on a mutual understanding of what is at stake, the environmental community and the oil and gas industry can create strong, sensible standards that reduce the risks of unconventional oil and gas development—and ensure that the economic windfall benefits the environment, too.

How Chinese Innovation is Changing Green Technology

Beijing's Big Gamble on Renewables

S. Julio Friedmann

For energy enthusiasts, China has become the main event. The country uses more energy and emits more greenhouse gas than any other on earth. Its production of power is booming, too. Every year, China generates nearly 100,000 megawatts more than the previous year—more than the total generated by California or Texas. The scale of the accompanying infrastructure change is staggering: every week, a new large coal plant opens somewhere in China. This has led to widespread pollution, health problems, and environmental degradation—to the cost to the Chinese economy of about 11 percent of GDP.

But this is not the same old cautionary tale of dirty development: China has taken these challenges, and the need for energy and 20 million new jobs per year, as an spur to invest in clean technology. Indeed, with the government putting over $50 billion into clean energy R&D every year, China has become a global hub for energy innovation.

The country's progress is driven by a combination of government mandate and direct investment. Examples are many. A 2007

S. JULIO FRIEDMANN is leader of the Carbon Management Program at Lawrence Livermore National Laboratory.

law required four percent gains in energy efficiency each year through 2012, including in the transportation and industrial sectors. Since then, total efficiency in the power sector has increased by nearly ten percent and is likely to continue rising. Such mandates have been matched by requirements for sulfur emissions control and cleaner water, the closure of many low-efficiency coal mines and cement plants, and new investment in solar, wind, and other renewable power.

To all this, China's twelfth five-year-plan, introduced earlier this year, added goals for developing clean technology indigenously. Mostly these innovations will be for domestic use, although there is growing interest in international export markets for clean tech. Many state-funded projects now require that 80 percent of the technology used be indigenous. Two agencies are responsible for overseeing compliance. First is the National Energy Administration (NEA), which approves the financing and construction of virtually every large energy project. Second, the Ministry of Science and Technology (MOST) runs the more than 100 Chinese academies that conduct clean tech research. In 2010, China funneled tens of billions for green innovation through these two organizations.

Massive state investment has allowed Beijing to do what private industry around the world cannot. Power and energy production requires massive upfront capital investments; the total cost for building individual novel solar, nuclear, or wind power facilities often exceeds one billion dollars. The high expense makes such projects risky for capital markets around the world, not to mention for most private firms. Often, private banks only want to be fast followers and invest in second-generation plants, not first-generation plants with a new design. NEA and MOST backing helps projects clear this hurdle.

A good example is Huaneng, the world's largest power company, which generates about 160,000 megawatts of power per year—30 percent more than Texas. Every year, it adds 13,000 megawatts of new generation—about the same as Massachusetts' current generation. To meet the government's many clean energy mandates,

Huaneng plans to install windmills capable of generating 10,000 megawatts per year (close to the total of U.S. wind power) and solar panels capable of generating 10,000 megawatts per year (greater than the U.S. total). By 2025, Huaneng expects to add more than 50,000 megawatts of hydropower and 10,000 megawatts of nuclear power. Meanwhile, it will continue to add nearly 50 megawatts of coal power.

Beyond producing energy, Huaneng innovates through its Clean Energy Research Institute, which is funded by its own revenues and NEA and MOST. It has designed and built two major indigenous clean coal technologies in the last decade. The first is a gasifier that turns coal into synthetic gas with high efficiency and ultra-low pollution. The second is a new capture technology that strips CO_2 out of coal plant emissions. It is apparently the world's largest post-combustion carbon capture facility—and its cheapest. The deadlines set by the government mandates brought these projects to life in just three years and have already led to international licensing agreements and new proposed projects in North America and Europe.

Other companies, too, are developing clean tech from scratch, both for domestic use and for export. The XinAo Group, Shenhua, State Grid, and CNOOC, all major Chinese energy firms, have created their own innovation enterprises undergirded by the financial power of their parent companies and the state. Their efforts include solar thin-films, biofuels, batteries, efficient vehicles, coal-to-liquids, shale gas, and smart grids. In many cases, Chinese companies have even formed joint ventures with firms in the United States to accelerate development and Western commercialization. For example, Lishen, one of the world's largest battery companies, has embarked on a $7 billion development drive to improve battery technology on its own, with licensing agreements in the United States.

At the same time, China has started to repatriate Western-educated Chinese nationals, especially those who have worked at Western energy firms (GE, Dow, DuPont, Areva) or are leading scientists and engineers at Western universities (Johns Hopkins, MIT, Stanford, and USC, among others). When they return to China, they are given staffs of hundreds, multimillion-dollar budgets, and aggressive delivery timelines. Sometimes called "sea turtles" (for returning to the shores of their birth), they bring a Western innovation strategy to Chinese design, and are paired with the intellectual and financial resources needed to bring designs to life.

In many ways, China's green dreams are good news.

Consider the impact on the environment. Together the United States and China account for 40 percent of emissions, 40 percent of energy consumption, and 50 percent of global coal use. Nothing other countries do on this issue can match the impact of the actions (or innaction) of the United States or China. Without Washington and Beijing leading the way, the world will not mitigate the worst consequences of climate change. In this context, any Chinese investment in clean tech is a global good.

Many U.S. businesses will benefit, too. For one, Chinese investment in green tech is already creating jobs in the United States. Thanks to Chinese partnerships with GE, Applied Materials, Duke Energy, and others, those companies have been able to build plants, hire people, demonstrate technology, and underwrite projects. Further, U.S. companies benefit directly from Chinese research. For example, FutureFuels, a U.S. company energy company in Pennsylvania, is deploying a novel clean-coal plant that Huaneng first tested and developed. Once operational, the plant could carry the smallest carbon footprint of any coal or gas plant in the eastern United States. And it would create with it thousands of jobs in southern Pennsylvania's Rust Belt, besides.

Beyond that, U.S. companies and consumers will benefit indirectly from having access to lower-cost technologies that have already been tested on a large commercial scale, speeding the implementation of more efficient and sustainable energy technologies in the United States. So, too, will partnerships between the two countries. These commercial agreements have already started to lay a foundation of trust, absolutely essential for future U.S.-China government agreements in trade, climate, and other key areas.

At the same time, China's green innovation raises questions about U.S. and European competitiveness. For years, the West believed that its economic advantage was its ability to invent products that could be sold to eastern markets. Successive governments sold innovation as a pathway to job creation and prowess in manufacturing. However, if the West buys Chinese clean tech, that narrative reverses. It also raises the specter of permanent loss manufacturing for some heavy equipment, technology development, and high-value innovation.

One might ask, as well, whether all this will truly address China's challenges. Air quality improvement is still localized and slow, and concerns about particulates and mercury remain. Fuel shortages of all kinds, including coal, gas, and gasoline, persist, raising local and global prices despite China's impressive gains. And some in China have tried to force burgeoning commercial partnerships to start committing to intellectual property agreements that chill innovation and trade. Trade and monetary imbalances could also be magnified by Chinese clean tech exports, as could concerns for worker safety.

Ultimately, China's clean energy investment and deployment will dominate climate and trade trajectories for decades—whatever the effects on commerce, industry, energy, and even human rights and monetary policy. The scale of its effort simply dwarfs every other on earth. That is good news for the oceans and the atmosphere, but also gives pause to the 5.5 billion people on this planet who don't live in China. For them, the economic and security implications of China's innovation drive are yet to be seen.

The First Cold War

The Environmental Lessons of the Little Ice Age

Deborah R. Coen

Reflecting on the "misery and misfortune" he had witnessed during the Thirty Years' War, Caspar Preis, a German farmer, was sure that "no one living in a better age would believe it." From 1618 to 1648, the population of Germany fell by as much as 40 percent. Roughly four million people were killed in the wars between Catholic and Protestant princes; many others died of starvation or disease; still others fled their homes in search of safety. The misery was worst in the 1640s, when summer frosts and storms wiped out crops and soldiers nearly froze to death. Towns were ruined, currencies depreciated, and people made meals of grass. As Denmark, Sweden, and France were drawn into the conflict, it looked as if all of Europe had fallen into civil war. Indeed, wars and revolutions were spreading chaos well beyond the view of a German peasant, throughout the British Isles and Russia, even in faraway China and the lands of the Ottoman Empire.

Historians have long debated whether these widespread upheavals were simply what passed for normal life in the premodern world or in fact constituted a decisive historical turning point: a "general crisis" that swept away an older order and cleared the ground for the emergence of modern states, economies, and

DEBORAH R. COEN is Associate Professor of History at Barnard College, Columbia University, and the author of *The Earthquake Observers: Disaster Science From Lisbon to Richter.*

systems of thought. From the start of this debate in the 1930s, scholars kept one eye on the present, using their research to reflect on the geopolitical and economic crises of the twentieth century. Now, the military historian Geoffrey Parker brings this history to bear on the environmental crisis of the twenty-first century.

In *Global Crisis: War, Climate Change, and Catastrophe in the Seventeenth Century*, Parker uncovers the environmental factors behind the seventeenth century's earthshaking events, from the English Civil Wars, to the collapse of the Polish-Lithuanian Commonwealth, to the Manchu conquest of China. The immediate cause of state breakdown in each case was often an impulsive decision by a shortsighted prince. But that, in Parker's terms, was merely the "tipping point." What brought each state to the brink of catastrophe, he argues, was instead a global environmental phenomenon: the Little Ice Age.

A wealth of scientific evidence shows that the seventeenth century was one of the more extreme periods in an era of global cooling that stretched from the fourteenth to the nineteenth century. Thanks to the telescopes that came into use around 1600, sunspot records indicate a low point in solar activity in the latter half of the seventeenth century. Following relatively mild conditions in the

1500s, the chill took seventeenth-century observers by surprise. "It is horribly cold," wrote the Marquise de Sévigné to her daughter in Provence in the summer of 1675. "We have the fires lit, just like you, which is very remarkable." She and her daughter agreed that "the behavior of the sun and of the seasons has changed."

Rivers that were usually navigable in winter froze solid, and the long winters were immortalized in the landscape paintings of the Dutch Golden Age. Seventeenth-century accounts of droughts, floods, insect infestations, famines, and epidemics trace the far-reaching effects of climate change. These scourges struck repeatedly and across vast regions, contributing to an estimated loss of one-third of the world's population.

Parker's book captures this century of upheaval in a political, economic, and cultural history of dozens of early modern states. Parker combed archives in six European countries, as well as India. His bibliographical essay modestly attests to a feat of research that would seem to call for an army of historians. Out of the details he uncovered, Parker weaves a gripping story that includes witch-hunts, palace intrigues (such as the travails of Osman II, the first Ottoman sultan ever to be killed by his subjects), and new distractions to cope with the misery: tobacco, coffee, tea, and chocolate. Parker has reconstructed the seventeenth-century crisis in a masterpiece of narrative history, which falters only when it turns to the present-day implications of climate change. By refusing to address the link between industrialization and global warming, Parker ultimately gives a skewed picture of the resolution of the crisis and a blinkered view of its implications for environmental policy today.

FROST, FIGHTS, AND FAMINE

The first section of Parker's book refutes the claim that the violence and instability of the seventeenth century were nothing new. Examining each revolutionary state, from Ming China to Stuart England, Parker concludes that "the 1640s saw more rebellions and revolutions than any comparable period in world history." Nowhere does he claim that the collapse or near collapse of an early modern

Deborah R. Coen

state was the direct result of climate change. He is no environmental determinist, but he does insist that many conflicts were fundamentally competitions over dwindling natural resources. Thus, he takes issue with the economist Amartya Sen, who has attributed famines not to food shortages in and of themselves but to flaws in the distribution of food. Parker suggests that Sen's argument has drawn the attention of historians and policymakers away from the environmental determinants of food crises.

Parker complements his narrative of the century's turmoil with an analysis of the strategies of those states that were able to stave off revolution and regime change. India, Japan, and Persia all avoided breakdown; Spain and the Italian lands restored order quickly; and the Americas, Australia, and sub-Saharan Africa saw little sign of crisis at all. All these countries and regions, Parker argues, entered the seventeenth century with relatively low population densities. Elsewhere, the warmer weather of the sixteenth century had led to overpopulation, with disastrous consequences once cooling set in. Among the most effective coping strategies during the crisis, Parker finds, were birth control and abortion, which reduced populations to more sustainable levels.

Japan under the Tokugawa shogunate emerges as the foremost success story. Parker attributes its stability in part to a centralized power structure that facilitated disaster preparedness, as well as to the avoidance of "foreign entanglements." But Japan also owed its stability to what the shogunate did not do: namely, raise taxes, punish the underreporting of harvests, or promote new ideas. Unlike the Stuarts in England and Scotland or the Habsburgs in Spain, Japan's leaders avoided imposing what Parker calls "burdens" and "innovations" on their subjects in the midst of an ecological crisis. But Japan's success had a high price, politically and environmentally: the repeal of vassals' rights, the exploitation of farmers and craftsmen, the destruction of forests, and the depletion of soils. Inertia paid off only in the short term.

KNOWLEDGE-BASED RECOVERY

Parker draws a fascinating conclusion from the fact that the political upheavals generally ended in the late seventeenth century while the global cooling did not. Stability, he claims, was achieved largely through two widespread innovations. In response to the crisis, every government hoped to regain some measure of control over its population and natural resources and to provide collective insurance against future threats. Particularly in China, England, France, and the Netherlands, the governments' efforts brought innovations such as statistical surveys, systems of quarantine, and granary maintenance. As Parker argues, the crisis brought "welfare states" into existence.

Just as important to economic recovery around the globe, Parker argues, were intellectual developments that resulted in new ways of thinking about the natural world. Parker compares the emphasis placed on observational and experimental methods in seventeenth-century Europe—what historians call "the scientific revolution"—with contemporaneous intellectual trends in China, India, and Japan. In many parts of Asia, as in much of Europe, the crisis prompted a turn to what Parker calls "practical" reasoning. But only in western Europe did governments encourage and incorporate this style of thought. Only there did monarchs sponsor scientific academies that allowed one discovery to build on another, ultimately generating the knowledge that fueled industrialization in the eighteenth and nineteenth centuries. Parker thus contends that the end of the general crisis laid the intellectual foundations for what the political scientist Samuel Huntington has called "the Great Divergence," the economic acceleration of Europe relative to the rest of the world.

Here, Parker overplays his hand. The first problem is his assumption that seventeenth-century science was a precondition for industrialization. Decades of research on the history of technology have shown that technological innovations tend to depend more on the skills and experience of technicians than on scientific theories. Moreover, as the historian Prasannan Parthasarathi argues in *Why*

Europe Grew Rich and Asia Did Not, the most important factors propelling British industrialization—the timber shortage, which drove the country's shift to coal, and the competition from Indian textiles, which inspired the mechanization of spinning—had little to do with science.

A second problem is Parker's characterization of the new currents in European thought as uniformly "practical," in the sense of being an aid to economic recovery and thus a source of social stability. After all, the idea that the seventeenth century was a time of general crisis originally referred to the critical, even radical thrust of the period's natural and moral philosophy. In *The Crisis of the European Mind*, published in 1935, the French historian Paul Hazard argued that this intellectual ferment was responsible for the political instability that culminated in the French Revolution of 1789. "Reason was no longer a well-balanced wisdom," he wrote "but a critical audacity."

More recent historians have distinguished between critical and conciliatory strains of the new science, but Parker ignores such distinctions. Disregarding the differences among Francis Bacon's empiricism, René Descartes' rationalism, and Galileo's heretical search for universal laws, Parker instead lumps all these thinkers together with the fictional Robinson Crusoe as proponents of a stolid "practical learning." But such a generalization ignores the fact that there is no evidence that philosophers such as Descartes and Galileo had anything to do with Europe's economic recovery. Their appeals to the authority of reason potentially threatened all elements of the existing order.

THE NEXT CRISIS

A more fundamental problem with the book's argument emerges in the epilogue, where Parker considers the present-day implications of this history. The principal lesson he draws concerns the need for disaster preparedness at the national level—on the model of the construction of the Thames Barrier, downstream from central London, in the 1970s and 1980s. Wealthy nations, Parker implies, should follow the example of Tokugawa Japan and "avoid foreign entanglements." But here, the seventeenth-century example loses relevance. Unlike in the seventeenth century, the causes of climate change are clear today, and there is also a clear collective global responsibility to reverse it.

Concerted international efforts, rather than isolation, are needed today to avoid or minimize catastrophes of the kind that Parker so skillfully portrays. Yet Parker insists on separating the question of the cause of global warming from the question of how to respond to it. He urges the use of technical ingenuity to protect against disasters but says nothing of alternative energy technologies that could help limit the greenhouse effect. He would have readers believe that climate change today is fundamentally the same phenomenon it was in the seventeenth century: a natural and inevitable check on population growth.

But this history looks different when viewed squarely through the lens of the most recent climate science. Scientists have come to see the last 250 years as a distinct geological epoch, called the Anthropocene, that is marked by the transformative effects of human activities on the very conditions of life on earth. From this perspective, the dawn of the industrial age in eighteenth-century Europe no longer looks like a happy ending to the general crisis but rather like the onset of a new and unprecedented crisis. The recognition of the unintended consequences of industrial development throws the very meaning of "practical" knowledge into question, since practicality must be judged by long-term costs, not only short-term benefits.

Discussing the impact of the Little Ice Age in Australia, Parker likens the adaptive behavior of seventeenth-century aboriginal people to the resilience of their continent's plants and animals. But historians in the Anthropocene should be wary of assuming that Englishmen learned more from the unusually cruel weather of the seventeenth century than Australians did. For a better example of truly practical lessons learned from the crisis, consider the German foresters who, faced with timber shortages in the wake of the Thirty

Deborah R. Coen

Years' War, first articulated the idea of sustainable development. Or consider the explorers who left a cold and hungry Europe in search of tropical riches, only to realize that their own rapacity could quickly exhaust the bounty of an island paradise. Despite the breadth and force of *Global Crisis*, the story of the lessons learned from the Little Ice Age calls for one more chapter: on the dawning of an ecological consciousness.

The Geoengineering Option

A Last Resort Against Global Warming?

David G. Victor, M. Granger Morgan,
Jay Apt, John Steinbrune

E ach year, the effects of climate change are coming into
sharper focus. Barely a month goes by without some fresh
bad news: ice sheets and glaciers are melting faster than
expected, sea levels are rising more rapidly than ever in recorded
history, plants are blooming earlier in the spring, water supplies
and habitats are in danger, birds are being forced to find new migratory patterns.

The odds that the global climate will reach a dangerous tipping
point are increasing. Over the course of the twenty-first century,

DAVID G. VICTOR is a Professor at Stanford Law School, Director of Stanford's
Program on Energy and Sustainable Development, and an Adjunct Senior Fellow at the Council on Foreign Relations.

M. GRANGER MORGAN is Head of Carnegie Mellon University's Department
of Engineering and Public Policy and Director of the Climate Decision Making
Center.

JAY APT is Professor of Engineering and Public Policy at Carnegie Mellon
University.

JOHN STEINBRUNER is Professor of Public Policy and Director of the Center
for International and Security Studies at the University of Maryland.

KATHARINE RICKE is a doctoral student at Carnegie Mellon University.
Additional materials are available online at www.cfr.org/geoengineering.

key ocean currents, such as the Gulf Stream, could shift radically, and thawing permafrost could release huge amounts of additional greenhouse gases into the atmosphere. Such scenarios, although still remote, would dramatically accelerate and compound the consequences of global warming. Scientists are taking these doomsday scenarios seriously because the steady accumulation of warming gases in the atmosphere is forcing change in the climate system at rates so rapid that the outcomes are extremely difficult to predict.

Eliminating all the risks of climate change is impossible because carbon dioxide emissions, the chief human contribution to global warming, are unlike conventional air pollutants, which stay in the atmosphere for only hours or days. Once carbon dioxide enters the atmosphere, much of it remains for over a hundred years. Emissions from anywhere on the planet contribute to the global problem, and once headed in the wrong direction, the climate system is slow to respond to attempts at reversal. As with a bathtub that has a large faucet and a small drain, the only practical way to lower the level is by dramatically cutting the inflow. Holding global warming steady at its current rate would require a worldwide 60-80 percent cut in emissions, and it would still take decades for the atmospheric concentration of carbon dioxide to stabilize.

Most human emissions of carbon dioxide come from burning fossil fuels, and most governments have been reluctant to force the radical changes necessary to reduce those emissions. Economic growth tends to trump vague and elusive global aspirations. The United States has yet to impose even a cap on its emissions, let alone a reduction. The European Union has adopted an emissions-trading scheme that, although promising in theory, has not yet had much real effect because carbon prices are still too low to cause any significant change in behavior. Even Norway, which in 1991 became one of the first nations to impose a stiff tax on emissions, has seen a net increase in its carbon dioxide emissions. Japan, too, has professed its commitment to taming global warming. Nevertheless, Tokyo is struggling to square the need for economic growth with continued dependence on an energy system powered mainly by

conventional fossil fuels. And China's emissions recently surpassed those of the United States, thanks to coal-fueled industrialization and a staggering pace of economic growth. The global economic crisis is stanching emissions a bit, but it will not come close to shutting off the faucet.

The world's slow progress in cutting carbon dioxide emissions and the looming danger that the climate could take a sudden turn for the worse require policymakers to take a closer look at emergency strategies for curbing the effects of global warming. These strategies, often called "geoengineering," envision deploying systems on a planetary scale, such as launching reflective particles into the atmosphere or positioning sunshades to cool the earth. These strategies could cool the planet, but they would not stop the buildup of carbon dioxide or lessen all its harmful impacts. For this reason, geoengineering has been widely shunned by those committed to reducing emissions.

Serious research on geoengineering is still in its infancy, and it has not received the attention it deserves from politicians. The time has come to take it seriously. Geoengineering could provide a useful defense for the planet—an emergency shield that could be deployed if surprisingly nasty climatic shifts put vital ecosystems and billions of people at risk. Actually raising the shield, however, would be a political choice. One nation's emergency can be another's opportunity, and it is unlikely that all countries will have similar assessments of how to balance the ills of unchecked climate change with the risk that geoengineering could do more harm than good. Governments should immediately begin to undertake serious research on geoengineering and help create international norms governing its use.

THE RAINMAKERS

Geoengineering is not a new idea. In 1965, when President Lyndon Johnson received the first-ever U.S. presidential briefing on the dangers of climate change, the only remedy prescribed to counter the effects of global warming was geoengineering. That advice reflected the scientific culture of the time, which imagined that engineering could fix almost any problem.

By the late 1940s, both the United States and the Soviet Union had begun exploring strategies for modifying the weather to gain battlefield advantage. Many schemes focused on "seeding" clouds with substances that would coax them to drop more rain. Despite offering no clear advantage to the military, "weather makers" were routinely employed (rarely with much effect) to squeeze more rain from clouds for thirsty crops. Starting in 1962, U.S. government researchers for Project Stormfury tried to make tropical hurricanes less intense through cloud seeding, but with no clear success. Military experts also dreamed of using nuclear explosions and other interventions to create a more advantageous climate. These applications were frightening enough that in 1976 the United Nations adopted the Convention on the Prohibition of Military or Any Other Hostile Use of Environmental Modification Techniques to bar such projects. By the 1970s, after a string of failures, the idea of weather modification for war and farming had largely faded away.

Today's proposals for geoengineering are more likely to have an impact because the interventions needed for global-scale geoengineering are much less subtle than those that sought to influence local weather patterns. The earth's climate is largely driven by the fine balance between the light energy with which the sun bathes the earth and the heat that the earth radiates back to space. On average, about 70 percent of the earth's incoming sunlight is absorbed by the atmosphere and the planet's surface; the remainder is reflected back into space. Increasing the reflectivity of the planet (known as the albedo) by about one percentage point could have an effect on the climate system large enough to offset the gross increase in warming that is likely over the next century as a result of a doubling of the amount of carbon dioxide in the atmosphere. Making such tweaks is much more straightforward than causing rain or fog at a particular location in the ways that the weather makers of the late 1940s and 1950s dreamed of doing.

In fact, every few decades, volcanoes validate the theory that it is possible to engineer the climate. When Mount Pinatubo, in the Philippines, erupted in 1991, it ejected plumes of sulfate and other fine particles into the atmosphere, which reflected a bit more sunlight and cooled the planet by about 0.5 degrees Celsius over the course of a year. Larger eruptions, such as the 1883 eruption of Krakatau, in Indonesia, have caused even greater cooling that lasted longer. Unlike efforts to control emissions of greenhouse gases, which will take many years to yield a noticeable effect, volcano-like strategies for cooling the planet would work relatively promptly.

Another lesson from volcanoes is that a geoengineering system would require frequent maintenance, since most particles lofted into the stratosphere would disappear after a year or two. Once a geoengineering project were under way, there would be strong incentives to continue it, since failure to keep the shield in place could allow particularly harmful changes in the earth's climate, such as warming so speedy that ecosystems would collapse because they had no time to adjust. By carefully measuring the climatic effects of the next major volcanic eruption with satellites and aircraft, geoengineers could design a number of climate-cooling technologies.

ALBEDO ENHANCERS

Today, the term "geoengineering" refers to a variety of strategies designed to cool the climate. Some, for example, would slowly remove carbon dioxide from the atmosphere, either by manipulating the biosphere (such as by fertilizing the ocean with nutrients that would allow plankton to grow faster and thus absorb more carbon)

David G. Victor, M. Granger Morgan, Jay Apt, John Steinbrune

or by directly scrubbing the air with devices that resemble big cooling towers. However, from what is known today, increasing the earth's albedo offers the most promising method for rapidly cooling the planet.

Most schemes that would alter the earth's albedo envision putting reflective particles into the upper atmosphere, much as volcanoes do already. Such schemes offer quick impacts with relatively little effort. For example, just one kilogram of sulfur well placed in the stratosphere would roughly offset the warming effect of several hundred thousand kilograms of carbon dioxide. Other schemes include seeding bright reflective clouds by blowing seawater or other substances into the lower atmosphere. Substantial reductions of global warming are also possible to achieve by converting dark places that absorb lots of sunlight to lighter shades—for example, by replacing dark forests with more reflective grasslands. (Engineered plants might be designed for the task.) More ambitious projects could include launching a huge cloud of thin refracting discs into a special space orbit that parks the discs between the sun and the earth in order to bend just a bit of sunlight away before it hits the planet.

So far, launching reflective materials into the upper stratosphere seems to be the easiest and most cost-effective option. This could be accomplished by using high-flying aircraft, naval guns, or giant balloons. The appropriate materials could include sulfate aerosols (which would be created by releasing sulfur dioxide gas), aluminum oxide dust, or even self-levitating and self-orienting designer particles engineered to migrate to the Polar Regions and remain in place for long periods. If it can be done, concentrating sunshades over the poles would be a particularly interesting option, since those latitudes appear to be the most sensitive to global warming. Most cost estimates for such geoengineering strategies are preliminary and unreliable. However, there is general agreement that the strategies are cheap; the total expense of the most cost-effective options would amount to perhaps as little as a few billion dollars, just one percent (or less) of the cost of dramatically cutting emissions.

Cooling the planet through geoengineering will not, however, fix all of the problems related to climate change. Offsetting warming by reflecting more sunlight back into space will not stop the rising concentration of carbon dioxide in the atmosphere. Sooner or later, much of that carbon dioxide ends up in the oceans, where it forms carbonic acid. Ocean acidification is a catastrophe for marine ecosystems, for the 100 million people who depend on coral reefs for their livelihoods, and for the many more who depend on them for coastal protection from storms and for biological support of the greater ocean food web. Over the last century, the oceans have become markedly more acidic, and current projections suggest that without a serious effort to control emissions, the concentration of carbon dioxide will be so high by the end of the century that many organisms that make shells will disappear and most coral reef ecosystems will collapse, devastating the marine fishing industry. Recent studies have also suggested that ocean acidification will increase the size and depth of "dead zones," areas of the sea that are so oxygen depleted that larger marine life, such as squid, are unable to breathe properly.

Altering the albedo of the earth would also affect atmospheric circulation, rainfall, and other aspects of the hydrologic cycle. In the six to 18 months following the eruption of Mount Pinatubo, rainfall and river flows dropped, particularly in the tropics. Understanding these dangers better would help convince government leaders in rainfall-sensitive regions, such as parts of China and India (along with North Africa, the Middle East, and the desert regions of the southwestern United States), not to prematurely deploy poorly designed geoengineering schemes that could wreak havoc on agricultural productivity. Indeed, some climate models already suggest that negative outcomes—decreased precipitation over land (especially in the tropics) and increased precipitation over the oceans—would accompany a geoengineering scheme that sought to lower average temperatures by raising the planet's albedo. Such changes could increase the risk of major droughts in some regions and have a major impact on agriculture and the supply of fresh water. Complementary policies—such as investing in better water-management schemes—may be needed.

The highly uncertain but possibly disastrous side effects of geoengineering interventions are difficult to compare to the dangers of unchecked global climate change. Chances are that if countries begin deploying geoengineering systems, it will be because calamitous climate change is near at hand. Yet the assignment of blame after a geoengineering disaster would be very different from the current debates over who is responsible for climate change, which is the result of centuries of accumulated emissions from activities across the world. By contrast, the side effects of geoengineering projects could be readily pinned on the geoengineers themselves. That is one reason why nations must begin building useful international norms to govern geoengineering in order to assess its dangers and decide when to act in the event of an impending climatic disaster.

LONE RANGERS

An effective foreign policy strategy for managing geoengineering is difficult to formulate because the technology involved turns the normal debate over climate change on its head. The best way to reduce the danger of global warming is, of course, to cut emissions of carbon dioxide and other greenhouse gases. But success in that venture will require all the major emitting countries, with their divergent interests, to cooperate for several decades in a sustained effort to develop and deploy completely new energy systems with much lower emissions. Incentives to defect and avoid the high cost of emissions controls will be strong.

By contrast, geoengineering is an option at the disposal of any reasonably advanced nation. A single country could deploy geoengineering systems from its own territory without consulting the rest of the planet. Geoengineers keen to alter their own country's climate might not assess or even care about the dangers their actions could create for climates, ecosystems, and economies elsewhere. A unilateral geoengineering project could impose costs on other countries, such as changes in precipitation patterns and river flows or adverse impacts on agriculture, marine fishing, and tourism. And merely knowing that geoengineering exists as an option may take the pressure off governments to implement the policies needed to cut emissions.

At some point in the near future, it is conceivable that a nation that has not done enough to confront climate change will conclude that global warming has become so harmful to its interests that it should unilaterally engage in geoengineering. Although it is hardly wise to mess with a poorly understood global climate system using instruments whose effects are also unknown, politicians must take geoengineering seriously because it is cheap, easy, and takes only one government with sufficient hubris or desperation to set it in motion. Except in the most dire climatic emergency, universal agreement on the best approach is highly unlikely. Unilateral action would create a crisis of legitimacy that could make it especially difficult to manage geoengineering schemes once they are under way.

Although governments are the most likely actors, some geoengineering options are cheap enough to be deployed by wealthy and capable individuals or corporations. Although it may sound like the stuff of a future James Bond movie, private-sector geoengineers might very well attempt to deploy affordable geoengineering schemes on their own. And even if governments manage to keep freelance geoengineers in check, the private sector could emerge as a potent force by becoming an interest group that pushes for deployment or drives the direction of geoengineering research and assessment. Already, private companies are running experiments on ocean fertilization in the hope of sequestering carbon dioxide and earning credits that they could trade in carbon markets. Private developers of technology for albedo modification could obstruct an open and transparent research environment as they jockey for position in the potentially lucrative market for testing and deploying geoengineering systems. To prevent such scenarios and to establish the rules that should govern the use of geoengineering technology for the good of the entire planet, a cooperative, inter-national research agenda is vital.

FROM SCIENCE FICTION TO FACTS

Despite years of speculation and vague talk, peer-reviewed research on geoengineering is remarkably scarce. Nearly the entire community of geoengineering scientists could fit comfortably in a single university seminar room, and the entire scientific literature on the subject could be read during the course of a transatlantic flight. Geoengineering continues to be considered a fringe topic.

Many scientists have been reluctant to raise the issue for fear that it might create a moral hazard: encouraging governments to deploy geoengineering rather than invest in cutting emissions. Indeed, geoengineering ventures will be viewed with particular suspicion if the nations funding geoengineering research are not also investing in dramatically reducing their emissions of carbon dioxide and other greenhouse gases.

Many scientists also rightly fear that grants for geoengineering research would be subtracted from the existing funds for urgently needed climate-science research and carbon-abatement technologies. But there is a pressing need for a better understanding of geoengineering, rooted in theoretical studies and empirical field measurements. The subject also requires the talents of engineers, few of whom have joined the small group of scientists studying these techniques.

The scientific academies in the leading industrialized and emerging countries—which often control the purse strings for major research grants—must orchestrate a serious and transparent international research effort funded by their governments. Although some work is already under way, a more comprehensive understanding of geoengineering options and of risk-assessment procedures would make countries less trigger-happy and more inclined to consider deploying geoengineering systems in concert rather than on their own. (The International Council for Science, which has a long and successful history of coordinating scientific assessments of technical topics, could also lend a helping hand.) Eventually, a dedicated international entity overseen by the leading academies, provided with a large budget, and suffused with the norms of transparency and peer review will be necessary.

In time, international institutions such as the Intergovernmental Panel on Climate Change could be expected to synthesize the findings from the published research. The IPCC, which shared the Nobel Peace Prize in 2007 for its pivotal role in building a consensus around climate science, has not considered geoengineering so far because the topic is politically radioactive and there is a dearth of peer-reviewed research on it. The IPCC's fifth assessment report on climate change, which is being planned right now, should promise to take a closer look at geoengineering. Attention from the IPCC and the world's major scientific academies would help encourage new research.

A broad and solid foundation of research would help on three fronts. First, it would transform the discussion about geoengineering from an abstract debate into one focused on real risk assessment. Second, a research program that was backed by the world's top scientific academies could secure funding and political cover for essential but controversial experiments. (Field trials of engineered aerosols, for example, could spark protests comparable to those that accompanied trials of genetically modified crops.) Such experiments will be seen as more acceptable if they are designed and overseen by the world's leading scientists and evaluated in a fully transparent fashion. Third, and what is crucial, a better understanding of the dangers of geoengineering would help nations craft the norms that should govern the testing and possible deployment of newly developed technologies. Scientists could be influential in creating these norms, just as nuclear scientists framed the options on nuclear testing and influenced pivotal governments during the Cold War.

If countries were actually to contemplate the deployment of geoengineering technologies, there would inevitably be questions raised about what triggers would compel the use of these systems. Today, nobody knows which climatic triggers are most important for geoengineering because research on the harmful effects of climate change has not been coupled tightly enough with research on whether and how geoengineering might offset those effects.

Although the international scientific community should take the lead in developing a research agenda, social scientists, international lawyers, and foreign policy experts will also have to play a role. Eventually, there will have to be international laws to ensure that globally credible and legitimate rules govern the deployment of geoengineering systems. But effective legal norms cannot be imperiously declared. They must be carefully developed by informed consensus in order to avoid encouraging the rogue forms of geoengineering they are intended to prevent.

Those who worry that such research will cause governments to abandon their efforts to control emissions, including much of the environmental community, are prone to seek a categorical prohibition against geoengineering. But a taboo would interfere with much-needed scientific research on an option that might be better for humanity and the world's ecosystems than allowing unchecked climate change or reckless unilateral geoengineering. Formal prohibition is unlikely to stop determined rogues, but a smart and scientifically sanctioned research program could gather data essential to understanding the risks of geoengineering strategies and to establishing responsible criteria for their testing and deployment.

BRAVE NEW WORLD

Fiddling with the climate to fix the climate strikes most people as a shockingly bad idea. Many worry that research on geoengineering will make governments less willing to regulate emissions. It is more likely, however, that serious study will reveal the many dangerous side effects of geoengineering, exposing it as a true option of last resort. But because the option exists, and might be used, it would be dangerous for scientists and policymakers to ignore it. Assessing and managing the risks of geoengineering may not require radically different approaches from those used for other seemingly risky endeavors, such as genetic engineering (research on which was paused in the 1970s as scientists worked out useful regulatory systems), the construction and use of high-energy particle accelerators (which a few physicists suggest could create black holes that might swallow the earth), and the development of nanotechnology (which some worry could unleash self-replicating nanomachines that could reduce the world to "gray goo"). The option of eliminating risk altogether does not exist. Countries have kept smallpox samples on hand, along with samples of many other diseases, such as the Ebola and Marburg viruses, despite the danger of their inadvertent release. All of these are potentially dangerous endeavors that governments, with scientific support, have been able to manage for the greater good.

Humans have already engaged in a dangerous geophysical experiment by pumping massive amounts of carbon dioxide and other greenhouse gases into the atmosphere. The best and safest strategy for reversing climate change is to halt this buildup of greenhouse gases, but this solution will take time, and it involves myriad practical and political difficulties. Meanwhile, the dangers are mounting. In a few decades, the option of geoengineering could look less ugly for some countries than unchecked changes in the climate. Nor is it impossible that later in the century the planet will experience a climatic disaster that puts ecosystems and human prosperity at risk. It is time to take geoengineering out of the closet—to better control the risk of unilateral action and also to know the costs and consequences of its use so that the nations of the world can collectively decide whether to raise the shield if they think the planet needs it.

The Truth About Geoengineering

Science Fiction and Science Fact

David G. Victor, M. Granger Morgan, Jay Apt, John Steinbrune

he failure to make much progress at the UN Climate Change Conference in Doha, Qatar this winter was yet another reminder that the world might soon face extreme climate shifts. In response, it is becoming increasingly likely that governments will adopt risky strategies, known as "geoengineering," to rapidly cool the planet. Four years ago, in order to raise awareness about geoengineering, we published "**The Geoengineering Option**" in *Foreign Affairs*. Almost nobody thought that such tactics—which included spraying particles into the upper atmosphere to make the earth more reflective, akin to how big volcanoes cool the planet—were a particularly good option. The risks were simply too great and the unknowns too many. Still, if reliable data and specific models

DAVID G. VICTOR is a professor at the School of International Relations and Pacific Studies and co-director of the School's new Laboratory on International Law and Regulation.

M. GRANGER MORGAN is a professor and head of the Department of Engineering and Public Policy at Carnegie Mellon University.

JAY APT is a professor and director of the Carnegie Mellon Electricity Industry Center.

JOHN D. STEINBRUNER is a professor and director of the Center for International and Security Studies at the University of Maryland.

KATHARINE RICKE is a postdoctoral fellow at Carnegie Institution for Science.

showed that climate change was about to get out of hand, we wrote, such drastic measures might start to look more appealing. The world could no longer ignore the geoengineering option, and we argued that a major science program should begin to explore it.

These days, barely a month goes by without new research that shows that the planet's climate could be more sensitive to global warming than experts previously thought. For example, some ice sheets now appear a lot less stable than scientists had imagined. And new estimates of how much the sea will rise when ice sheets melt far surpass the best estimates of just a few years ago. It is clear that, unchecked, climate change won't just menace natural ecosystems; it will also cause severe harm to humans and could even threaten national security. And, because governments have made barely any progress in controlling the emissions that cause global warming—the 2000s saw the most rapid growth in emissions of carbon dioxide and other warming gases since the 1970s—it's not so crazy to imagine that some nation will launch an emergency geoengineering scheme, perhaps before its viability and consequences are understood.

Since we wrote our essay, press coverage of geoengineering has exploded. The topic makes for good copy: it is weird, sexy, and steeped in exotic science. The term is also incredibly vague, including both techniques for removing carbon dioxide from the air and technology that could rapidly change the amount of sunlight reflected back to space and cool the planet. That method is often termed solar radiation management (SRM).

Carbon dioxide removal schemes include everything from planting trees to fertilizing the oceans in an attempt to cajole great blooms of phytoplankton. Both hinge on photosynthesis, which sucks carbon dioxide from the air; carbon dioxide is the chief long-term cause of global warming. These techniques also include installing scrubbers almost anywhere on the planet, which can strip carbon dioxide out of the atmosphere. Such removal strategies are intriguing, but seem likely to cost hundreds of billions of dollars a year and would take decades to have much of an effect.

In contrast, SRM technologies could cool the planet in just a few months by tinkering with the planet's energy balance. The usual proposals involve spraying material into the stratosphere, where it would turn into reflective clouds, or blowing seawater into the air, with a similar effect. The clouds could deflect just enough incoming sunlight to offset, crudely, the number of degrees human emissions have warmed the planet. Flying a fleet of high-altitude aircraft that spray particles into the upper atmosphere would cost perhaps ten billion dollars per year—a pittance for a country that is suffering from severe climate change and seeks a quick solution.

Most carbon dioxide removal schemes appear relatively safe, although tinkering with a fragile ecosystem by fertilizing the ocean does involve risks. In contrast, SRM raises serious political and policy questions. Although quick and cheap, messing with the complex and imperfectly understood climate system, which is already stressed by warming gases, could end badly. Severe side effects might, for example, include a shift in the seasonal monsoons that many countries rely on for rainfall and agriculture, or accelerate the destruction of the ozone layer. No one knows whether it would be possible to predict and offset all such harmful side effects or how much it might cost. Further, once an SRM system is deployed for an extended period of time, stopping it suddenly would lead to even more rapid and severe climate change as the mask is lifted. Another wrinkle is that some aspects of climate change, such as degraded coral reefs, might be irreversible, and, since the driving forces behind the destruction would remain, it would be particularly irresponsible to deploy SRM without an accompanying program to control carbon emissions.

Given the real and imagined dangers, a movement to regulate geoengineering has been gaining momentum. In the fall of 2010, 193 governments adopted a nonbinding decision under the United Nations Convention on Biological Diversity that would all but ban testing of geoengineering systems. Most environmental NGOs seem to be opposed to even talking about geoengineering out of fear that it might distract from the urgent task of controlling emissions or encourage governments to go ahead with their own projects.

The missing ingredient in all this controversy, though, is arguably the most important: the science. Since 2009, there has been a significant increase in geoengineering research. So far, however, the research is almost exclusively devoted to modeling. It has not yet really moved on to the next stages—careful monitoring nature's own geoengineering processes (for example, volcanic eruptions) and small-scale field tests. There has been some limited field work on ocean fertilization, with less than encouraging results.

The result is that the scientific community knows little more than it did four years ago about how geoengineering would actually work or what its consequences would be. These technologies might not be well understood when and if they are needed, and could be deployed prematurely. In the growing efforts to regulate geoengineering, governments and activists are flying blind as they conjure up new regulations.

Since 2009, several proposals have been made for new SRM research, including by the United Kingdom's Royal Society, the U.S. Bipartisan Policy Center, and a variety of other scientific groups. Yet funding for serious laboratory, modeling, and field study has not followed, in part because government officials fear the political spotlight that follows this kind of research. Indeed, when White House science adviser John Holdren broached the topic some years ago, he quickly retreated after a blizzard of controversy.

Getting started on serious research need not be expensive. When managed correctly, a well-designed scientific research program also needn't be that controversial if government funders and scientists follow some simple guidelines. Small-scale field trials in the upper atmosphere to test components of an SRM system are particularly urgent. The countries with the leading atmospheric research programs already have the rockets, satellites, and aircraft technologies needed to deploy, instrument, and gather data from tests. For now, research doesn't even require much new investment, since better knowledge of the upper atmosphere overlaps heavily with broader needs of climate research.

The key is to draw a sharp line between studies that are small enough to avoid any noticeable or durable impact on the climate or weather and those that are larger and, accordingly, carry larger risks. (In a recent **paper**, Ted Parson, a scientist at the Emmett Center for Climate Change and Law, and David Keith, an engineer at Harvard, suggested some reasonable limits.) A smart research program begins with small tests, for example to study whether and how very fine particles in the stratosphere might clump together and how long they will persist. Results would be essential to develop guidelines for larger experiments down the road.

Such small-scale tests should not be viewed as the camel's nose under the tent. As the results are analyzed, it is likely that deficiencies of SRM will become more apparent. And the public, far from seeing SRM as a silver bullet, could become yet more concerned about climate change and about the fact that failures to control emissions have made even terribly risky options plausible.

In 1891, Sir Arthur Conan Doyle's Sherlock Holmes admonished Dr. Watson, "It is a capital mistake to theorize before one has data." And right now, the politics of geoengineering are far ahead of the science. As the 2010 decision within the Conventional on Biological Diversity shows, fears about geoengineering are leading to counterproductive policy schemes. More practical understanding of what is at stake could help reorient the debate, and if the science is funded and published openly, then best practices and norms for behavior will emerge. In time, those norms and new information will make it easier to focus treaty negotiations—if they prove necessary at all—on the aspects of geoengineering that actually need formal intergovernmental regulation.

That nations are talking seriously about climate engineering is a sign of just how sick the planet has become. In 2009, we presented geoengineering as an intriguing research project that had potentially profound political consequences. Since then, the politics and public discourse have run quickly, but the research has not. Until the science gets serious, the politics won't reflect what's really at stake. Meanwhile, the planet keeps warming and the day when geoengineering might be needed draws nearer.

The Climate Threat We Can Beat

What It Is and How to Deal With It

David G. Victor, Charles F. Kennel,
Veerabhadran Ramanathan

For more than two decades, diplomats have struggled to slow global warming. They have negotiated two major treaties to achieve that goal, the 1992 UN Framework Convention on Climate Change and the 1997 Kyoto Protocol. And last year, at the UN Climate Change Conference in Durban, South Africa, they agreed to start talking about yet another treaty. A small group of countries, including Japan and the members of the European Union, now regulate their emissions in accord with the existing agreements. But most states, including the largest emitters of greenhouse gases, China and the United States, have failed to make much progress. As a result, total emissions of carbon dioxide, the leading long-term cause of global warming, have risen by more than 50 percent since the 1980s and are poised to rise by more than 30 percent in the next two to three decades.

DAVID G. VICTOR is a Professor at the School of International Relations and Pacific Studies at the University of California, San Diego.

CHARLES F. KENNEL is Distinguished Professor and Director Emeritus at the Scripps Institution of Oceanography.

VEERABHADRAN RAMANATHAN is Distinguished Professor of Atmospheric and Climate Sciences at the Scripps Institution of Oceanography.

The ever-increasing quantity of emissions could render moot the aim that has guided international climate diplomacy for nearly a decade: preventing the global temperature from rising by more than two degrees Celsius above its preindustrial level. In fact, in the absence of significant international action, the planet is now on track to warm by at least 2.5 degrees during the current century—and maybe even more. The known effects of this continued warming are deeply troubling: rising sea levels, a thinning Arctic icecap, extreme weather events, ocean acidification, loss of natural habitats, and many others. Perhaps even more fearsome, however, are the effects whose odds and consequences are unknown, such as the danger that melting permafrost in the Arctic could release still more gases, leading to a vicious cycle of still more warming.

All these risks are rising sharply because the traditional approach to international climate diplomacy has failed. For too long, climate science and policymaking have focused almost exclusively on emissions of carbon dioxide, most of which come from burning fossil fuels. Weaning the planet off fossil fuels has proved difficult, partly because expensive and rapid shifts to new energy systems could have negative effects on the competitiveness of modern economies. What is more, carbon dioxide inconveniently remains in the atmosphere for centuries, and so even keeping carbon dioxide at current levels would require deep cuts sustained over many decades—with economic consequences that states are unlikely to be willing to bear unless they are confident that their competitors will do the same. No permanent solution to the climate problem is feasible without tackling carbon dioxide, but the economic and geophysical realities of carbon dioxide emissions almost guarantee political gridlock.

A fresh start to climate diplomacy would emphasize that carbon dioxide is not the only warming pollutant. At least 40 percent of current global warming can be blamed on four other types of pollutants: dark soot particles called black carbon, methane, lower atmospheric ozone, and industrial gases such as chlorofluorocarbons (CFCs) and hydrofluorocarbons (HFCs), which are used as coolants in refrigerators. Nearly all these pollutants have life spans of just a few weeks to a decade—much shorter than that of carbon dioxide. But although their tenure is brief, they are potent warmers. Emitting just one ton of black carbon, for example, has the same immediate effect on warming as emitting 500-2,000 tons of carbon dioxide. Because the impacts of these short-lived pollutants on the climate are severe and swift, limiting them could curb warming quickly, allowing more time for serious efforts to reduce carbon dioxide.

ALIGNING INTERESTS

Luckily, reducing short-lived pollutants poses fewer political hurdles than cutting carbon dioxide, for two reasons. First, existing technologies and policies, if properly applied, readily allow for deep cuts in these pollutants. Second, unlike reducing carbon dioxide, the main benefits of which arrive only after decades of costly efforts, controlling these pollutants would actually serve the immediate interests of developing countries, where pollutants such as soot and ozone damage vital crops and cause respiratory and heart diseases. A few hundred million tons of crops are lost to ozone smog every year; in India, air pollutants have decreased the production of rice by about ten million tons per year, compared with annual output in the 1980s. Globally, the inhalation of soot produced by cooking indoors already kills about two million people each year, mostly women and children living in extreme poverty. And because soot is dark, it traps heat from sunlight and thus speeds melting when it settles on mountain glaciers—a direct threat to drinking-water supplies and agricultural lands that depend on glacier-fed river systems in China and India, such as the Ganges, the Indus, and the Yangtze. Owing to these near-term economic and public health risks, even countries that have been skittish about costly long-term efforts to regulate carbon dioxide are already proving more willing to confront short-lived pollutants.

A plan to reduce short-lived pollutants would align the self-interests of the three largest polluting nations: China, India, and the United States, all of which have conspicuously failed to do much about climate change. It would also engage Europe, which has long been committed to the Kyoto Protocol but has struggled to find willing partners. The United States and a few other countries are in the early stages of building a coalition to address short-lived pollutants; China and India must find constructive ways to join. Limiting these pollutants could cut the pace of climate change in half over the next few decades. Visible success in fighting them would also restore credibility to climate-change diplomacy, which is essential for progress on the more daunting task of limiting carbon dioxide. And taken together, immediate action on short-lived pollutants and serious efforts to control carbon dioxide could achieve the goal of stopping warming at two degrees—just barely.

Still, even those combined efforts cannot reverse the warming that will inevitably occur. Thus, all countries will need to adapt to some of the effects of climate change, especially poorer countries whose economies depend heavily on agriculture and other industries that are especially sensitive to the climate. International cooperation can help these places adapt, but not principally through targets set by diplomats in New York and Geneva, or through the kinds of large-scale, expensive projects directed by wealthy countries and international organizations that have been the mainstay of climate diplomacy to date. Instead, effective adaptation will require bottom-up institution building at the local level to engage people on the frontlines of climate change, such as city planners responding to the risk of rising seas and agricultural ministries helping farmers anticipate how a changing climate will affect their crops. The next era of climate diplomacy should revolve around connecting international experts to those local officials, so that information about best practices can spread more readily.

BEYOND CARBON DIOXIDE

As climate science matured in the late 1970s, all eyes were focused on carbon dioxide. Other gases were known to affect the climate, but human activities emit more carbon dioxide than any other greenhouse gas. Because carbon dioxide came mainly from fossil fuels, which governments tracked closely, its emissions were easy to quantify; other pollutants, by contrast, were much harder to pin down. When policymakers first began to pay attention to global warming, they, too, concentrated on carbon dioxide. The UN Framework Convention on Climate Change and the Kyoto Protocol recognized that other gases also cause warming, and the Kyoto Protocol created a scheme through which countries could meet their emissions-reduction obligations by substituting other gases for carbon dioxide at UN-established exchange rates. But the diplomats set the exchange rates in ways that emphasized long-term climate change, creating incentives to cut carbon dioxide and other long-lived warming gases and effectively penalizing attempts to reduce short-lived pollutants. Some of these, notably soot particles, were omitted from these treaties altogether, because, at the time, their precise warming effects were difficult to quantify.

In the background, however, climatologists started to pay attention to a longer list of greenhouse gases. In the 1970s, CFCs became the first to attract scrutiny. Adding one molecule of these hyperwarmers to the atmosphere has the same climate effect as the addition of more than 10,000 molecules of carbon dioxide. Policymakers, however, were more concerned about the role that CFCs played in depleting the ozone layer, which caused skin cancers, damaged crops, and threatened natural ecosystems. Those risks inspired the Montreal Protocol, a 1987 treaty that banned CFCs and many other ozone depleters. Because the Montreal Protocol focused on pollutants that had little effect on national economic competitiveness, it has been the most successful environmental treaty in history. It set the stage for the ozone layer to heal, and because CFCs are also warming gases, it had the helpful side effect of slowing climate change. In fact, studies have shown that the reduction of CFC emissions since the late 1980s has done more to reduce global warming than all the climate treaties focused on carbon dioxide to date. Unfortunately, HFCs and some of the other gases that have been used to replace CFCs are also strong warming agents; adding them to the list of pollutants covered by the Montreal Protocol, a policy now under consideration, could help phase them out speedily.

As climate science has progressed, researchers have become aware of more warming agents. For the most part, emissions of these pollutants result from primitive energy technologies, mostly in emerging economies. Most black carbon, for example, is emitted by old-fashioned cookstoves, improperly maintained and poorly regulated diesel engines, and outdated power plants. Emissions from all three of these sources could be reduced with available technologies, market-based incentives, and low-cost government regulation. Between 1989 and 2007, California cut its black carbon emissions from diesel engines nearly in half by mandating the use of better fuels and filters.

Similar steps would have an even greater impact in the developing world, where pollution controls are much more primitive. In 2008, a group of scientists working for the United Nations Environment Program (UNEP) estimated that roughly 60 percent of India's soot emissions could be eliminated by replacing traditional stoves that burn unprocessed firewood and dung with cleaner stoves that burn more efficiently by using pellet forms of those fuels. India and other South Asian countries could lower their soot levels even further by switching from the primitive kilns used to manufacture bricks to more efficient modern varieties. Similarly, eliminating the burning of solid coal for heating homes in China could reduce black carbon emissions there by more than 50 percent. Developing countries could achieve further soot reductions by installing better insulation in homes (to reduce the need for heating) and by using alternative fuels for heat, such as natural gas, which yields essentially no soot when burned. Making these changes would require governments to subsidize the initial costs of the new technologies. But those expenses would be offset relatively quickly by gains in public health and agricultural productivity.

The strategy for reducing soot from power plants also involves shifting to more efficient technologies, along with switching to natural gas and installing pollution-control equipment, such as scrubbers and filters, in coal-burning plants. In most places, market-friendly reforms could spur these changes. In India, deregulation and the restructuring of state-owned companies led to increased competition among technology suppliers and power plant operators; as a result, the country's newest coal plants are dramatically more efficient.

During the last 15 years, dozens of research teams have documented effective, low-cost methods of reducing levels of soot and the three other short-lived warming pollutants. Last year, the UNEP summarized their work, highlighting the potential benefits of installing new cookstoves, building more efficient power plants, and plugging the leaks that occur when natural gas is extracted from wells. The UNEP concluded that such steps would make it possible to cut 40 percent of global man-made methane emissions and almost 75 percent of global black carbon emissions by 2030. Those reductions could ultimately prevent as many as five million deaths every year and safeguard as many as 140 million tons of corn, rice, and soybeans every year—the equivalent of four percent of annual global production. These measures would also halve the global warming expected to occur between now and 2050 and sharply raise the odds that total warming could be limited to two degrees.

These aims are ambitious but not unrealistic. Driven by short-term national interests unrelated to climate change, China and India are already trying to cut the air pollution that sullies their cities and undermines their agricultural productivity. China has put in place an elaborate program to document the national economic costs of local pollution and has made energy efficiency a centerpiece of its most recent five-year plans. In India, courts are forcing the national government to take stronger action to control air pollution.

In February, the United States announced that it would lead a group of countries including Bangladesh, Canada, and Sweden in a new strategy to reduce short-lived pollutants. Working with the

UNEP, this initiative aims to help countries make the deepest cuts possible by leveraging a form of peer pressure and by sharing information on best practices. For years, major polluters have criticized UN climate talks as too rigid; this initiative could represent a practical complement. But for it to succeed, China and India must find a way to become involved. Both countries have been wary of diplomatic initiatives that could lead to binding emissions controls, and they have been suspicious that efforts to control short-lived pollutants represent a way for the industrialized nations to avoid taking responsibility for decades of carbon dioxide emissions. Chinese and Indian policymakers need to realize that, in fact, a new focus on short-lived pollutants would allow them to shift climate negotiations to their own terms. It would reduce global warming while letting China and India focus on the pollutants that they are most inclined and able to control.

Success on short-lived pollutants could also help recharge climate diplomacy more generally. Most of the world's governments and big industrial firms—players whose policies and investments are crucial to solving the climate problem—are growing weary of climate talks that have dragged on for decades yet produced few tangible results. A relatively quick and easy victory over short-lived pollutants could help reverse those sentiments and reinvigorate efforts to manage the much harder task of coordinating cuts in carbon dioxide emissions.

EMBRACING ADAPTATION

But even an effective international effort on short-lived pollutants cannot avoid the increase in the earth's temperature that will be the inevitable consequence of the emissions that are still accumulating in the atmosphere. Yet until just a few years ago, even discussing adaptation to climate change was taboo, because activists and policymakers alike wrongly believed that simply talking about preparing to cope with a warmer planet would make averting its arrival seem somehow less urgent. Most of them now realize that adaptation is essential; still missing, however, is a strategy to guide international diplomacy around the issue.

Poor countries are the most vulnerable to the changing climate, and it would be unconscionable for the international community not to help them deal with it. Historically, discussions of foreign aid for dealing with climate change have focused on large-scale projects or on helping government officials from poor countries attend international meetings. Ultimately, those approaches will fail, because adaptation is an intrinsically local activity. Aid must play a role, but countries will have to take control of their own fates. And even in the poorest countries, internationally funded projects—for example, building seawalls in places threatened by rising oceans—will play only marginal roles, at best. What international organizations can do, however, is fund networks to connect local authorities all over the world to one another, which would allow them to share information about best practices. Such networks could also connect local authorities to international experts who can help them assess and respond to climate vulnerabilities in their areas.

Until recently, most climate-risk assessments were done at the global level; very few countries or localities were willing to invest in translating abstract global dangers into practical local actions. But the best adaptation plans draw on the more detailed kind of information about conditions on the ground that is available only to locals. For example, in 2006, California conducted a thorough assessment of its vulnerability to a range of climate-change effects, including more frequent or severe wildfires and a possible 90 percent decline by the end of the century in snow cover in the northern Sierra Nevada mountain range, which would threaten all the state's major rivers. In turn, local officials used those studies to guide their planning. Similar assessments are being performed across the United States—for example, in states along the Gulf of Mexico, where officials and firms that operate the region's infrastructure are now preparing for the higher sea levels and stronger storms that are likely in a warmer world.

Many governments in the developing world are also doing serious assessments, including those in Brazil, China, and India. But locally directed assessments are not occurring in the most vulnerable, poorest places, such as rural Africa, where climate-sensitive agriculture is the dominant economic activity, and low-lying Pacific island nations, where rising sea levels and stronger storms will redraw coastlines. Places such as these would benefit the most from the establishment of collaborative networks of government officials, private-sector firms, and nongovernmental organizations that can share information and expertise, thereby cutting the cost and speeding the implementation of adaptations.

Such connections are already making a difference. For example, in 2004, a team of 300 scientists that included representatives from all eight countries with territory in the Arctic published the *Arctic Climate Impact Assessment*, which synthesized international and local research on the likely effects of global warming on the region. The report is part of a larger, collective effort by the Arctic countries to prepare for those effects and minimize them through controls on pollutants such as soot. With its combination of international funding and local expertise, the Arctic assessment project should serve as a model for how to connect high-level climate diplomacy with ground-level policymaking.

AFTER DURBAN

As with most global challenges, climate change requires policymakers and activists to align international goals with national interests. The Durban conference witnessed some progress on that front. Delegates there agreed to the so-called Durban Platform, which offers a framework for new climate talks that could reduce the divisions between wealthy and poor countries that have frequently impeded progress. In the past, poor countries have refused to agree to emissions controls and demanded that rich countries alone make all the effort. For their part, rich countries have worried that reducing their own emissions would limit their ability to compete with emerging economic power-houses such as China.

David G. Victor, Charles F. Kennel, Veerabhadran Ramanathan

Unlike earlier frameworks that put all the burden for emissions controls on rich countries, the Durban Platform requires all the major emitters to make a serious effort.

That is a good first step, but the practical details that will define any new talks remain unsettled. The largest emitters of short-lived warming gases—China, India, the United States, and the countries of the EU—should demonstrate leadership by putting those pollutants at the center of the next round of diplomacy. In Durban, diplomats also agreed to devote a significant amount (probably several billion dollars a year) to projects relating to adaptation. They should use those funds to build networks to connect people who are developing practical, location-specific ways to adapt.

For the last 20 years, any proposal that de-emphasized the long-term mitigation of carbon dioxide or advocated adapting to irreversible warming was considered a dangerous distraction from the goal of permanently solving the climate problem. But an unrealistic focus on permanence has proved counterproductive, obscuring practical steps that are already attainable and politically attractive to the countries that matter most. The best way to restore faith in climate diplomacy is to make tangible progress on those measures. After all, only once countries revive climate diplomacy can they take on the much harder challenge of taming carbon dioxide emissions.

How Big Business Can Save the Climate

Multinational Corporations Can Succeed Where Governments Have Failed

Jerry Patchell and Roger Hayter

In September 1987, representatives of 24 countries met in Montreal and accomplished a rare feat in international politics: a successful environmental accord. The Montreal Protocol on Substances that Deplete the Ozone Layer, which UN Secretary-General Kofi Annan later called "perhaps the single most successful international agreement to date," set the ambitious goal of phasing out chlorofluorocarbons (CFCs) and other dangerous chemicals. It worked: by 1996, developed countries had stopped their production and consumption of CFCs, and by 2006, the 191 countries that had ratified the protocol had eliminated 95 percent of global ozone-depleting emissions.

On its surface, the Montreal Protocol was an agreement among countries. Each signatory agreed to report its emissions and face trade sanctions for failing to meet reduction targets. Developed countries committed to help developing countries meet their targets with side payments and technological support. The treaty's

JERRY PATCHELL is Professor of Geography in the Division of Social Science at the Hong Kong University of Science and Technology.

ROGER HAYTER is Professor of Geography at Simon Fraser University.

main targets, however, were companies. By preventing the production and consumption of ozone-depleting substances within countries, as well as the trade of those substances between countries, the treaty gave multinational corporations a clear and short deadline to find substitutes for the chemicals or face being forced out of the world market. The results were dramatic: the companies responded to the pressure by developing alternative methods, going a long way toward solving the problem at its root.

Unfortunately, this success has not been matched when it comes to the world's greatest collective challenge: stopping climate change. For 20 years, national governments have sought to slow the heating of the planet and the rise of the oceans by apportioning blame and attempting to spread the financial burden. The vehicle for their efforts, the UN Framework Convention on Climate Change (UNFCCC), is a negotiating process aimed at getting countries to commit to reducing their emissions of heat-trapping greenhouse gases, the main cause of global warming. But the UNFCCC has floundered because of disagreements between developed and developing countries; difficulties in credibly measuring, reporting, and verifying emissions reductions; and the power of vested interests in the energy sector.

Above all, the UNFCCC has failed because it does not provide powerful enough directives for companies to develop and use technologies that could radically reduce their greenhouse gas emissions. Unlike the Montreal Protocol, the UNFCCC does not focus on specific internationally traded products that generate harmful emissions. Instead, countries with little power to enforce how products are made are expected to reduce their greenhouse gas emissions on a national basis, leading to quarrels among a wide range of stakeholders and industry sectors. The framework's reliance on emissions-trading schemes, meanwhile, offers countries and companies a cheap out, allowing them to forestall investments in clean technologies.

Climate diplomacy urgently needs a new approach. Borrowing from Montreal's playbook, the international community should shift its focus from setting targets that countries cannot meet to setting directives that multinational corporations have to follow. Relying on the threat of sanctions, the UN should compel the multinational corporations that dominate important sectors to define and adopt ambitious targets for driving down their greenhouse gas emissions. Third parties would evaluate the reductions throughout the corporations' supply and distribution channels.

Individual countries contain multitudes of competing voices and interests, which complicate efforts to get them to change their behavior. But corporations are authoritative organizations that can channel extraordinary levels of human, technical, and fiscal resources toward specific problems and missions. Multinational corporations dominate markets, trade, investment, research and development, and the spread of technology. To fight climate change, the international community needs to harness this power.

WHY MULTINATIONALS?

It is worth taking a look back at the Montreal Protocol to consider just why it was so successful. What really sealed the deal was oligopoly. At the time, several large multinational corporations—most notably the chemical giants DuPont and what was then Imperial Chemical Industries—produced a majority of the world's CFCs. Even as the Montreal Protocol was being negotiated, DuPont began to develop alternatives to the problematic chemicals and rapidly scaled up its production of those substitutes, forcing its rivals to follow suit. Just as important, corporations that consumed ozone-depleting substances in large quantities figured out how to eliminate processes that depended on them and thus reduce their emissions of CFCs. Within a couple years, these companies created alternative refrigerants, aerosols, and electronics-processing methods. In turn, the U.S. Environmental Protection Agency awarded and provided technical support to a diverse range of compliant firms, including SC Johnson, AT&T, Ford, Nissan, and Coca-Cola.

The fact that most of the world's ozone-depleting substances were produced and consumed by a relatively small number of mammoth corporations led to a straightforward solution: when those companies devised substitutes, much of the problem was eliminated. Scientists helped develop technical solutions, nongovernmental organizations advocated change, and local and national governments made important regulatory demands. But it was profit-motivated, competitive multinational corporations that actually implemented the technologies required to stop ozone depletion on a large scale.

Unlike the small number of similar companies that accounted for most CFC emissions, a huge number and wide array of businesses contribute to the emissions of greenhouse gases that drive climate change. But only a relatively small number of companies account for a very large proportion of the research and development of new technology, which most experts see as the most important aspect of addressing climate change. In an influential 2004 study, the Princeton scholars Robert Socolow and Stephen Pacala showed how the world could stabilize its emissions simply by increasing the use of seven groups of existing technologies. More recently, in a 2009 report, the consulting firm McKinsey & Company concluded that by switching to technologies that already exist or are being developed, the world could reduce its greenhouse gas emissions by 35 percent below 1990 levels with an increase of only five to six percent in business costs. The hard part is implementing the right policies—specifically, finding ways to ensure that climate-friendly technologies are adopted on a large scale.

This is where multinational corporations come in. Their global reach and tremendous capacity for the research, development, demonstration, and diffusion of new technologies offer the best chance of addressing climate change. In the United States, McKinsey estimates that multinational corporations account for 74 percent of private-sector research-and-development spending. And the biggest 700 multinational corporations—just one percent of the world's roughly 70,000 multinationals—make up half of global research-and-development spending and two-thirds of research-and-development spending in the private sector.

Of course, what matters most is how that research and development is put to work. Profit-hungry corporations tend to waste little time in creating, patenting, and exporting new products. Each year, they invest hundreds of billions of dollars in production processes, product development, factories, offices, transportation, and stores. By themselves, multinational corporations account for a quarter of global GDP—$16 trillion in 2010—and well over $1 trillion of yearly global investment. If every large multinational corporation demanded that its facilities and those of its suppliers reduced their greenhouse gas emissions by just five percent each year, or by some other substantial, self-determined goal, the results would ripple across the global economy. Moreover, the corporations' efforts would generate reduction technologies that could be adopted broadly.

Compare the ability of multinational corporations to make use of their research and development with the technology-transfer schemes built into the current climate change framework. Under the UN's Clean Development Mechanism, developed countries wishing to offset their own emissions can transfer money to the developing world, so long as the funds are used to reduce greenhouse gas emissions in some manner. From 2006 to 2012, the program channeled somewhere between $22 billion and $43 billion to the development of new technologies, including plants that turn manure into electricity. But all this work has led to only modest emissions reductions and no significant research and development. A far more promising approach would be to make sure that greenhouse-gas-reduction technologies and practices were integrated into all the massive investments that multinational corporations undertake each year.

CHOOSING THE RIGHT TARGETS

One sensible-sounding proposal to reform the UNFCCC would target specific industry sectors that contribute the most to climate change, require them to invest in new greenhouse-gas-reduction technologies, measure their progress, and force them to pay for carbon reductions elsewhere. This is, in essence, what the European Union has done, developing an emissions-trading scheme involving electricity- and heat-generating plants; oil refineries; coke ovens; metal ore and steel installations; cement kilns; glass and ceramics manufacturing; and pulp, paper, and board mills. Such facilities account for about half of the EU's carbon dioxide emissions and thus seem like the smartest targets for stricter rules.

But lining up the usual suspects may not be the best way to regulate the climate. Some industries are inherently dependent on emitting greenhouse gases—and not even the most clever environmental rules will change that. The petroleum, gas, and coal sectors, for example, might discover new ways to reduce emissions during production and distribution, but they prosper only by selling more carbon. Cement and steel are not much different. Asking firms in these sectors to make incremental reductions in the emissions they produce, even by smacking them with carbon taxes or offsetting requirements, would do little to stimulate the development of renewable energy. That approach would only lock in technologies that would continue to produce unsustainable levels of emissions for decades to come.

It would make more sense to concentrate not on the industries that produce fossil fuels but on those that consume energy—and can thus more realistically make changes. Most multinational corporations make goods or offer services that are not dependent on any one type of energy or energy-intensive material. Moreover, since they respond to the needs of consumers, they do not have to support vested interests (of which there are plenty in energy sectors) the way that governments do. For these companies, energy expenses are minor, and it would cost relatively little for them to switch to renewable energy and environmentally friendly materials. Doing so would also help them avoid the increasing regulatory penalties on fossil fuel usage and, at the same time, improve public perceptions of their behavior.

To be sure, multinational corporations are not altruistic organizations and will not want to pay for these changes themselves. Today, corporations make countries compete for their investments by offering flexible working conditions, low wages and taxes, infrastructure subsidies, and limited environmental regulation. But if multinationals were compelled to reduce their greenhouse gas emissions, countries and regions would have to compete to attract them by providing clean energy, research-and-development support, and workers and consumers who were dedicated to a low-carbon future.

HOW IT WORKS

Collective action against climate change has proved elusive because it requires cooperation among deeply divided camps. Developing countries such as China and India—the first- and third-largest emitters of carbon dioxide, respectively—argue that developed countries are responsible for historical emissions and are most able to afford contemporary reductions. They expect rich countries to lead by reducing their own emissions and paying for reductions in the developing world, while excusing themselves from environmental constraints. Meanwhile, developed countries want poorer states to rein in their increasing emissions before receiving funding.

The impasse runs even deeper, however. It originates in governments' fear that attempting to stop climate change will harm economic growth and reduce standards of living, all with a regressive distribution of costs and benefits among rich and poor countries and among rich and poor people within countries. This fear is what prevented the UNFCCC from trying to secure direct funding for emissions reduction from developed countries and what led it to rely instead on the Clean Development Mechanism. This approach was supposed to be market-driven and efficient, but it has been hampered by bureaucracy.

To avoid these obstacles, the climate diplomacy expert David Victor has suggested that the UN should set aside its quixotic attempt to create a global set of rules acceptable to so many divergent countries. Instead, he argues, countries with a similar commitment to and capacity for governance and socioeconomic change should form "carbon clubs" that reward members for sound climate change policies and penalize inaction.

But since countries differ wildly in terms of their interests and capacities, an even more effective and equitable approach would be for the international community to compel similar multinational corporations, the oligopolies of global industry, to form climate clubs that would set targets for emissions reduction and standards for product design and share knowledge about renewable energy technologies. The clubs would comprise not only multinationals from established rich countries but also the rapidly emerging businesses of the developing world. As a result, the clubs would draw developing countries into the global climate change framework by enlisting companies capable of acting rather than making demands of people who are not.

The UN could delegate governing the system to the World Trade Organization, taking advantage of the WTO's established dispute-resolution mechanism. However, since the WTO mediates trade disputes only between national governments, its procedures would need to be modified for the direct evaluation of multinational corporations. (Such a shift would be rather simple to implement, since many multinational corporations already adhere to common standards, particularly those of the Greenhouse Gas Protocol, and the WTO could enlist the help of many recognized third parties to do the evaluations.) Large multinationals would need to meet deadlines to establish clubs and regulations, and smaller corporations would be expected to join the clubs once they hit a certain level of international production or imports. Penalties for noncompliant companies could include taxes paid to countries or fees paid to the UN.

The greatest difference between this proposal and the status quo is the role played by national governments. At the moment, the UNFCCC sets carbon targets and asks each country to figure out how it will meet them. The pressure to do so leads countries to focus on carbon-dependent industries—for the most part, energy producers—which are inherently disinclined to reduce their greenhouse gas emissions. Moreover, most governments lack the capacity to credibly monitor carbon emissions across their countries. That task is better performed by individual corporations, which can benefit from combining carbon audits with the quality-control and supplier audits that they use to control their supply chains.

Focusing on multinational corporations is also a more equitable approach to dealing with climate change. Less developed countries and the less well-off within countries would not have to pay a higher price for energy. Nor would farmers and small businesses be saddled with the higher energy costs that would come from a carbon tax or carbon trading. The people around the world who buy products made by major corporations—the relatively and absolutely wealthy—would end up paying the true costs of their carbon consumption. Multinationals would have to account for environmental damage in their production costs, creating an incentive for them to eliminate or reduce the source of any additional costs rather than charge their customers higher prices.

The system would also avoid the problem of "carbon leakage," whereby one country's setting tighter limits on emissions simply leads emitters to move elsewhere. Corporations can be held responsible for emissions anywhere along their supply chains, regardless of which countries host the more pollution-heavy aspects of their businesses.

As the world continues to climb out of a recession, multinational corporations are far better placed to tackle climate change than deficit-ridden or poor governments. The concentration of immense power in a small number of corporations—long a fear of concerned citizens everywhere—might turn out to be just what is needed to save the planet.